WHAT HIGH SCHOOLS DON'T TELL YOU

WHAT HIGH SCHOOLS DON'T TELL YOU

300+ SECRETS

TO MAKE YOUR KID IRRESISTIBLE TO COLLEGES BY SENIOR YEAR

Elizabeth Wissner-Gross

HUDSON
STREET
PRESS

HUDSON STREET PRESS
Published by Penguin Group
Penguin Group (USA) Inc., 375 Hudson Street, New York, New York 10014, U.S.A. •
Penguin Group (Canada), 90 Eglinton Avenue East, Suite 700, Toronto, Ontario, Canada M4P
2Y3 (a division of Pearson Penguin Canada Inc.) • Penguin Books Ltd., 80 Strand, London
WC2R 0RL, England • Penguin Ireland, 25 St. Stephen's Green, Dublin 2, Ireland (a division of
Penguin Books Ltd.) • Penguin Group (Australia), 250 Camberwell Road, Camberwell, Victoria
3124, Australia (a division of Pearson Australia Group Pty. Ltd.) • Penguin Books India Pvt. Ltd.,
11 Community Centre, Panchsheel Park, New Delhi – 110 017, India • Penguin Group (NZ), 67
Apollo Drive, Rosedale, North Shore 0745, Auckland, New Zealand (a division of Pearson New
Zealand Ltd.) • Penguin Books (South Africa) (Pty.) Ltd., 24 Sturdee Avenue, Rosebank, Johan-
nesburg 2196, South Africa

Penguin Books Ltd., Registered Offices: 80 Strand, London WC2R 0RL, England

First published by Hudson Street Press, a member of Penguin Group (USA) Inc.

First Printing, August 2007
10 9 8 7 6 5 4 3 2 1

REGISTERED TRADEMARK—MARCA REGISTRADA

HUDSON
STREET
PRESS

LIBRARY OF CONGRESS CATALOGING-IN-PUBLICATION DATA

Wissner-Gross, Elizabeth.
    What high schools don't tell you : 300+ secrets to make your kid irresistible to colleges by sen-
ior year / Elizabeth Wissner-Gross.
        p. cm.
    Includes index.
    ISBN 978-1-59463-037-8 (hardcover)
    1. Universities and colleges—United States—Admission. 2. College student orientation.
    3. Education—Parent participation. I. Title.

    LB2351.2.W574 2007
    378.1'610973—dc22

                                                                                    2007016685

Printed in the United States of America
Set in Bembo
Designed by Eve L. Kirch

To my grandmother
Florence Hollander
who made studying fun

ACKNOWLEDGMENTS

In writing my previous book, *What Colleges Don't Tell You (and Other Parents Don't Want You to Know)*, I heard so many college admissions officers comment that the majority of parents of applicants to the top colleges are out of touch with "the depth of the applicant pool out there" and the strong credentials that *other* candidates bring to the table.

What those credentials are and how to access them has been a best-kept secret in America for decades. (The relatively few parents who know what it takes to get in don't share their information—to maintain the competitive edge for their own kids.) But it's time to spill the beans. So I've written this book—a guide to some of the most outstanding opportunities that build those credentials that dazzle colleges—a book that I wished had existed when I was raising my own two sons.

To learn the inside secrets of building the most sought-after credentials over the course of four years of high school, I interviewed teachers, college admissions officers, parents of nationally recognized high school students, directors of some of the most prestigious summer programs, and creators and administrators of inspiring high school contests and other opportunities. So many people contributed generously to the wealth of options provided in this book, and I thank them all.

In addition, *What High Schools Don't Tell You* would not have been possible without the vision and upbeat approach of publisher Laureen Rowland, the continued commitment of Luke Dempsey and Clare Ferraro, and the thoughtful queries and contagious enthusiasm of my editor, Danielle Friedman. Thanks to Liz Keenan, Marie Coolman, Abigail Powers, Susan

Schwartz, Eve Kirch, Melissa Jacoby, and everyone else at Hudson Street Press for their work on the book. I also want to acknowledge Leda Schein-taub, for very astute copyediting. I especially want to thank my literary agent, Susan Ginsburg, for continuing to live up to her image of being "the best agent in New York," and Emily Saladino, for all her help.

I express gratitude to my patient friends and family, who were most understanding when I had to tune out for weeks at a time or miss social gatherings, to have this book ready just a year after *What Colleges Don't Tell You*.

Most of all, I want to acknowledge the hundreds of students with whom I've had the privilege to work—the young scientists, mathematicians, artists, scholars, journalists, advocates, and leaders—for their willingness to dream and help pioneer paths to achieve those dreams. They are what this book is all about.

CONTENTS

What High Schools Don't Tell You, But This Book Will　　　　　　xi

**Part I: The Secret to College Admissions Success?
You Have to Have a Game Plan**

CHAPTER 1: You Can't Exceed Your Goals If You Don't Have Any:
Helping Your Child to Identify Her Passions　　　3

CHAPTER 2: Strategic Summers: The Time to Gain the Advantage
for College　　　21

CHAPTER 3: Designing the Four-Year Academic Plan: What Colleges
Mean When They Say They Prefer Kids Who
Challenge Themselves to the Fullest　　　47

CHAPTER 4: Coordinating the Game Plan with Your Child's School:
Inviting the Faculty to Join Your Team　　　76

**Part II: The Amazing Array: Finding the Best
Opportunities for Your Kid**

Note to the Reader　　　85

CHAPTER 5: Mathematics: The Triad—Three Pedigrees
for Math Students　　　87

CHAPTER 6: Science and Engineering, Part I:
             Raising a Science Olympian   111

CHAPTER 7: Science and Engineering, Part II: Launching Inventors
             and Explorers on the Research Track   125

CHAPTER 8: The Arts: Spotlighting the Creative Applicant   163

CHAPTER 9: The Humanities: The Scholar Every College Wants   197

CHAPTER 10: Journalism, Media, and Advocacy: Headlining
             the Front-Page Kid   215

CHAPTER 11: Government: Building a Political Leader from
             the Ground Up   233

CHAPTER 12: Business: Marketing the Future Mogul   246

A Final Note   257

Appendix: Four-Year Summer Plans for Forty Different Interests   259

Index   291

About the Author   301

WHAT HIGH SCHOOLS DON'T TELL YOU, BUT THIS BOOK WILL

When people ask me what I *do* exactly, I'm sometimes tempted to tell them that I make kids' dreams come true, because that's where clients say my true talent lics. But I realize that people unfamiliar with my work would be suspicious of that claim, so I give them a more mundane title: educational strategist. What I really do, however, is try to uncover kids' greatest aspirations and then help them to achieve them. The plan focuses heavily on empowering kids during high school so that by the time they apply to their dream colleges they are so outstandingly accomplished in their fields of interest and so overwhelmingly appealing that every college wants them. I work with kids from 8th grade on, some of whom are able to articulate clearly what they aspire to do, others who claim they have no clue. Within a two-hour meeting, I'm generally able to unearth these kids' dreams and passions and give them a concrete plan—informing them of some of the top opportunities available—to help them achieve their goals.

They tell me: astronaut, rock star, film producer, physicist, novelist, inventor, medical wizard, Olympic athlete, business mogul, or even president. What I do that nobody else seems to do is take these dreams seriously. Together we map out a road to get there, starting when they are thirteen and fourteen years old. Even in today's ultracompetitive times, gaining admission into the most sought-after colleges can become a relatively simple task when a student is filled with energy and ambition and is vigorously pursuing a dream. Just as students have dream colleges, I have found that colleges also have dream students. I help students become those dream students.

Nothing is more exciting to me than meeting with a supposedly turned-off kid, and then during my visit suddenly seeing an amazing glint, an academic or artistic passion ignited—an inner spark that excites her about education and the world. Parents often tell me that I leave a very different child behind—and even a different family. Not by tutoring, but by helping a teenager rediscover his childhood dream. Not by therapy, but just by showing the teenager the doable, concrete plans that I have spent years researching obsessively. For most teenagers, I find that their dreams are often buried just below the surface.

Through my years of working with children, I have found that involved parents can play a key role in delivering their kids' dreams—even with kids who are hesitant to accept help from adults. If your son wanted to become a songwriter, for example, and you had a concrete, surefire, step-by-step path to get him there, don't you think he would be eager to follow it? And if your daughter wanted to be a national politician, and you knew the steps she could take to succeed, starting from 8th grade, don't you think she would be ready to work with you?

I believe that, if done right, the teenage years can be filled with exuberance, unmitigated energy, uncensored aspiration, and intense academic passion: the dream to outsmart Einstein, to outwrite Shakespeare, to outpaint Rembrandt, to outdo Mother Teresa. Teenagers should be rarin' to go. But in my experience as an educational strategist, I have seen that a large percentage of teenagers—even those at the top of their class—feel directionless, jaded, or depressed, and only work when badgered or bribed. There's little correlation between school and fun in their lives. And they see so little hope of achieving their dreams that most have simply abandoned them or emotionally settled for something less.

It's my job and this book's mission to bring those dreams back. To show teenagers (and their parents) that their innermost career aspirations are realistic, and to provide them with a proven path for achieving their goals. Of course, there are many side benefits to this process for parents as well. Kids who pursue their academic, artistic, or athletic passions can be a lot more fun to raise—every day is an adventure, with more to learn and more to accomplish. And colleges adore these kids, so the application process becomes easier. In fact, these are the kids that every college finds irresistible.

In this book, I share the secrets I have discovered as an educational strategist by working with hundreds of middle school and high school students, including my own two sons, Alex and Zach—one of whom is currently finishing his PhD in physics at Harvard, and the other who is just starting a combined PhD program in biophysics at Harvard and MIT. When Alex and Zach were still in high school, I met parents of their competitors—some of the nation's top-achieving students. Many of these parents generously shared their strategies with me in casual conversations and formal interviews. In the process, I accumulated enough information to be able to advise other families of aspiring academic superstars, and decided to make educational strategy my career.

The students I have worked with have gone on to become Intel Science Talent Search finalists and winners. They've won national medals and awards at the International Science and Engineering Fair and at the middle school–level Discovery Challenge. They've been inducted into the National Gallery for America's Young Inventors, and have been named international winners of the First Step to the Nobel Prize in Physics. They've gotten roles in the New York City Opera and in TV commercials. They've gotten exciting assignments as crew members in our national parks for the Student Conservation Association. They've had their writing published in journals, newspapers, and other national venues, and have been awarded patents for their discoveries while still in high school. They've trained with the U.S. Math Olympiad team and Computer Olympiad team and have been named national semifinalists and finalists in other academic Olympiads. They've stood before Congress to receive Congressional Awards for outstanding community service. And they've participated in Junior Olympics and won national recognition in their sport, organized vaudeville-show fund-raisers for terminally ill children, presented their original work before national conferences, led overseas missions to help earthquake victims, and helped provide medical assistance in hurricane-ravaged New Orleans. They have led the organization of a New York City recycling program, and have organized used sports equipment drives to provide baseball bats, sports helmets, and other supplies to needy children. They have been offered admission into Harvard, MIT, Yale, Princeton, Stanford, Caltech, Duke, and other top colleges.

I wrote this book, in part, because the information I have uncovered in my ten-plus years of working with students is found nowhere else. This is the only book of its kind. I organized it into "secrets" because much of the information has been kept hush-hush by other ambitious parents who prefer not to share their approaches with parents of kids competing for college—and guidance counselors, principals, and teachers generally don't even *know* about many of the opportunities discussed. *How did you find out all this information?* parents of my students commonly ask. I have acquired this information over years of exploration. I interviewed heads of admissions at colleges, studied credentials and résumés of the most successful students, interviewed parents of some of the nation's most outstanding students, and, most importantly, worked with my own sons.

This book fills in the gaps, giving parents (and educators) the inside scoop on how to create a solid game plan for their kids, according to their kids' own artistic, athletic, and academic passions—a long-term strategy that will deliver on your child's dreams and create camaraderie and exciting teamwork within families. In a time when getting into a top college *has never been more competitive*, parents and kids need to band together and, ideally, begin planning when the kids are still in 8th or 9th grade in order to get the most out of their high school years, and appeal most to colleges.

My hope is that *What High Schools Don't Tell You* will empower parents by revealing how and where to find the best opportunities for your children. In taking advantage of these opportunities, your children will become the movers and shakers of whichever fields they choose—and as a result become shoo-ins to many of the country's top colleges.

What's Inside?

The 309 secrets you will find in this book will help to improve your teenager's chances of success (both in college admission and career aspirations), regardless of your own education, economic background, ethnicity, religion, and politics; the quality of your kid's high school; or even whether or not she is already the highest achiever. While it is targeted to parents of early high school students and students in their final year of middle school, even if your child is already in her junior year of high school, this book will provide you with plenty of useful tips—it's not too late to stack the deck in her favor.

Part 1 of the book addresses how to help your kids formulate exciting goals and set up a concrete game plan for achieving them. It covers everything from how to make the most of your child's summers to coordinating your child's plan with his school.

Part 2 delves into specific opportunities available in a wide range of subjects to make your kids stand out. Entire chapters are devoted to discussing the pedigrees in mathematics, science research, and science contests, revealing many secrets to catapult students into math and science stardom. Similarly, chapters on the arts (including fine arts, drama, music, dance, and creative writing), humanities (including classics, history, and literature), journalism and advocacy, government, and business give parents insider advice on what activities appeal most to colleges and how to guarantee their kids' success. (Should what appeals to colleges be the determining factor of what activities your child ultimately chooses? No. But *knowing* what appeals to colleges can certainly help parents and students make informed decisions.) In part 2, focus first on the chapters that address your children's interests, but don't be afraid to explore some of the other chapters that discuss areas that might *potentially* interest them. If they seriously pursue any of the tracks described in this book, they will become extremely desirable to colleges.

Finally, the appendix at the back of this book provides forty four-summer plans, listed by interest, ranging from more popular subjects, such as computer game design and fashion, to more abstract fields like anthropology and philosophy.

But don't these programs and plans only work for kids who are exceptionally gifted from the get-go? some parents ask at our first meeting. No, I tell them. In my experience, it really comes down to the age-old question "Is it nature or nurture (that makes a student highly motivated and successful)?" The more I have worked with families, the more convinced I have become that, although nature controls the equipment we start out with, nurture is the big winner— how you treat your children; how involved you are in their lives; how much direction you're able to provide; and, most importantly, *how much attention you pay to your child's dreams, and aspirations.* Most parents don't realize how influential their involvement is in bringing about their kids' successes. Children with supportive parents to guide the way tend to become far more capable and achieve more—once they set their minds to a passion/dream and put in the work.

Perhaps surprisingly, some parents of supposed superstar clients of mine (and the kids themselves) have confided that when the children started along their academic journeys back in elementary school, they were not necessarily considered the most outstanding students: the novelist who was not initially the top reader in 1st grade, the chemist who in 4th grade preferred to do his arithmetic slowly, the actress who was shy. Much of their later success is attributed to parents taking the time to understand their children's dreams and being willing to work with them to see those dreams come true.

Since I can't meet with every kid in America to unearth his or her goals and aspirations, I have written this book to clue you in so that you, too, can enjoy the magic of raising kids who are heading somewhere wonderful. You, too, can be the deliverer of opportunities. For any parent who has ever dreamed of playing Mary Poppins, Santa Claus, or any other deliverer of dreams, this book is meant to show you tangibly how to play the role well— to benefit your teenage kids and in the process to put them on track for the college that will help deliver those dreams.

Go ahead. Give your daughter the background to become the medical scientist who will someday find the cure. Help your son become that show-stopping artist. Support your son's effort to lead a record-breaking community service fund-raiser to feed the hungry. You as a parent have the power to help make your child's dreams a reality, and *What High Schools Don't Tell You* shows you how.

PART I

THE SECRET TO COLLEGE ADMISSIONS SUCCESS? YOU HAVE TO HAVE A GAME PLAN

CHAPTER 1

You Can't Exceed Your Goals If You Don't Have Any

Helping Your Child to Identify Her Passions

Forget what other parents may tell you about the value of just "letting kids be kids." Fun, play, and relaxation are important for kids and adults alike, but most would agree that being engaged in an educational activity that they're passionate about *is* fun and also has long-term benefits for getting into college and ultimately enhancing one's career.

I tell parents of children preparing to start high school (and those with kids in their freshman or sophomore years) that working with teenagers can be the most exciting, enjoyable, and rewarding parenting experience—for both them and their kids. You get to play the role of opportunity scout and assistant navigator. Your child still has her entire high school career ahead of her, which means there's time for you to help her explore her personality, skills, talents, likes, and dislikes. Most importantly, early high school is the time to set long-range goals. It's the time when you get to ask your child what he would like to accomplish as a teenager before going off to college, and then to help him plan out a strategy. This chapter will help you and your child to pinpoint some of his own interests and give you both some direction as he embarks on this exciting and intense journey.

SECRET 1 Interacting with your kids, helping them set goals, helping them scout out the best opportunities to develop their talents and passions—and helping them develop a solid strategy for success in the subjects that intrigue them most—will almost *guarantee* college admissions success. All colleges are seeking students who are energetic, self-motivated, talented, accomplished, inquisitive, enthusiastic, and hard working. (Remember those adjectives when it comes time to fill out college applications that ask students to list a few words that describe them!) And parents can play a significant role in cultivating those qualities in their teenage kids by helping their children to aspire.

SECRET 2	**One of the biggest secrets that high school guidance counselors, teachers, and administrators don't**

tell you is that the "game" begins in 8th or 9th grade. Waiting until the end of your child's junior year or beginning of senior year to figure out his goals or college choices is coming late to the competition, and, in today's hypercompetitive environment, simply won't cut it. If your child aspires to attend college with superstar students, he has to establish himself as a superstar well before the 12th grade.

That said, the aim here is not to have you feed or join the current college admissions frenzy, but rather to transcend the frenzy by helping you help your kid become so "over-the-top" that no college will want to turn him away. High schools generally won't tell you how to make your kid *more* competitive for college. Instead, most will tell you and your kid to not even think about college until at least the end of junior year. "Enjoy high school," they advise your children. "Focus on the prom and getting your driver's license." Yet by the end of junior year it becomes significantly harder to groom your child for the top science, math, art, music, dance, language, and even business contests and experiences that make the very top competitors so much more appealing to colleges.

In addition to helping you and your child articulate his passions and dreams, this chapter will help you begin to design an exciting four-year strategy that will help make him irresistible to the country's best colleges. Don't worry if your thirteen-year-old isn't completely sure at this age what he really wants to do with his life in the long term. Have him choose something that intrigues him now, and stick with it for as long as he's *reasonably* passionate about it (reasonably, because every pursuit has its ups and downs). If he drops it in six months, he will have gained six months' valuable experience that will most likely enhance whichever academic passion he chooses to pursue next. (The experience gained from one quality activity should translate to multiple pursuits. A well-taught summer course in any particular subject, for instance, should provide your kid with the study skills, hands-on technique, and focus to contribute to any other field if his interests evolve.)

| SECRET 3 | **To enter the game, you need a game plan.** Creating a game plan for your child will include five |

elements:

1. Identifying an overall vision or dream (discussed in this chapter).
2. Creating a four-summer plan that directly speaks to that vision and that forms the skeleton or shell of the overall strategy for your child (discussed in chapter 2).
3. Developing a four-year, year-round plan that directly relates to that vision (covered in chapter 3).
4. Developing an appealing résumé (also discussed in chapter 3).
5. Planning out six-month (or more frequent) shorter-range goals to help fill in the gaps—the mini-steps to accomplishing the larger long-term goals (also in chapter 3).

If you're coming to this book later than 8th grade, don't fret—opportunities will still exist for your child to pursue in 9th, 10th, even 11th grade to help her win admission into her choice colleges. But the sooner you start, the more time she'll have to avail herself of more opportunities and the more credentials she will be able to build.

Start with a Dream

"My kid doesn't have any motivation," I hear constantly from parents. "I have the laziest kid on earth. If I didn't go into his room to wake him up, he would sleep twenty-four hours a day." Others say, "I can try to motivate my daughter until I'm blue in the face, and she still won't listen to a thing I say."

| SECRET 4 | **The most important secret to motivating a teenager (or anyone, for that matter) is to es-** |

tablish a set of goals and dreams—and a game plan to make those goals reachable. In my experience, we all have an easier time working hard when we know that our work serves some *greater purpose* or cause that interests us and when we know that our work is likely to be appreciated. It's far more gratifying to practice the cello when you know that your musical skills will be enjoyed by an audience, while it's a chore to memorize dates of battles that we don't believe we'll ever use again. When we feel that we are wasting time on mindless busy work or that we're going to be criticized constantly or not appreciated for our work, most of us become apathetic and nearly impossible to motivate. But when we're in touch with our goals, we are better able to see how or if the task will further our aspirations. Seeing that connection and purpose is very motivating.

| SECRET 5 | **At thirteen or fourteen years old, your child's personal goals should include but not consist entirely** |

of college admission. When a child is just entering high school, you don't want her to become fixated on getting into *one* particular college, nor do you want her to believe that college is the end in itself. Her dreams should extend far beyond college, and college should be viewed merely as a stepping-stone to reach a larger goal. No one college (or dozen colleges) holds a monopoly on success.

That said, ideally you should start looking at colleges at the very beginning of high school or end of middle school as a motivator for hard work and general achievement in high school. Seeing a school or schools in person can give a child a concrete vision of something to strive for; the college environment alone can be invigorating. Ignore the folks who tell you that there's no need to look at colleges until the end of junior year, when your kid is getting ready to apply. You want your child revved up early to help her focus her interests, set goals, and gain incentive.

In 8th grade, before grades officially count, or in early 9th grade, visit campuses of some of the most inspiring colleges that accommodate your child's interests as you best perceive them. (Later in this chapter, I will provide exercises to help you and your child define just what her interests are at this stage.) Take your engineering/science-bent daughter, for example, to see MIT, Caltech, Harvey Mudd, Rice, Olin, Cooper Union, Cornell Engineering, Berkeley, or Stanford. Take your premed or pre-vet aspirant to see Washington University, Johns Hopkins, Northwestern, Brown, or Tufts. Bring your artist/musician/filmmaker son to visit Juilliard, Curtis, USC, UCLA, Rhode Island School of Design, Oberlin, NYU Tisch, CalArts, SUNY Purchase, Parsons, Pratt, or Yale. Show your future statesman Harvard's Kennedy School, Georgetown, Princeton's Woodrow Wilson School, Tufts's Fletcher Graduate School, Claremont McKenna, or Chicago. Show your someday–business executive Wharton, NYU Stern, Baruch, Babson,

Michigan, or Duke. The idea is to show your child that these wonderful avenues are open to him if he works hard.

SECRET 6	**Make the initial college trip fun. Be a tourist.**

Sample the campus cafeterias. Take pictures. Buy a T-shirt in the gift shop. Don't make the trip stressful. There's no need to say, "You see? If you work really, really hard, you may have some nice options." Assume that that concept is self-evident based on the experience. At the same time, point out the fact that no one college has a monopoly on education (or success after college)—and if your child does not get into this or that college, many other exciting opportunities also await.

SECRET 7	**Checking out colleges early makes the college visit experience more enjoyable (and less anxiety pro-**

ducing). It is much easier and much more inspiring to make the first exploratory visit during the summer after 8th or 9th grade. Campuses tend to be most attractive at that time of year—Frisbee players and bicycle riders abound, the foliage is in bloom, and the campuses are less crowded and less stressed. People will gladly stop to answer questions or take you on informal walking tours. Also, your child will be less self-conscious and resistant about trekking across campuses with Mom and Dad at a younger age. As he nears college age and becomes a bit more self-conscious (and potentially stressed out about getting in), visits become more difficult for many teenagers. Parents tell horror stories about arriving at a campus during the summer before their child's senior year, when their young scholars are too self-conscious (or intimidated, in some cases) to even step out of the car to look. You'll face a lot less resistance in the summers before 8th and 9th grade.

Many guidance counselors will say that there's no need for your child to start visiting colleges until his junior or senior year. But college information sessions (that are offered along with college tours on most campuses) can be extremely valuable for an early high school student: Most will tell you that they prefer applicants with strong academic interests accompanied by track records that reflect those interests—and the earlier your child embarks on this track, the stronger and more convincing his application will eventually be.

Is One Passion or Track More Attractive to Colleges Than Another?

The first step in creating a track record for your child is to help her identify her academic or artistic passions. What are some of the interests considered "best" or most sought-after by colleges?

SECRET 8	**Colleges most desire students with demonstrated talent in mathematics, science, engineering, hu-**

manities, the arts, journalism, community service, leadership, and business. Depending on the college activities and majors offered, other fields of expertise—including nonacademic fields like community service and sports—might impress the school as well. When helping your child to explore potential interests, think of subjects and activities that are generally accommodated on college campuses. (Find a listing of subjects offered by looking online at each college's Web site—under "Academics" or "Student Life." Presume that if a college offers ancient Greek, for example, that the college will value ancient Greek lessons as an activity. Likewise, if the college has a top football team, it's likely to value applicants who are star football players. I often tell parents, somewhat tongue-in-cheek, to think of college admissions as selfish entities—colleges look to fill their own needs first and the students' needs second. (Note that a college's specific "needs" might change from year to year. A school might need an oboe player this year and more cross-country runners next, or more classics majors one year and civil engineers the next.)

How can you predict in advance what spots they'll be looking to fill?

The truth is, you often can't. Few admissions officers openly reveal this information—which is one of the reasons why, instead of attempting to cater your child's résumé to a particular school's needs, I ultimately advise that you encourage your children to pursue the activities that truly interest them and steer kids who are unsure or flexible toward subjects that aren't "crowded." (Subjects that are less familiar to high school students—anthropology, ancient Greek, bassoon, nuclear engineering, and food science, for example—can increase your child's odds of getting in.)

The Totally Apathetic Teenager

SECRET 9	Identifying an apathetic teen's interests may take a little creative thinking—but the challenge is

worth your energy. Always work with your child's interests. If you try to force interests on your child, she will tire or bore easily, and you'll find that the only means of motivation will be badgering, turning the whole parent-child relationship sour. Many students complain to me that their parents always badger them; many parents complain to me that they hate the role of badgerer. Most kids, I have found, *have* interests; you just need to be willing to recognize them. Your child likes parties? Get him involved in planning parties for organizations that raise money for cancer research or other causes. Your son trades baseball cards? Translate that interest into monitoring stock market statistics. Your daughter watches rock TV day and night? Get her some training in TV production so she could get a studio internship by the time she's a high school senior. Your son is addicted to computer games? Sign him up for a computer gaming summer program where he'll learn to create his own computer games. Utilize your child's natural interests—whatever they may be—and self-motivation and help her discover that there is life and opportunity outside of school.

Is It Wrong to "Create" a Passion?

"Tell your children, 'Do what you love,'" a liberal arts college admissions dean said when I interviewed her at her office in New England. "If you love the triangle, play triangle." Running with your child's passion is not to say that passions can't also be created and nurtured, however. Savvy parents can help expand an interest in the triangle (to use her example) to create interest in additional percussion instruments, for instance, to make the kid's skills more versatile and valuable to bands and ensembles. Use your child's love of gardening to help create a passion for botany. One parent I worked with helped channel her daughter's constant phone conversations (solving problems for friends) toward a fascination with psychology. The girl went on to major in psychology at a top university. Help find new and related opportunities for your child, but be careful not to push unwanted interests on her.

Helping the Kid with No Clear-Cut Passion
Identify His Interests

Some kids may *want* to develop interests, but nothing jumps out at them. These children need a bit more encouragement and guidance to identify their passions. Field trips (accompanied by parents) become extremely important to help these kids get a better sense of what's out there. Destinations should be varied—an airport, a national park, a museum, a concert, a university, a factory, a major corporation, a small claims court, a local newspaper office, an animal shelter, a zoo. Encourage discussion about the kinds of work that people do. In addition to leading field trips, parents have to be very observant, noticing the kinds of activities that the child seems drawn to and good at. Float some overly simplistic statements past your daughter (testing the waters) like "You've always seemed to love reading science fiction—I bet you'd love to be an inventor." Or "I've noticed that you like to rearrange the furniture; I bet you'd make a really creative interior designer." If your kid has unusual interests (e.g., collecting toy soldiers or doodling), be liberal and creative with the way you receive them and in the way you assign potential applications to these interests (e.g., becoming a battle historian or a film animator) as long as you do not find the activity objectionable or somehow in conflict with your family religion or philosophy.

It's not necessary to limit a child to one academic field or art or sport in the 8th and 9th grades. Let her explore three or four interests, with the aim of combining them and narrowing the interests down to one or two by junior year. One student whom I worked with, for example, loved archeology, Latin, Greek drama, and Italy, and applied to (and was offered admission into) several Ivy League colleges as a classics major. Another adored American history, attended summer training in intensive debating, and was active in Model U.N. at school, and was admitted into a college international affairs program.

| SECRET 10 | **Younger students often are happier when they are pursuing multiple interests or activities.** Not only |

does this allow for an easier transition if and when their interests change, but on a day when one area of interest doesn't go so well they have another to pull them up emotionally.

For parents who are just starting to explore long-term goals with their children, I usually recommend one art/music, one sport/game, and one academic/research subject. Ask your child to identify goals in each subject and then incorporate three diverse aspirations into a single sentence. For example, "I want to master the art of portraiture, win an Olympic medal in diving, and gain expertise in stem cell research." Or "I want to publish my poetry, dance well enough to perform with a professional ballet company, and study African history." The aim in getting your child to articulate goals is to get both you and your child *tuned into* his goals.

SECRET 11 | **Long-term goals should always be dazzling and very ambitious.** The more ambitious the goal, the harder the child will want to work in order to reach that goal. Long-term goals should not be dull or too nearsighted: "I want to learn algebra." "I want to learn how to ski." "I want to volunteer in a hospital." Such goals should instead be viewed as stepping-stones to larger goals. While lofty goals potentially may sound intimidating, your job as a parent will be to show your child the route to reach those goals. (This book reveals a wide array of enticing paths in part 2.)

SECRET 12 | **In helping a child to select goals, do not choose a noun label; instead, encourage her to use verbs in a full sentence to describe what she would like to accomplish.** Do not have the kid say, for example, "I want to be <u>a doctor</u>," "I want to be <u>president</u>," or "I want to be <u>a movie star</u>." Such goals, no matter how lofty, may feel too confining to a teenager, who should be at the peak of ambition.

Instead, encourage sentences like "I want <u>to discover a cure</u> for cancer using the ice plants on the Channel Islands." Or "I want <u>to train for an Olympic medal</u> for luge." Or "I want <u>to solve the hunger problem</u> in Somalia." The aim is to encourage your child to express what she aspires to *do,* rather than which label she wants to attain. Aspirations that entail action are far more motivating than job-label aspirations.

To broach the subject with your child, be direct. In the same kind of upbeat tone you would use when you ask, "What would you like for your birthday?" ask, "What would you like to do in this world if you could do anything at all?" Kids generally don't feel threatened by this topic, since it provides an opportunity to dream.

SECRET 13 | **By always being aware of your child's goals, the two of you can work together, as a team, to reach**

those goals. If you have no idea what your child's secret ambitions are, you are bound to eventually be perceived as an impediment rather than a team player, and that's when parent-child relationships fall apart.

Before our first meeting, the mother of a girl I worked with told me that her daughter, whom she was not getting along with, wanted to pursue medicine. When I looked at the girl's extracurricular activities list, I noticed that she was active in high school and regional debate competitions and student government.

"Where is this medical interest?" I asked the girl when I met her. "Nothing in your background even hints at the slightest interest in medicine."

"I just don't have any room in my schedule to add any medicine-related activities," the girl said, somewhat apologetically. "Debate and student government take up all my time."

Clearly, the girl had no interest in medicine. And once the mother and daughter realized this, their relationship was on the mend, and the girl was ultimately accepted as a public policy major at a top university.

SECRET 14	**In order to help further your child's goals, you will need to demonstrate that you will (1) take your**

child's stated goals seriously, and (2) dedicate yourself to bringing the selected goals within your child's reach. The family motto should be "We're all in this together."

Not all children are able to articulate goals easily, even when they know that their parents will be supportive. When I meet with new students in 8th, 9th, or 10th grade, I generally give them a fifty-choice list of sample goals to help them identify their wishes and dreams. I tell them to look through the list to see if anything appeals to them. If nothing does, I encourage them to create and list three of their own original goals instead.

If you find that you are unable to elicit lofty goals from your children, ask them to rank the top three goals from the following list. Look for patterns in their choices. Let them choose more goals if they want to, but don't let them choose fewer than three. Let them create goals if they prefer some goals that are not mentioned, but make sure that their goals are equally ambitious. By striving and pushing for seemingly unreachable goals, they will develop passions and success. (Contrary to what some parents may fear about ambitious goals making a child feel defeated, I have found that lofty goals backed by parental commitment to help deliver the goals create an almost magical bond between parent and child and a much stronger chance of attaining those goals. Everybody likes the person who can help deliver their dreams.)

What Are Your Goals?

Directions: If you could choose any of these goals to accomplish before you complete high school, select your three top choices in priority order.

1. I would like to star on Broadway or in Hollywood.
2. I would like to write a novel.
3. I would like to win the Intel or another national science recognition.
4. I would like to earn my first patent on something I invent.
5. I would like to create my own designer clothing label.
6. I would like to speak at an important political rally.
7. I would like to design an exhibit at a museum or theme park.
8. I would like to have my own comic strip or political cartoon published.
9. I would like to publish an article in a major daily newspaper.
10. I would like to have a musical debut at Carnegie Hall.
11. I would like to choreograph a ballet or compose a symphony.
12. I would like to make a movie and have a public screening.
13. I would like to lead an environmental campaign.
14. I would like to train animals and enter them in a show.
15. I would like to win an Olympic medal in my favorite sport.
16. I would like to see all the countries on another continent.
17. I would like to make a major medical discovery.
18. I would like to rewrite the curriculum for a high school class.
19. I would like to take gourmet cooking classes and write a cookbook.
20. I would like to paint a great work of art and have it exhibited.
21. I would like to run for office in an actual real–world election.
22. I would like to get my pilot's license and fly a plane.
23. I would like to create a puppet theater and book my own tours.
24. I would like to become known as the nation's top math student.
25. I would like to learn farming and become completely self-sufficient.
26. I would like to climb Mount Everest or Mount McKinley.

27.   I would like to build a boat and learn how to sail it.
28.   I would like to volunteer to help build trails in a national park.
29.   I would like to conduct research for NASA.
30.   I would like to become a self-made millionaire by the time I'm twenty.
31.   I would like to immerse myself in a new language and culture.
32.   I would like to sing in an opera or dance in a ballet.
33.   I would like to landscape a great estate or park.
34.   I would like to make a new astronomical discovery.
35.   I would like to create a new method to teach younger children to read.
36.   I would like to do an internship in a restoration or reenactment.
37.   I would like to work with a scientist investigating time travel.
38.   I would like to get EMT certification to help in emergencies.
39.   I would like to swim with dolphins and go snorkeling or diving.
40.   I would like to learn to ski or surf.
41.   I would like to photograph people and have my photos exhibited.
42.   I would like to write an opera or musical and have it performed.
43.   I would like to design a new toy and try to market it nationally.
44.   I would like to go on an archaeological dig.
45.   I would like to start my own band and perform in competitions.
46.   I would like to write poetry and give readings at a coffeehouse.
47.   I would like to host a fund-raiser ball for cancer research.
48.   I would like to arrange an ethnic music and arts celebration.
49.   I would like to become a chess or bridge champion.
50.   I would like to host a news show about high school for local TV.
Other: _____.

Believe it or not, teenagers have accomplished all of the things on this list. Granted, all require enormous family encouragement.

When asked what they would dream of doing if they could do anything at all, many children will turn to their parents to ask what they "should" do—what the right answer is. Yet there is no right answer as such.

| SECRET 15 | **There is no wrong answer to the question of what a child could aspire to do, with the exception of** |

criminal acts, acts that violate family beliefs, or acts that aim to hurt one's self or others. For children who are unable to select a goal or only want to pursue goals of which the parents do not approve, parents might suggest goals that they think might captivate the child. A child who only wants to gamble, for example, might be introduced to investment. A child who spends hours applying makeup might be introduced to theater costuming and makeup lessons or courses in cosmetology and chemistry to develop an original line of cosmetics.

Occasionally I will work with children who simply cannot relate to the idea of choosing goals—and are unable to fill out the list above. In these cases, I present them with the following list of celebrities and ask them if they could be anyone, who would they prefer to be? (I also let them make up conglomerates of people if they prefer that. For example, a child may say, "I want to make movies like Steven Spielberg, but I want to have the political influence of the president of the United States.") The aim is the same—to determine your child's aspirations—but sometimes tangible people are easier to envision than intangible areas of interest.

Who Would You Like to Be?

Directions: If you could be any of the following people—past or present—who would you be?

1. Madonna
2. President of the United States
3. Atticus in *To Kill a Mockingbird*
4. Jon Stewart (comedian)
5. Robert Redford
6. Oprah Winfrey
7. Agent Jack Bauer
8. Editor of *The New York Times*
9. Bill Gates
10. Donald Trump
11. Martin Luther King or Mother Teresa
12. I. M. Pei (architect) or Picasso
13. Olympic athlete
14. Thomas Edison or Albert Einstein
15. Hillary Clinton
16. John Williams (composer)

17. Jane Goodall
18. Steven Spielberg
19. Walt Disney
20. Jonas Salk (polio vaccine inventor)

Add to the list thirty more people who might be of interest to your child. If she suggests two or more people, discuss the qualities about them that she admires most. Talk about how she can strive to become a conglomerate of the people she admires.

Motivating Your Child

Be enthusiastic when your child writes her first story, paints his first picture, attempts her first physics experiment, or writes his first math proof. Stay supportive when she sticks with something she likes, regardless of how much talent you see or don't see, and regardless of whether you find the topic of interest. If your child seems to lack "natural talent" but seems determined to pursue an interest anyway, speak to an expert in the field (perhaps his teacher) to find out how to help him gain the skills to help compensate for the supposed lack of talent. A child whose talent is not immediately recognizable may develop ability with hard work. Embrace the Thomas Edison philosophy: "Genius is one per cent inspiration and ninety-nine per cent perspiration." If your child is unwilling to work hard, address this apathy from a supportive perspective. Perhaps the presumed aspiration isn't something to which he aspires after all.

If you're asked your opinion of an artwork, performance, or experiment, be fast to point out the highlights (and not in a sarcastic or patronizing way)—genuinely attempt to find the virtues (e.g., "I liked the way you incorporated shading in the drawing" or "I'm impressed that you were able to memorize all that choreography"). Let your child be the one to point out deficiencies if any are to be noticed.

Once goals have been selected or created, it's time to put something in writing.

Creating a Time Capsule

| SECRET 16 |

Create a time capsule with your 8th or 9th grader to get a sense of his newly articulated ambitions, and to help him plan a high school strategy.* The capsule should consist of a letter from the child, addressed to the child. The purpose is to make her aware of her own ambitions (and inspire her to achieve them), to define her goals in writing, and to clue the parents in to her mind-set (you'll be better able to deliver her dreams if you know what those dreams are). Once the letter is written, seal it in an envelope and store it somewhere safe (a parent's sock drawer works well); neither you nor your child should open the envelope or read the letter again until his senior year of high school.

The letter should start this way: "Dear [name of child], I am writing this letter to myself in 8th grade. By the time I graduate from high school, I am hoping to be known as the kid who _____. In order to get there, I am hoping to study _____. I am hoping to win _____. I am planning to join _____."

Steer your child away from social ambitions (e.g., "I will be the most popular guy in the school"). It's also important to keep in mind and understand that, throughout the next four years, your child may change his ambitions along the way. The purpose of the capsule is to get your child to aspire and to develop personal expectations, and to think in advance about long-term time utilization and planning—not to commit your kid to any one pursuit. Whether or not your kid ultimately achieves the goal he set out to accomplish, reading the capsule in senior year can be both enlightening and stimulating. Did he find newer, more alluring goals? Did she know her aspirations well back in 8th or 9th grade? Was he successful in reaching the goals he set for himself? Armed with this experience with goal setting, he is ready to set goals in college.

---

*Are you too late if you're coming to this after your child has completed 9th grade? You're never too late; however, the exercise of creating a high school time capsule can be more effective if your child is younger.

Once a Passion Is Identified

Once your child states and embraces an interest (or interests), you can offer support in many ways.

SECRET 17 **Each different field of interest has its own "culture"—familiarize yourself with the culture in your child's field of interest.** Understanding the practices and opportunities within the culture can reinforce your child's interest enormously. For example, if your daughter is interested in mathematics, you'll want to find out if her high school has a math team, whether parents come to meets, if the successful kids get private training, if there's a local varsity team, how the superstars of American mathematics train, and so on. Likewise, if your kid's interest is in furniture design, you'll want to find out if there's a design course offered locally, if internships can be arranged in local furniture design firms, if any design contests exist for students, and how the famous furniture designers got started.

SECRET 18 **Once your child fully embraces an interest, do not just dump materials and resources on him—*share the interest.*** If your kid is interested in astronomy, tune in to what interests him—black holes, dark matter, etc. Sharing is affirming. Welcome each new interest as if a new career were brought into the family. Find out what books exist on the topic and bring some into your home. Research what magazines and journals address the topic and subscribe. Read some to be able to discuss the topic intelligently. Pay attention to the ads in those publications to find out what related events are taking place that might interest your child. Accompany your child to these events and to related sites—conventions, lectures, etc. Seek out internships, summer jobs, and volunteer work that will give your child more experience and credentials in her field of choice. Also, look online for related contests and competitions to demonstrate her new knowledge.

What If Your Kid Wants to Abandon a Goal?

Often a child will decide after 9th grade that a chosen interest no longer appeals to her—that she'd prefer to take less art and more music. It bears repeating that you should be flexible and allow your children to have many changes of goals throughout their first few years of high school. Perhaps, after taking a single art class, your daughter may decide that the school's art department is weak, and she may be right. Or she may be struggling with a difficult art project and worry that she doesn't have the ability. Find out why she wants to abandon a particular goal, but at the same time make her feel free to do so.

If parents are able to help ease their child through a difficult time or project, sometimes she may choose to stay in the course after all. This can often be accomplished by discussing the interest change with a teacher—a valuable member of the child's "team," who may have additional insights into any sudden interest changes. Has the kid legitimately lost interest in chemistry? Or is he really just struggling with one concept? Is the kid really no longer enjoying Spanish? Or are classmates making fun of her accent?

Sometimes, however, the kid legitimately wants out, and parents can be very helpful in drawing up a new plan with the child. Don't lecture your kid about struggling through difficult situations if you're sure that he has genuinely lost interest. Avoid speeches about how much time or money you've invested. Rest assured that if he pursued worthwhile activities— even if the specific field no longer interests him—the money and time were well invested. He will bring this gained knowledge to his next endeavors.

Designing a Plan

Once your child's larger goals have been established, it's time for parents to devise a workable, strategic game plan for the child to follow to success-fully reach those goals. The plan should be designed in consultation with the child and should be coordinated with her school curriculum. It should include summer activities, academic courses, after-school activities, intern-ships, and jobs, and, most importantly, it should provide a viable way for her to build a track record for college applications and other opportunities and a means to showcase her creativity, intelligence, inventiveness, and, ulti-mately, her leadership in her chosen field.

Although it may feel a bit out of order, I recommend that you focus *first* on your child's summer plans, since summers provide a chance for him to pursue some of the nation's best learning opportunities specifically catered to his career goals—opportunities that look stellar on a college application.

During the school year, you're limited to local offerings. In summer, you're not. Look at the grander scale of opportunities available to make your kid stand out nationally and make her irresistible to even the most competitive colleges. (Locating such opportunities is discussed in the next chapter.)

As mentioned earlier, a four-summer plan of stimulating summer activities should act as the skeleton for your child's game plan, later to be filled in by school-year courses, after-school and weekend extracurriculars, internships, and jobs. Think of school as a supplement to summer rather than just thinking of summer as enrichment to school.

CHAPTER 2

Strategic Summers

The Time to Gain the Advantage for College

Summer school. For most of us, the words conjure up images of tedium and punishment. Hot summer days in unair-conditioned classrooms, struggling through dull and difficult material that wasn't mastered the first time around—while other kids are out playing, swimming, and pursuing carefree summer activities at resorts and summer camps.

Now imagine summer courses that include diving to photograph coral reefs off the coast of Belize, dancing in a national arts festival in the mountains, living on an island off the coast of Maine and studying sea star populations, helping to build a day care center in Costa Rica, participating in a nationally recognized computer game design competition, studying anthropology by living in the Navajo Nation, designing one's own fashion label, writing a screenplay to submit to Hollywood film studios. Summers are meant to be thrilling—even for the highest achieving and most academically driven students.

| SECRET 19 | **Summers are the best-kept secret of superstars— the time for your child to stand out from the pack** |

and gain an edge both for college admission and her future career. So many parents ignore the phenomenal opportunities that eight empty months can provide over four years. Also, many just don't know these activities/ opportunities exist. In this chapter, you will learn how to find and participate in some of the country's best opportunities, based on your children's interests. While many kids just hang out for weeks with no structured plans, top achievers—and those who aspire to become top achievers—are busily gaining exposure to new places and ideas that feed their own interests and look great on college applications.

A child should emerge from a summer excited, fired up, and eager for a new school year, having accomplished or surpassed his summer goals and knowing that he is on his way to achieving his dreams. At what other time in life (before retirement!) do you get such blocks of time to explore and pursue whatever it is that inspires you most?

In creating the summer portion of a multiyear strategy, start with your child's top goals and craft an *ideal* plan. If you could design four perfect summers to enhance your child's interests, regardless of geographical distances, financial costs, or other barriers, what programs, family trips, and opportunities would that plan include? Be expansive. Think big. And take advantage of some of the opportunities discussed in this chapter and listed in the appendix. After reading this chapter, you will be equipped to design an ideal four-summer plan to use as the skeleton of your overall game plan.

Creating a Track Record

If you're skeptical about the idea of planning out four summers in advance, pick up any college application. Note that college applications ask each applicant to list and briefly describe activities pursued during the three or four summers leading up to college. The task is much easier when the response has been planned from the get-go with a specific academic, artistic, or athletic direction.

A father of one of my students told me that his son, a senior, was passionate about business and wanted to apply to Wharton. I looked over the boy's résumé.

"Wharton? Business?" I asked. "The résumé shows that he spent every spare moment participating in drama. Each summer, he attended theater camps."

"But he's *really* interested in business," the father insisted, adding that the boy talked about owning a big company someday.

"But he has no track record. Business schools aren't impressed with even the very top students if they don't show any evidence of a passion for business. He isn't even a member of his high school's DECA club,"* I said. "Nothing in his record indicates any interest in business."

"But we were told to let him run with his passion during the summer and not worry about picking up formal credentials."

"And that's just what you did," I responded. "You let him run with his *passion,* which clearly turned out to be drama, not business."

This whole concept seems very difficult for a lot of parents. Colleges care very much about the applicant's track record in the field that the student claims to want to study. Your daughter won't impress an admissions officer at Juilliard by saying that she intends to become a concert violinist in college if she's never played the violin. Nor can your son impress an admissions officer at business school if he has no prior business-related activities. Many people seem to understand how experience is required in music and dance, but somehow they don't always see the connection in other fields. Pharmacy colleges prefer students who have worked in pharmacies. Combined college dental programs are drawn to students who have done internships or paid work for dentists. Even liberal arts colleges prefer students who have strong background in the subjects in which the students claim (on the application) to want to major.

Does every summer activity your child participates in need to be enriching and focused on his goals? In my experience, the students who are most successful in securing a place in their top-choice colleges are the ones who have devoted the vast majority of their summers to activities that reinforce their primary interests. But consider some complexities. Let's say your child's long-term dream is to become a political leader. And he's decided that in order to reach that goal he wants to attend Yale. Your child is also athletic and is sure that if he works at crew during the summer, he'll be so much in demand by crew teams that Yale will want to admit him for his impressive athletic abilities alone. That child would be smart to devote some summer weeks to intensive crew practice rather than taking political science or government studies programs exclusively.

"But whatever happened to old-fashioned summers where children were free of pressure? Shouldn't summers just be devoted to unwinding

*DECA (Delta Epsilon Chi) is an international association of high school and college students studying marketing, management, and entrepreneurship in business, finance, hospitality, and marketing sales and service.

and pure leisure after a busy school year?" some parents ask. "Won't relaxation ultimately produce the most academic success when the child goes back to school?" The very top students in the country whose parents I interviewed for this book *consistently* told me that they deliberately filled their children's summers with the most enriching activities they could find—courses, day trips, vacations, internships, and jobs—and because these activities were inspired by the students' genuine passions, the kids saw them as fun, not work. Summer, these parents agreed, is one of the only times children can develop an edge over the competition while exploring what interests them.

| SECRET 20 | **Contrary to pop psychology, down time need not be unstructured to be relaxing and to help a stu-** |

dent decompress. Many parents wrongly equate decompressing with sitting idly with no planned activities. But sometimes the structure of either an organized program or scheduled plan of activities can be far more relaxing and fulfilling than whiling away time or simply hanging out. For a child who is seriously interested in sculpture, for example, summer could include weeks attending multiple studio art programs, some with small groups, others in large classrooms, arranging exhibits at a local bank or library, plus informal museum trips. There's no reason to assume that hanging out by the pool—and only occasionally devoting time to sculpting—is the most productive or relaxing way for your young artist to spend an entire summer.

| SECRET 21 | **Regardless of how appealing unstructured summers may sound, summers without an overall plan** |

or goal tend to be frustrating for both the child and the parents. While other teenagers are eagerly gaining an edge in academics, the arts, or even work experience or sports training, many children without plans start to feel like they're in a summertime rut—unfocused, unproductive, and less able to compete on the debate team or math team, in play auditions, or to try for first seat in the orchestra when school starts up again. Not only is the idle kid missing out on gaining an advantage over the competition, but he is actually falling behind. And if that falling-behind kid did not like school in the spring, he is even less likely to like school when it reopens at the end of an unproductive summer, when he has nothing to show for his summer and no new place to excel. Not all parents get this.

The father of one of my students chided his ambitious son for wanting to register for back-to-back summer programs. "For dessert, you only get chocolate cake or apple pie. You can't have both." The man was trying to draw an analogy between pastry and summer activities. He wanted his son to pick just one, fearing that otherwise the boy would become spoiled. But the boy, living in a very competitive community, was *excited* to attend three programs to help maximize his summer learning. He wanted to take a college course in Native American archaeology for four weeks, volunteer for a one-week dig at a nearby archeological site, and also work as a paid intern in a nearby natural history museum. How many enrichment activities should a parent allow a child to cram into a single summer? As many as your child is willing to participate in.

| SECRET 22 | **Cram your child's summers with *multiple* enriching activities and opportunities, as long as the** |

child is eager to pursue them, the programs have something to offer, and the combination of programs is affordable. Speak to your child about a realistic budget for your family, and present her with enough choices (within your budget) to maximize her summer months. Not all activities cost money. By high school, many internships even *pay* money and are far more prestigious (and more helpful for college admissions) than expensive teen tours, sleepaway camps, and other costly high school programs. And some very competitive programs are free.

Down Time

"Should students have no down time at all?" some parents ask.

Down time is necessary, but it should not make up the bulk of your child's summer. It probably will exist between programs or activities, just before school starts up again, and if the family takes a vacation together. In addition, busy families also often view summer as catch-up time to take care of medical checkups, buy school supplies for the fall, sleep in (without being scolded for late-night habits), or get together with friends. This is all fine, of course. But don't let down time monopolize your child's summer.

Summer Jobs and Internships

Goal-related jobs and internships sometimes provide the most valuable and exciting experiences for students—lab work for scientists, studio work for artists, tutoring for potential teachers, environmental work for future natural resource managers—and help them gain credentials valued by colleges and future employers. Most of these are arranged on an individual basis by labs, studios, tutoring centers, parks, universities, and businesses. Specifics regarding how to go about making these arrangements is discussed according to interest area in part 2.

| SECRET 23 | **If your child plans to take a job for the summer, try to help him secure a job that is relevant in some** |

way to his ultimate goals. If your child plans a future in business or in fashion, for example, working in a local retail store might make a valuable experience. But if your child plans to become a physicist, working on original research in a physics laboratory would be more valuable. If your child aspires to work as a teacher or recreation director, a job as a camp counselor would provide valuable training. But don't send the kid who is interested in business or physics to be a CIT—no matter how big of an honor the camp tells you it will be to become a CIT. Having to work or wanting to make money is not a good enough excuse for wasting valuable summer time on tasks that do not enhance or contribute in any way to your child's long-term goals. Help your child find something that not only pays but also brings him one step closer to achieving his dreams.

"Shouldn't a child experiment with different kinds of jobs during the summers of high school?" parents ask. Yes, but only *within* fields that interest them. A student who wants to pursue a career in science, for example, might spend one summer conducting research in a government lab, another at a university, and another in a science-related corporation. A student interested in law and government might spend one summer working on a political campaign, another in a government agency, and a third summer in a law office.

Scouting Out Summer Activities

| SECRET 24 | **Before you settle on summer plans with your child, have a discussion with him about which skills he** |

hopes to pick up that summer. Be specific to help him maximize his time. Even if he is planning to attend a traditional summer camp (during the summer before 8th grade, let's say), specify the skills that he might strive to acquire: learning how to water ski, canoe, rope climb, rock climb, pass a

Red Cross swim test, and so on. You want your child to learn the overall message that time is valuable and should be utilized in such a way as to empower him with new skills and abilities. All summer plans should be designed with the acquisition of new skills and experiences in mind. You and your child should together decide which skills she wants to learn and then design a summer plan around those skills and lessons.

Summer Camps

"My granddaughter attends the most prestigious camp," the grandmother of a client of mine boasted, as she proudly recited the camp's name.

"What makes it prestigious?" I asked.

"It's very old. Established. It has a top name."

"What will your granddaughter do there?"

"Oh, it's not what she *does* there. It's the social connections that she'll make. The children from that camp become the leaders of everything."

If that was once true, it is rarely the case nowadays. Boating, swimming, hiking, and arts and crafts do not necessarily produce leaders. If you're convinced that your child must go to sleepaway camp to learn leadership or to gain valuable connections or social skills, ask the camp which leaders they have trained before paying them money. And ask the camp which leadership skills they teach.

SECRET 25 Colleges don't particularly value attendance at one camp over another on a student's record, and few summer camps impress them, unless your child manages to get into one of the academic or athletic Olympiad training camps, camps that specialize in a single sought-after sport or a handful of extremely competitive academic programs: **RSI, TASP, Ojai, Ross, Socorro, Clay.** (These are discussed in more depth in chapters 5 to 9.) The notion of "connecting" at camp was popular in the 1930s, '40s, '50s, and '60s (in many cases, connecting meant finding a suitable spouse), and camps still may play a role in bringing children together religiously or ethnically. For parents who want their children to focus their summers on cultural heritage, a traditional camp may indeed be beneficial, provided that the program includes more than just "hanging" together. Speak to the camp directors and ask if the child will learn rites, traditions, folk music, and folk arts and sample traditional foods. If you want this kind of enrichment for your child, do not expect these programs to impress colleges—unless you're planning to send your child to a religious or ethnic school or if the camp represents the gathering of an underrepresented minority.

Organized Teen Programs and Teen Tours

One of my high school senior students asked me if she should focus her college application essay on the four-week America teen tour she had just taken.

"What new skills or knowledge did you gain from the trip?" I asked her.

"Well," she said, "we got to see all of America, and I think the colleges will be impressed by that."

"What was the most interesting thing you saw, and how did it influence you?" I asked, trying to assess the essay's potential.

"Actually, my friends and I stayed at the hotel most of the time. I wasn't really curious to see what they were showing us. And we were having fun at the hotel. The kids were really great."

This is every parent's nightmare—or, if it's not, it should be. It's safe to say that *no* college would be impressed with an essay based on a trip in which she didn't see anything.

| SECRET 26 | **Very few teen tours or summer teen programs give your child the tangible edge of experience** |

that she should be seeking to gain during the summer. Many programs view their job as one of entertaining or babysitting a bunch of otherwise bored teenagers—a catch-all place to send directionless kids who are too young to find a job or whose parents have money to burn. Be very, very wary of these programs. Do not judge the tour by how many sights the tour bus is scheduled to see. In some tours (such as the one described above), the young travelers see nothing, despite an elaborate itinerary. Instead, try to determine how your child will experience each sight—will it be passive exposure (sitting on a bus being lectured to about the cultural significance) or hands-on learning (participating in a dig, climb, or expedition or doing community service)? Passive tours will give your child nothing to write about when it comes time for college essays, but more importantly, they lead to the least growth. Note that even some programs that claim to be active are only active for a day or two of the long-term experience—a one-day hike, a one-day community service, and one day of rafting, for example. Find out in advance what specific skills your child will gain from the program or tour.

| SECRET 27 | **In seeking summer programs, never assume that the most costly are the best or even the most** |

prestigious. In fact, quite the opposite is often true, particularly as the child reaches the junior and senior years of high school. The most prestigious opportunities are often free summer internships, free academic programs, or volunteer jobs in laboratories, companies, or studios. And in many cases, students are paid for their participation, rather than vice versa.

Don't be jealous of the parent who sends her kid on a fancy, exotic, high-priced teen tour or teen course program. As discussed above, that's not what impresses colleges. Colleges want to know what applicants actually *did* over the four summers leading up to the senior year of high school— not where they went. In the new age of meritocracy, the kid who helped hurricane victims for three weeks is much more impressive than the kid who took a bus tour of France. The kid who stayed home and wrote a complete novel is much more impressive than the kid who spent the summer at a trendy resort with his or her family. The kid who worked in a local laboratory and made an original discovery is far more desired than the kid who went to the most prestigious sleepaway camp with her friends, even if previous attendees include famous people.

Talent Searches

| SECRET 28 | **Four major universities offer talent searches and talent-search summer programs that remain among** |

the best-kept American secrets, and parents often learn about them only after it's too late. These programs identify gifted learners and provide a valuable college-recognized stamp of giftedness for participants. In addition, these talent searches sponsor three-week summer talent search camps to qualifying rising 8th, 9th, and 10th graders. The programs include the Johns Hopkins Center for Talented Youth (CTY), Duke's Talent Identification Program (TIP), Northwestern's Center for Talent Development (CTD), and University of Denver's Rocky Mountain Talent Search. In addition to these four, Stanford also offers an Education Program for Gifted Youth (EPGY) that includes residential summer institutes (ages thirteen to seventeen), a residential middle school program (ages eleven to fourteen), and e-learning (online computer) courses (ages five to eighteen). Participation in any of the five programs mentioned represents an impressive starting credential for most of the country's top colleges.*

To qualify for the major talent searches, participants take the SAT or ACT exam as far back as 7th grade. (Young CTY and other programs for grades 2 through 6 are now offered as well at campuses of prep schools and colleges, mostly on the East Coast and West Coast. They require different entrance exams—the SCATs—and 5th and 6th graders may opt to also take the Spatial Test Battery to support their application. But participants in these younger programs are not automatically grandfathered into CTY or the other talent searches. To gain admission into regular CTY, they must retest in 7th grade to qualify.) College admissions officers say they look for that 7th grade quali-fying credential when the student applies for undergraduate admission; ac-ceptance into these talent search programs indicates that the student was academically focused, "on track," and a mature student from a young age.

Each year, about 120,000 7th and 8th graders nationally take the quali-fying SAT. Yet, somehow, few "outsiders" seem to know about the pro-gram. For the Johns Hopkins CTY and CAA (Center for Academic Advancement, a slightly less competitive version of CTY, with slightly lower SAT qualifying scores) alone, about 44,000 take the qualifying exam (choice of SAT or ACT). Of those, only about 26 percent qualify for CTY, and about 71 percent qualify for CAA. These programs are known for their rigor and for the camaraderie of the serious students that they attract. And they play a significant role for bright kids in that middle age group—not old enough for jobs and internships, and too intellectually sophisticated for most traditional summer camps. These summer programs include challeng-ing course work (occupying the mornings) and an array of social and leisure activities (afternoons and evenings).

| SECRET 29 | The talent searches act as the earliest stamps of achievement you can help your child attain in |

---

*Another national talent search worth mentioning, although it's extremely small and se-lective, is the Davidson THINK Summer Institute. This three-week program at the Univer-sity of Nevada, Reno, only accommodates up to sixty students twelve to fifteen years old, so don't expect to hear it talked up at school (or anywhere else). For more information about the program, visit www.davidsonacademy.unr.edu.

middle school and early high school, opening doors to a lot of other opportunities. When your child applies to research programs, contests, and other academic opportunities for rising 11th and 12th graders later on, many applications and interviewers specifically ask if your child ever participated in a talent search. Just taking the test and qualifying means participating in the search. Many of the nation's superstar students attend the talent search summer programs, particularly in the summers before 8th and 9th grades. That's why you need to know this information *before* your child hits the later years of high school.

Schools are hesitant to inform parents about these talent search summer programs for several reasons. Many public schools, as a policy, do not tell parents about privately run programs, not out of negligence, but more out of refusal to help promote programs that they perceive to be expensive, elitist, or targeted for "talented" youth. Public schools don't want to be responsible for making parents feel obligated to pay for expensive private programs, even though many such programs offer significant scholarships to those who qualify financially. Also, public schools don't want to be held accountable if your child doesn't like one of the talent search programs (they don't want to be blamed for recommending it) or doesn't get accepted into these programs. Another rationale is that many public schools believe that they should not promote one private program over another. Instead, many schools—both public and private—want to promote the image that they can offer everything a child needs academically—no need to go elsewhere. No need for private after-school lessons. No need for tutoring. No need for fancy summer programs. Their idea is that a child who attends school daily, does her homework daily, and participates in class gets all the education she needs.

As a result, many public and private schools adopt a policy of not informing parents about out-of-school opportunities—or even deliberately keeping parents in the dark—unless a parent directly asks a guidance officer, advisor, or administrator about a specific program. This causes fewer political hassles, but it's not necessarily best for motivated kids.

So, where do you find out about opportunities? Don't count on other parents whose children may be in competition with yours. Parents are often the last ones to want to share information—especially if they've devoted significant time to scouting out information for their own children. In most cases, caring parents are left to scout out their own opportunities for their children—or to read this book!

SECRET 30   Whether or not you or your child is interested in the courses or programs offered by any of the talent searches, have your child take the SAT in 7th grade. If nothing else, taking the SAT this early provides good practice. And good results will give your child one more credential to help him get future opportunities. While it would be ideal for a 7th grader to score 800 on either section of the SAT (and it's been done, although it's rare), a best-kept secret is that many of the talent searches are only looking for a 7th grader to get 520 verbal or 530 math in order to qualify, or even 410 verbal or 430 math to qualify for a less competitive version of the program. The Johns Hopkins Talent Search offers summer classes for both levels through its Center for Talented Youth (CTY) and Center for Academic Advancement (CAA) respectively.

SECRET 31   Students who qualify for any one of the four major talent searches are likely to be eligible for the other three programs as well, though they may not be notified of this. The minimum qualifying scores are very similar—but not identical—for Hopkins, Duke, Northwestern, and Denver. Parents willing to send their children to other regions of the United States should examine the offerings of the other programs to see if anything offered elsewhere appeals more. The summer after 7th grade, your child can attend one program for three weeks and the same or a different program for the next three weeks.

SECRET 32   Have your child do formal test preparation and practice for the SATs in 7th grade. In short: The highest American academic pedigree starts with students scoring well on the SATs in 7th grade. If your child doesn't, there are other ways to get on track. But by then you're already backpedaling.

Nobody else will tell you that many 7th graders are tutored for the SATs. Not the programs that invite high scorers or honor them. Not your child's school. Not other parents. But there is no shame in enrolling your 7th grader in a prep course—regardless of how pushy the neighbors may think you are for doing so. Both you and your child will be glad you did.

SECRET 33   Try to find an SAT prep course specifically targeted for your 7th grader's age group. Parents can be extremely helpful in locating suitable tutoring for their 7th graders and encouraging their children to practice at this age for the SATs. While it might take a bit of research to locate a prep course targeted specifically toward middle schoolers, they do exist.

Is your daughter doomed to a life of failure if she doesn't make the cutoff? Of course not. Depending on her aspirations, she can be extremely successful even if she doesn't sit for the test or if she doesn't do well. She could become a successful doctor, lawyer, or business executive or president of the United States. However, many of the most sought-after internships and college program applications ask if your kid qualified for a talent search program. Make it easier on yourself and your child by arranging for her to undergo test preparation in 7th grade, whether through a formal course or self-structured home study.

For students who miss the opportunity in 7th grade or who take the test and don't qualify, the talent searches generally offer means of retesting for 8th and 9th graders, but by then the students are expected to achieve somewhat higher scores in order to qualify. If you think your child may be able to do it and he hasn't qualified in 7th grade, have him retake the test. Note that the College Board (which administers the exams) does not list the scores received prior to high school on a child's ultimate college-bound SAT transcript years later.

Be aware that encouraging your child to retake the exam may be perceived by some to be pressuring your "underachiever." If your child doesn't do well the first time around, most who know will respond by saying, "It won't really affect your child's future. I would not bother retesting." Many parents follow that advice, worrying that as bad as not making the mark was the first time, failure to reach the minimum score the second time is even worse. In my opinion, however, if you think your child stands a chance of earning a qualifying score, you should have him take the test again.

Talent searches (and their related summer programs) aren't the only reasons to take the SAT in 7th grade, as the following story illustrates:

A girl's score of 690 on the math part of the December SAT I was certainly high enough to guarantee her acceptance into the Johns Hopkins CTY program in 7th grade. But at the next administration of the exam in January (and the last qualifying exam for the year), another parent spotted the girl there once again for the test.

"Why is your daughter retaking it?" the parent asked the girl's mother.

"Just for practice," the mother responded casually.

Turned out, the 690 scorer's mother knew that if her daughter could just jump up another 10 points to reach a score of 700, the girl would qualify for the Students with Exceptional Talent (SET) program, which could open up additional doors. But this mother did not want other local parents to know, lest their children might try to qualify for the highly competitive and prestigious program.

SECRET 34 **For the highest qualifiers, those who score above a 700 on the math or verbal portion of the SAT I, Students with Exceptional Talent (SET) offers free academic guidance throughout middle and high school, and another even more impressive stamp of achievement.** Within top academic circles, it's very prestigious to be identified as an "SET student" and to have demonstrated your academic capabilities at an early age. If your kid scores a 650 or 670 or even a 690 on the December SAT I in 7th grade, however, don't expect anyone to tell you that he should retake the test to try for a 700 in January. The 600s score will look impressive to most local high school officials; your child may be congratulated. But you won't be told a word about SET. Many school officials don't know about it, and many others don't think it's their business to tell the parent of a child who has already scored a 680, let's say, that there is more to strive for.

SECRET 35 **Although the talent searches let you choose between having your child take the SAT I in December or January, have your child take it in December, so that if his score falls just below the talent search or SET numbers, he will get a second chance.** Lots of well-intending parents wait until January to have their child first tested. The advantage is that the child gets an extra month, plus school vacation, to prepare for the test. But if he scores poorly on the December exam and well on the January exam, only the highest score will count anyway. You have nothing to lose by encouraging your child to take the test both times.

Where Talent Searches Fit In with the Big Picture

I should add a disclaimer that the talent search summer courses do not necessarily appeal to every child who is accepted into them. Depending upon your child's long-range goals, many other excellent programs exist that may appeal more.

SECRET 36 Talent searches should be viewed as launching points for middle school and early high school students and not ends in themselves. They are not enough to guarantee that a child will get into a top college, even when combined with top grades and top SATs later in high school. They are just one added credential. Many parents mistakenly think that once their child has attended a talent search program, she no longer needs to apply herself during the remaining summers in order to get into top colleges later on. This is a common misconception of parents whose children are the only ones from their middle school to qualify. Note there are, in fact, middle schools where twenty or thirty children qualify each year.

SECRET 37 Colleges want to see continuity. Students are generally finished with the talent search course programs by 10th grade and are then expected to use the background they obtained to go on to demonstrate continued achievements and actually *produce* something if they want to impress the most competitive colleges. They should conduct original research, for example, or write publishable stories, spend summers working at orphanages abroad, have paintings exhibited, sponsor an innovative fund-raiser.

Life After the Talent Search

SECRET 38 The summers before 11th and 12th grades should, ideally, be devoted to project-oriented endeavors such as composing a sonata, conducting science research, writing a screenplay, or creating a sports tournament fund-raiser, rather than classroom-based talent programs. An ideal four-year summer plan (based on ten weeks' annual summer vacation, starting with the summer before 9th grade) might consist of the following:

Summer 1 (pre-9th grade): Two talent search three-week courses (no credit; total six weeks), two-week family vacation, and two weeks of down time

Summer 2 (pre-10th grade): College course (credit) six weeks, two weeks of starting a science,

	art, community service, athletic, business, or humanities project, and two-week family vacation
Summer 3 (pre–11th grade):	Eight-week project and two-week family vacation
Summer 4 (pre–12th grade):	Eight-week project and two-week family vacation

The ideal four-summer plan should aim for the first summer to include no-credit courses; the second summer, college credit courses; the third summer, studio or laboratory experience; and the fourth summer, completed studio or laboratory projects. To maximize this type of program, a rising 9th grader should no longer be going to sleepaway camp unless that camp teaches specific skills that the student is hoping to gain as part of or her long-range goal (computer camp, math camp, etc.) or if she is considering an eventual major in recreation management, a serious major offered at a number of excellent colleges, including SUNY Cortland, Indiana University, University of Maine (Machias), University of Vermont, Northern Arizona University, North Dakota State, University of Pittsburgh (Bradford), Southeastern University, Carroll College, and Ithaca.

The projects pursued in 11th and 12th grades should be active (not passive) endeavors. Passive projects include taking a tour of an impoverished area, handing out leaflets for a cause, singing in a chorus, sending out mailings, babysitting, making phone calls as part of a phone pool, etc. Passive projects, no matter how noble the cause, or how much time invested, are not impressive to top colleges, in that they merely entail being another easily replaceable body in a long line. More impressive are active projects that demonstrate original, creative, independent thinking or leadership: designing a new fashion and creating a prototype, creating a sales promotion for a store, creating an innovative computer game, or producing a short animated movie.

Summer Courses

In addition to courses offered by talent searches, many excellent summer courses are offered by universities and other enrichment programs. When exploring these opportunities, parents should carefully compare the options.

| SECRET 39 | **If your child pursues summer coursework, don't be afraid to have him be the "least qualified" kid at** |

the program. As a rule, it's better to be the youngest child with the least background than to be the know-it-all oldest, who may be attending to show off or build confidence. If your child feels that she must always be the smartest to be comfortable, she will never use the summer to adequately challenge herself. Even the most exciting summers should not be spent in the comfort zone. Nor should they serve merely as reinforcement or confidence builders for knowledge already attained. Summers are for exploration and advancement.

If your child has mastered all the information that a particular program has to offer—or all the information that he needs for his intended long-range goals—don't send him back to the program the next summer. Even though he knows his way around. Even though he's offered a CIT position. Move on. The next summer should pose a new adventure for him. Let him be the least qualified at the next program.

| SECRET 40 | **Avoid enrolling your child in dull courses that she could just as well take during the school year.** |

Summer is when she should be encouraged to explore beyond the cookie-cutter student program. A well-arranged summer should enhance school-work in the fall rather than be redundant.

| SECRET 41 | **Not all summer programs on college campuses are affiliated with the universities that house them, and** |

they may not be as rigorous. The program directors themselves won't tell you this—they'd rather you assume that they *are* affiliated. Just because a program meets on a college or prep school campus or bears the name of the prestigious school, it does not mean that the program is *part* of the university or prep school. The main indicators of whether the program is part of the school are (1) if high school/college credit is offered and (2) if the school's highly reputed faculty members are teaching the courses (or if outsiders are brought in). *These indicators are not universal, however. Sometimes more qualified experts may be brought in for special summer programs that require expertise.* To locate some of the programs and courses that impress admissions officers most, see chapters 5 to 12, each of which focuses on a different grouping of interests.

When programs are not affiliated with the school whose campus they're using, the level or commitment of fellow students may be less competitive and less stimulating. If your child is seeking an authentic experience attending *that* school with *those* students, make sure that the program you select provides *that* experience. Ask yourself: What are the qualifications for summer entry? How serious are the other students likely to be?

SECRET 42	**One tip-off to the rigor of a program can be the course titles.**

Less rigorous programs often try to hard-sell teenagers with cutesy (supposedly nonthreatening) names like Figaro! Figaro! instead of calling the course Opera, or Skin and Bones instead of Anatomy.

SECRET 43	**By the time a high school student reaches senior year, she should be ready for actual college-level**

courses in her field of academic passion—rather than college-simulating courses. The most competitive colleges are not impressed with the high-priced teach-to-the-lowest-common-denominator, uncredited courses, which many admissions officers equate with sleepaway camp or entertainment rather than realistic explorations in academia. Even if the program claims to be for talented students. Far more impressive are for-credit college courses, academic Olympiad training courses, studio courses that result in quality portfolios, and research courses that result in original research projects.

SECRET 44	**Raw talent is no longer enough in these competitive times—colleges want to know what the child**

has *done* with the raw talent. What has the student achieved or accomplished? Has he *produced* anything? A journal research paper? A movie? A sculpture? A collection of poems? A successful fund-raiser? The theory is that if she has *done* something while still in high school, she is more likely to continue to *do* things in college—and beyond. Colleges want movers and shakers—forward-thinking young leaders with imagination and energy—not kids who only *dream* of becoming movers and shakers.

Should this be cause for angina? No. Parents who have 8th, 9th, or even 10th graders have two to four years to create *producers*. This should be viewed as an exciting challenge rather than a threat. (Specific guidance for programs that will help your kids embark on these projects can be found in the appendix.)

Do College Summer Programs Guarantee an "In" to the Colleges Where They're Held?

A girl who spent two summers conducting research at an Ivy League college asked her research mentor to write her a recommendation for admission into that school. The mentor agreed and even showed the girl the glowing recommendation. Yet the girl, who had top standardized test scores and A-plus grades, was not admitted.

SECRET 45	**Contrary to popular expectation, college summer programs are not back doors into the most com-**

petitive colleges. Colleges generally tell you this up front. For example, the following statement appears on Georgetown's summer program Web site: "Admissions into the International Relations Program does not ensure acceptance into the undergraduate schools of Georgetown." And Brown's summer program site states that "The Pre-College summer program attendance does not affect admission as a degree candidate to Brown University." Penn's Web site says that "Candidates should note that participation in the LEAD Program at Wharton does not guarantee admission into Penn."

Could they be any clearer?

Why didn't they take the girl who did research on their campus? The rationale was that they thought it would be better for her to vary her experience on additional campuses. Many colleges would agree. (For the same diversity of experience rationale, many universities or college departments don't accept their own top undergraduate alumni for graduate work. One of the most prominent examples of this was the Nobel Prize–winning physicist Richard Feynman, who was denied admission to MIT's graduate physics program after completing his bachelor's degree there. He ended up at Princeton instead.) The message here is: Encourage your child to attend multiple programs and gain multiple experiences during the four summers leading up to college. Don't be fooled into thinking that if your child spends three summers at Harvard or Yale, he will be more desirable to Harvard or Yale. It's better to have him sweep up every credential out there in his field than to profess loyalty to any one campus or program while in high school.

Some students foolishly write in their college application that they want to attend this college or that because they "know their way around" after having spent so many summers there, or that they have become "very comfortable with the campus." This type of familiarity doesn't impress anyone.

Still, many parents think that if their kid spends a summer at a most-competitive college, that college will see that their kid fits in and pays her tuition on time, and that this will make the college want to grab the kid. It bears repeating: Investing in college summer programs—even if you do A work at the college—is no guarantee of getting in. While some of the smaller, remote colleges may look with favor at students who have spent the summer on their campuses, particularly if these students are pursuing some of the least popular majors that a particular college offers—let's say, entomology (the study of insects)—the most-competitive colleges tend only to be impressed with the most qualified candidates, regardless of whether they've ever set foot on campus.

Summers Are Not the Time for Remediation

| SECRET 46 |

If you stay on top of your child's school-year course situation, you should know sooner rather than later if he needs tutoring. If this is the case, get him tutoring *during the school year*—there should be no need for him to have to repeat a course during the summer. Few kids learn to enjoy the repeated subject the second time around. If anything, their resentment for the subject grows, particularly if it makes them cancel their other, more interest-driven, summer plans. The backpedaling summer tends to offer little fulfillment.

That said, if your child somehow is stuck retaking a course over the summer, try to make the experience as pleasant as possible. Do not make her feel that she should be punished for it—even if summer school has caused the rest of the family to cancel some much-awaited vacation. She wants summer school even less than you do. She knows that the rest of the family is disappointed. Try to help her see that the subject matter is interesting despite this major setback. If you're not convinced that the subject is interesting, try to rediscover it with her to seek out what is interesting about the subject. Study with your child. Hire a tutor if tutoring is necessary. Make sure she aces the course this time. If you're offered a choice of sites to retake the course, choose the most attractive or most exotic to give her a break from regular school. Avoid letting her take the course with the same teacher who failed to teach her the first go-round. (Repeating a course with the same teacher, aside from being nonproductive, also tends to be humiliating and embarrassing.) And if you feel that your child is really trying her best, remind her that it's the teacher who failed her rather than the other way around.

Finally, make sure that some enjoyment and some academic, artistic, or athletic advancement is also built into your child's summer schedule. Don't make remediation the sole "advancing" activity of the summer. Balancing it with stimulating, enriching activities is important vis-à-vis boosting her confidence for the coming year (as opposed to having her enter the year feeling like a failure or that she's served a term of punishment).

Spending the Summer with Friends

A mother talked of how her son, Justin, was looking to find a stimulating summer program in aeronautics. She found some exciting programs for him that included flight lessons for high school students, but Justin argued, "I don't want to go alone. I want to spend the summer with a friend."

His friend Brett was going to an eight-week intensive computer course, but programming didn't interest Justin. His friend Brandon was going to baseball camp, but Justin was not nearly as good at baseball as Brandon and would not qualify. His friend Mike was going on a camping and cycling trip in Cape Cod, but Justin did not want to spend four weeks living outdoors. He tried, unsuccessfully, to convince his friends to study aeronautics with him at one of the programs his mother had recommended, because he dreamed of learning how to fly an airplane—but ended up going with Mike on the cycling trip, complaining all the way.

At the end of the program, Mike wanted nothing to do with Justin the complainer, and Justin had gained no appreciation of Cape Cod or camping. The moral here is that every child tends to have different interests that must be respected. And being with friends does not constitute an interest.

SECRET 47 **Children who insist on hanging out only with already-known friends during the summer often miss out on wonderful opportunities that would help them reach their own goals.** A child like Justin arrives home from the summer and, most likely, hears about other kids who spent the summer taking the aeronautics course he wished he had taken. And perhaps by next year, he is too old for the program or unable to participate in it for other reasons. Parents can learn a lesson from

Justin. Encourage your own kids to pursue the opportunities that most interest them rather than following other kids' interests, and to seize the best opportunities while they exist.

Assure your child that there will be time beyond the program to spend with his home friends, and that he will likely also make new friends with similar interests at the program. Summer provides a wonderful opportunity for teenagers to branch out and meet people from other schools and other parts of the country.

Sample Summer Plans

If you're still convinced that children need two months of unscheduled, unstructured down time, compare four high school summers of hanging with friends to the following four-summer academic plans.

Scouting Out Specific Summer Opportunities for Your Child

In the appendix, which begins on page 259, you will find forty detailed sample plans for students with the following wide range of interests: aeronautics and aerospace, anthropology, archaeology, architecture, art (drawing and painting), art history, business entrepreneurship, business finance and investment, choreography and dance, codes and encryption, debate, drama, energy, engineering, fashion design, forensic science, game programming, genetics, government, industrial design, international relations, journalism, landscape design, law, literature, marine biology and ocean science, math Olympics training, medicine, meteorology, mythology and folktales, neuroscience, paleontology, philosophy, poetry, psychology, religion (comparative), robotics, rock and roll, science fiction, and screenplay writing.

While the plans in the appendix obviously are not the only topics that interest students, the ideal four-summer plans provided are meant to help spark parents' thinking about creative ways to help their children plan out summers. Courses, research programs, academic Olympiad training, conservation internships, archaeological digs, art studio experiences, debate boot camps, science expeditions, and business simulation programs are all among the rich array of opportunities listed in the appendix.

The following is a sample four-summer plan for a child whose passion is computer games. Ask yourself which child you would accept into your college if you were on an admissions committee: the child who spent four summers playing computer games or the kid who actively designed computer games?

The purpose of these sample plans is to get you started in brainstorming (and researching) the possibilities that exist for your own children, and to give you an idea of how constructive a summer can be. This plan assumes an unlimited budget, so obviously you'll want to use the sample plan merely as an ideal. The plan only mentions a sampling of opportunities. There may be hundreds more programs for each of these interest areas—some equally as good or even better—that are not listed here, since the point is not to be exhaustive but inspirational. Some of the courses and programs listed may have prerequisites or significant application requirements. Parents should agree to be responsible for helping to see to it that their children prepare those prerequisites *and* for helping with all applications.

While the following summer courses and programs were offered at the time of publication, all may be subject to change annually as new courses are introduced and previous opportunities are sometimes discontinued. Also, depending upon scheduling, each year some programs may overlap others and make attending both prohibitive. The quality of programs may change, and cannot be guaranteed. And for readers' convenience, all four-year summer plans are listed alphabetically—more fully, with more options—in the appendix.

Computer Game Design

Summer 1 (pre–9th grade):   Penn State Introduction to 2-D Game Design, Animation, and Web Development

Summer 2 (pre–10th grade):   Case Western CTD Equinox, Introduction to Computer Game Design

Summer 3 (pre–11th grade):   UCLA Design/Media Arts Summer Institute, Game Design

Summer 4 (pre–12th grade):   Carnegie Mellon, National High School Game Academy

With this four-summer program, in contrast to children who boast, "I beat that game," your child will be able to claim, "Yes, but I *created* this game." A student who pursues this rigorous computer game design four-year plan should graduate from high school with authorship of multiple games—which will be very impressive to colleges.

To illustrate a very different four-summer plan, below is an ideal plan for a student who is interested in marine biology and oceanography and who would especially enjoy spending four summers outdoors. Compare this program to four summers of tanning at the beach or lifeguarding at the community pool.

Marine Biology and Ocean Science

Summer 1 (pre–9th grade): Johns Hopkins CTY and CAA, Oceanography, the Hawaiian Pacific

Johns Hopkins CTY and CAA, The Life Cycle of an Island: Hawaii

Summer 2 (pre–10th grade): Earthwatch, Belize Reef Survey

Students on Ice, Youth Whale Watch, Gulf of St. Lawrence

Duke University TIP, Marine Zoology, in North Carolina Outer Banks

Summer 3 (pre–11th grade): Stanford University, The Oceans: Introduction to the Marine Environment

Earthwatch, Grey Whale Migrations, family trip to British Columbia

Summer 4 (pre–12th grade): Cornell University, Oceanography of the Gulf of Maine (living aboard a ship and conducting research on an island)

Student Conservation Society, volunteer for one month for at Kenai Fjords National Park in Alaska

Family Vacations

SECRET 48

Vacations ideally should reinforce your children's summer learning without being repetitious. This doesn't necessarily mean a costly vacation. If a student is interested in geology, for example, the vacation could include a visit to a geological site, a relevant museum, and a quarry. If the student is focusing on sculpture, the family could spend some time visiting local art museums, galleries, or sculpture gardens. Let the child be the family docent, sharing his or her newly gained expertise on the trip.

Independent Summer Plans

Not all game plans entail course work, internships, or employment. Sometimes a student might prefer a summer in which he or she attempts to write a novel, choreograph a ballet, create a documentary, or design a stained-glass window. Any summer in which a student learns relevant new skills and emerges with a completed project furthering his career goals can be worthwhile (and impressive to colleges). If you're planning such a summer and don't want your child to be disappointed, writing up a daily, weekly, and full-summer schedule can be extremely important to guarantee that the child is not distracted along the way.

SECRET 49

Before embarking on an independent summer plan (writing, painting, practicing an instrument, etc.), strict respect for scheduling between parent and child must be agreed upon. At the beginning of the summer or earlier, the family should be clear on the child's expectations, and vice versa, so nobody schedules a great summer outing or party during the child's agreed work time. Weekdays might be devoted to conducting research or accomplishing artistic goals and evenings and weekends might be reserved for outings and social events, for example. It might also be useful for the family to work out an agreed way of checking in to confirm that progress is indeed being made.

SECRET 50

All breaks need to be established and agreed upon in advance when a child is pursuing an independent summer project so the parent and child can give full respect to

leisure time. People are much more productive when they know that there is a boundary to the amount of time in which they are expected to produce. It's much easier for a teenager to write or paint or compose, for example, from 9:00 a.m. to 4:00 p.m. if the child knows that work comes to a strictly observed halt at 4:00—no matter what—and dinner starts at 6:00, and a social evening or leisure is planned.

SECRET 51	**Throughout the workday, ten-minute breaks should be strictly observed each hour.** The child should

walk away from her work. Grab a snack or get ten minutes of exercise. Talk to people. At the end of the ten minutes, the end of break should also be strictly observed.

SECRET 52	**When a student is on a planned schedule to reach his or her goals, no other chores should be as-**

signed by the family. Completing work on schedule is chore enough.

What If Everyone Follows This Advice?

Will the best summer opportunities crowd over? Will everyone have written a novel by summer's end? I have had people ask me to keep my strategies secret—"just for one more year until my child graduates!" A father I met at a book signing threatened tongue-in-cheek to buy up all the copies of my book in Manhattan so that his child's competitors wouldn't crowd up his kids' programs. Many committed parents worry that if too many of their competitors follow the advice in this book, college admissions will become even more impossibly unattainable. "Are you just feeding the so-called college-admission frenzy?" they ask.

No. My aim is to help parents transcend the frenzy. If you help your kid to become so overwhelmingly qualified by his senior year that colleges are competing to recruit him, you're *freed* from having to panic with the masses. Since the plans I outline are based on areas of interest as diverse as the students themselves, there should be no concern over too many students applying for the same spot. If your kid ignores her own interests, however, and just applies for the same programs as the pack, she'll find space limited. Even in today's hypercompetitive climate, many programs, opportunities, and scholarships go undersubscribed, and part of my mission is to help students find those opportunities.

CHAPTER 3

Designing the Four-Year Academic Plan

What Colleges Mean When They Say They Prefer Kids Who Challenge Themselves to the Fullest

Once you have a clear idea of how your child ideally will spend all four high school summers, it's time to fill in the months in between by crafting a four-year school plan that first focuses on getting optimal grades (not overloading) in high school courses, and then adding outside courses, challenging competitions, internships, volunteer work, paid jobs, independent projects, and after-school extracurricular activities tailored to enhance her two or three academic interests. Start by selecting the right in-school courses.

Parents need to familiarize themselves with the high school's general course requirements so they can figure out how their children will fill those requirements. Ask at the high school guidance office (preferably when your child is still in 8th grade or when your child officially enrolls in the high school) to get a copy of the high school's course listing showing the course offerings and requirements. In laying out a four-year bare bones plan, note the prerequisites for each course (e.g., Are you allowed to take U.S. Constitution if you haven't taken American History yet? Are you allowed to take AP Art History if you haven't taken Studio Art?) Then write out your child's ideal four-year plan, fitting in the courses she most wants to take. Don't overcrowd the schedule with work-intensive courses for freshman year if possible. And try to leave the "iffiest" elective courses (the courses that your child feels she's most likely to get the lowest grades in) till senior year.

SECRET 53	**Keep in mind that grades are the currency by which opportunities are bought in today's meritoc-**

racy. No matter how many after-school activities or advanced level courses your child has on his résumé, no most-competitive college or selective summer program will be impressed if you kid earns less-than-top grades.

| SECRET 54 | **Grades count right from the beginning of high school.** Don't let anyone tell you otherwise. Some |

teachers announce at Open School Night that they will "low-grade" their students as an initial inducement to make them work harder, work to potential, and eventually earn higher grades. Don't allow this. If you see your child's grades inexplicably dipping in one course, encourage her to question her grades to find out if there is any deliberate grade deflation. Colleges don't ignore those "in-the-meantime low grades" or only look at the later high grades, even if your daughter writes a whole song and dance about how she's matured and her grades have improved. (Granted, a few colleges, including Princeton and Stanford, claim to look only at grades earned *after* 9th grade. But those colleges are the exceptions.)

If you were a college admissions officer and you had to choose between a child who started out with a C average and gradually worked toward an A average by senior year and a child who earned solid As starting in freshman year, which child would you prefer (assuming that the child with the initial C did not have some learning disability, family trauma, or language difference to overcome)? Yes, you'll occasionally hear about colleges that accepted kids who, having fallen, gradually picked themselves up and learned great life lessons as a result. But this is a rarity, and if your kid doesn't have a very compelling excuse for underachievement in the 9th and 10th grades, lower grades will only work against him.

What this means is that in planning out four years of courses, parents need to keep in mind that the student who aspires to attend a most-competitive college needs to be able to earn top grades throughout. Unfortunately, this often means that students must avoid extra (beyond the minimum requirement) courses known for giving subjective grades. (Often art, music, creative writing, and social studies electives are included in this subjective category.)

Parents also need to be aware that some students carry with them (on their transcripts) grades from middle school advanced math and science courses that have been awarded high school credit, meaning they're to be averaged into the high school GPA. This can be an albatross to a beginning high school student if he enters high school with a B or C average from the get-go, while other supposedly less advanced students enter high school with clean slates. If such grades appear on your child's high school record (from middle school), you might want to try to negotiate a clean-slate-start with your child's high school—to have the grades annulled or converted to pass-fail.

| SECRET 55 | **Public high schools are no longer the great grounds of academic and artistic experimentation that they** |

once were for students who want to attend the country's most-competitive colleges. For better or for worse, high school is no longer the place for your kid to dabble in art, music, and science, since grades have become the single most important criterion in the college admission process. If your child wants to dabble, have him do that through unaccredited classes taken outside of school—the local dance school, the online writing academy, the nearby music conservatory. He should aim to preserve his high school transcript.

Staying On Track and Avoiding Derailments

| SECRET 56 | **In choosing courses with your child, don't let anyone force her onto a slower academic track so she** |

can better focus on her passion or dream. For example, the fact that your daughter is a concert clarinetist should not be a reason for the administration to remove her from AP Calculus ("to allow her more practice time") if she qualifies and is able to handle the course load. Even if they tell you it's only temporary and that colleges won't notice if she spends a year in a less challenging curriculum. Colleges *will* notice. And it will be harder to get back onto a more rigorous track once she is derailed from the most challenging one.

Instead, when the going gets tough, encourage her to stay the course. Find tutoring if necessary. Help with homework. Do what you can to keep your kid in. (In the next chapter, coordination of game plans with school is discussed.)

| SECRET 57 | **Derailments spill over. Students whose tracks get derailed in one subject often end up suffering in** |

others. A mother I worked with had convinced her busy daughter, for example, not to take AP American History the following school year, because she knew that the course required hours of homework, and her daughter's special interest was biology. So the girl preregistered for a more basic version of American History, figuring that this would allow her more time to delve into AP Biology. Despite the mother's good intentions, this ultimately proved to be a bad move. Months later, when the new school year began, the AP Biology course was scheduled to coincide with basic American History. The school figured that this would not affect most kids' schedules, reasoning that AP Biology would be available to most of the students wanting to take it, since AP students in one subject are most likely to enroll in AP courses in another. So, after removing herself from AP American History, the girl was then shut out of AP Biology, since it met at the same time as her history class. In order to get in, her daughter had to agree to take AP American History, which luckily had one space left in the class. Before you pull your child off track in any subject, find out how such a move might affect the child's entire program—and college preparation. The most competitive colleges prefer applicants who accrue multiple advanced courses.

| SECRET 58 | **When a child is derailed in a subject, it is often nearly impossible to get back into the most chal-** |

lenging courses in that subject. At many schools, gaining access to the most challenging courses is competitive—there's limited space. Once your child drops down a level, another student often takes his place so the class remains full—and it's hard to move back in, because that would mean displacing someone else or convincing the teacher to take in an additional student voluntarily.

In addition, if your son decides to remove himself from, say, AP English for a year, the following year, when he wants to reenter, the school might tell you that he lost a year of English at the AP level. They'll argue that he is no longer at the level of the other students—he hasn't written as many papers or read as many challenging books—so he is no longer qualified for the course.

If your child is considering dropping down a level, many schools won't tell you that it's nearly impossible to get back in, particularly if other parents are clamoring to get their kids in. Faculty will be accommodating and even sympathetic if you're considering dropping your child down a level, where there's usually plenty of space available. It's important to note, however, that they may not be as nice the other way around, where space may be tight.

In light of this one-way traffic scenario, I recommend that parents become aware of when their kids are struggling with a subject and get extra support (tutoring or other help) in advance to prevent ambitious kids from having to drop down a level. High schools and colleges may talk about seeking to eliminate the ever-increasing pressure on high school students, but they still count the number of AP and IB courses your child is taking and are impressed by high AP or IB exam scores. My ultimate recommendation is: Do everything you can to help your child hang in there if she aspires to attend a most-competitive college.

How Many AP Courses Should Your Child Accumulate?

Colleges say in their literature that they want students who take the most rigorous curriculum available to them at their high school. This puts public school students, whose schools offer many more AP courses, under far more pressure than their counterparts at some private schools that deliberately offer fewer AP courses. In some of the most-competitive public high schools, students apply to college having aced thirteen or more AP courses. In contrast, I have seen students from fancy prep schools gain admission to top colleges with a total of only three or four AP courses—because that's all that their schools offer. The correct number of APs to take is dependent on the number offered at your child's school. But note that if your child is in a public school where no or few AP courses are offered, the top colleges will likely skip over applicants from the school entirely, preferring students from nearby districts with similar demographics and a more rigorous curriculum.

How Does IB Compare?

Some American high schools offer International Baccalaureate (IB) Diploma programs that serve as an alternative to AP courses. IB offers its diploma program in 1,465 schools in 123 countries. (In comparison, more than 14,000 schools offer the AP exams to more than 380,000 students each year.) The Switzerland-based IB program entails community service and athletics requirements in addition to academics. Is it superior to AP? No. It's generally considered equivalent by colleges.

The IB program entails completing six IB courses taken over two years. Students choose six subjects from six defined subject groups: language

(English), second language (foreign), individuals and societies (social studies), experimental sciences, mathematics and computer science, and the arts. As part of the program, students are required to complete a four thousand word essay, take a Theory of Knowledge course, and participate in "creativity, action, service" (a choice of arts, sports, and community service projects).

Use Local College Courses to Supplement High School

SECRET 59
In addition to AP or IB courses, while your child is still in high school, consider enrolling him at a local or community college to take simultaneous college courses. Many colleges allow select high school students to take college classes alongside college students. ("Select" often means any reasonably good high school student willing to enroll and pay the tuition.) In terms of schedule, many colleges offer evening courses that meet one evening a week and are targeted for people who work full time and students with other commitments (including full-time high school students).

There are several benefits to taking college courses:

- Grading is sometimes *kinder* in college courses than in the equivalent AP course (e.g., I've seen high school students who were struggling with AP Biology drop the high school course to ace community college Biology instead).
- In some high schools, any courses taken at a community college can be averaged into the high school average to help raise the student's GPA. In other high schools, the college grade does not get averaged in to the high school GPA, and the college course thus provides the high school student a chance to explore an advanced topic without affecting the high school transcript.
- College courses taken during high school look even better on a college application than high school AP courses. Most colleges ask up front on their applications if the student has taken any honors, AP/IB, or college courses (in ascending order of prestige) during high school.
- Local colleges tend to offer more subjects and can fill in the gaps with a course equivalent if your child wants to take an AP course

that isn't offered at his high school, or that's offered at a time that conflicts with another course, or if your child isn't admitted into AP.

- If the high school student doesn't do well at an enrichment course taken at a nearby college, the final grade need not be reported to the high school or colleges to which the student is applying. That said, if the student is taking more than one course and wants credit for at least one, she can't pick and choose which college grades to reveal. But if she's only taking one course and not doing well in it, there is no need to report it unless it is fulfilling some high school requirement.

| SECRET 60 | **When the most-competitive colleges state in their information sessions and literature that they pre-** |

fer students who have taken "the most rigorous courses available to them," they expect students who attend high schools that offer few AP courses to investigate (and take advantage of) the opportunities offered through nearby colleges to supplement the high school curriculum. Parents interested in college courses for their children can pick up copies of the local college course offerings brochure and find out what the procedure is for registering their high school students for courses. Colleges have different procedures for high school registrants. Some require the high school students to go through a formal interview and mini-application. Others let the students just sign up without any formal procedures.

Does the prestige of the local college matter on a college application? Depending upon the course, it generally doesn't. For example, a standard math course like Multivariable Calculus taken anywhere generally will be credited by liberal arts or tech colleges—even the most prestigious colleges—if the student proves that she has mastered the topic. (Some colleges require a placement exam as proof.)

If the student's high school doesn't give the student credit for the local college course and doesn't include the college grade in the transcript or GPA, the college that the student eventually attends after high school most likely *will* credit the local college course if the student seeks credit from the college. When the child ultimately graduates from high school and enrolls in college full time, the local-college letter *grade* itself may not appear on the child's college transcript. Instead, the A at a community college may simply appear as a pass or credit on the transcript (not all colleges directly transfer actual grades).

In general, doing well in a college course will impress colleges and contribute to getting in, and may mean being able to skip ahead to take more advanced level courses upon arrival at college.

School-Year College Programs for Gifted High School Students

Some universities go out of their way to welcome or even recruit gifted high school students to take college-level courses among their students. At these universities, "gifted" varies in meaning and shouldn't scare parents who worry that they have no documentation to prove that their children are in some way gifted. At many of these colleges, the mere act of your child enrolling in a gifted program is enough to convince them that he can handle the work involved. Many of these programs offer free advising—meetings with advisors for course recommendations and other guidance to ease your child's experience at the college. Such advisers can be valuable sources when creating your child's four-year plan. (Parents within range of the University of Wisconsin, for example, rave about the high school gifted program there and the helpful long-term advice offered by individual university faculty members. I have heard similar rave reviews from parents working with the University of Texas in Austin.)

Once you're aware of the basic high school course requirements and prerequisites, the honors, AP, or IB courses offered, and the local college courses available, you're ready to start planning the four-year course schedule.

Start Early

| SECRET 61 | **Ideally you should begin creating your child's four-year game plan when she is in 8th grade. (If she is** |

already in 9th or 10th grade, start now!) Working with your child, figure out what she wants to achieve before she graduates. What courses will she need to take to help her achieve her greater goals?

A child who sees the big picture from a young age has a definite advantage over his peers. Many students arrive at senior year and suddenly realize that they were not able to take all the science APs required to set them apart when applying to a prestigious college or university. Or, junior year, they learn that only the kids who took journalism as sophomores are considered for newspaper editor positions senior year, or that only the ones who took drama freshman and sophomore year are offered auditions for the big school musical at the end of junior year.

Note that the plan will need updating several times each year (when selecting courses for the following year, just before each new school year, and when making summer plans, which preferably should happen in November), allowing interests to evolve. Each year, try to get a hold of that year's listing of the high school's course offerings so you can stay on top of what is available.

| SECRET 62 | **Educate yourself in advance regarding what requirements exist in your child's school for the subjects and even extracurricular activities that interest your child—and plan accordingly.** |

To find this information, speak to the parents of older kids who have focused on similar activities or courses. Once your child enrolls in high school, make a point of meeting his guidance counselor to discuss your child's goals and ask about prerequisites. Encourage your child to ask faculty advisors about positions he someday aspires to pursue. Sometimes merely asking a teacher how to pursue an editorship or a part in a theatrical production can inspire the faculty member to give that child an extra look.

It bears repeating that any curriculum plan must remain tentative. High schools frequently change their course offerings, and some course selections may conflict in schedule with others in different years. So, even if the four-year plan you devise when your child is in 8th or 9th grade seems perfect on paper, be aware—and make your child aware—that flexibility is essential.

Skipping and Single-Subject Acceleration

Many parents ask me if, to help their kid stand out, they should encourage him to skip a course or two. In my experience, I've found that skipping can either be beneficial or detrimental depending on the student's mastery of the skipped material. *Preparation, rather than brilliance, is the key.* Successful skipping entails learning and thoroughly understanding all of the material in the skipped course. This requires parental or other outside teaching. No *material* should actually be skipped.

| SECRET 63 | As a general rule, colleges aren't terribly impressed if your kid skips a course or course level and |

doesn't earn top scores in the skipped-into class. And skipping an entire grade—all courses—is generally frowned upon unless there are some extenuating circumstances in which it's better to leave home a year early. While skipping may give your kid some boasting rights among peers, high school is not a game of tag in which your child wins by touching base first.

What's more important are the grades earned and the challenging nature of the courses taken. If your child is able to maintain high As while skipping into a challenging course, that could be impressive. If her grades slip because of it, however (and she would have gotten higher grades had she not skipped), that's a detriment.

How the skipped year is accounted for can also be impressive (e.g., Did your son teach himself the entire Honors Chemistry curriculum to place into AP Chemistry? Did your daughter skip the easier AP Calculus to take the harder AP Calculus BC and read the textbook over the summer?).

To maximize the value of skipping, your child should explain the skip in the college application section where it invites the applicant to reveal "anything else you want to tell us about yourself," specifying how the skipped material was mastered outside the classroom and how the student fared gradewise as a result.

If your child is thinking of skipping and you're not sure of your child's ability to ace the higher-level course, the gamble may be too big. High schools often don't allow a student to repeat a skipped course or skipped-into course. And skipping can also be difficult if the child is less mature than his classmates—if nobody wants to be his lab partner or nobody will allow her onto his committee. If you do ultimately decide that your child can score a top grade in a higher-level course, parents can smooth over potential edges with the teacher in advance by alerting the teacher that the child skipped and is younger than the other students.

| SECRET 64 | If you decide to let your child skip in a subject, don't let her miss an entire year's worth of cur- |

riculum, resulting in holes in her education. When designing your child's four-year plan, include all intentions or even fantasies of skipping grades— and be sure to check the textbook for the course your child is skipping into to ensure that she acquires any missing lessons. If you don't want to get this involved or are unable to, don't let your child skip.

| SECRET 65 | **The primary benefit of skipping is to qualify for some of the more competitive high school contests** |

that assume a complete mastery of high school material *before* senior year. (And this is a major benefit, since, with some of the contests, winning means being able to write one's own ticket to any college.) Most high schools' programs are arranged so that students complete the entire curriculum in all subjects by the *end* of senior year, when it's too late to qualify for these most prestigious contests. At most high schools, the general curriculum does not include taking all the AP sciences or a full range of AP social studies classes—but rather choosing a selection of one or two advanced courses in each subject over the course of high school.

For students who want to complete all of the AP sciences and social studies, not only before they graduate, but also in time to compete in some of the major science competitions during their junior or senior year of high school (e.g., USA Biology Olympiad, International Science and Engineering Fair, Intel Science Talent Search), or to experience the high school's full array of social science offerings, significant acceleration is necessary. If you think your child might like to compete in national contests such as these (or others of their ilk), you should help design a path for her while she is still in 7th or 8th grade, whereby she can accomplish this acceleration.

Using Middle School to Jump-Start the Program

The courses your child takes in middle school can affect the options she will have during her senior year of high school. And middle school is often the best time to have your child start the acceleration process, since the courses tend to be less demanding. Because there is no nationally recognized skipping system, parents should expect to negotiate their own children's course-by-course skipping individually with school administrators. Start with the middle school guidance office—if the school's guidance counselors have any power in determining placement. Be prepared to suggest a way for your child to make up skipped material. And provide a good reason for your child to skip (e.g., to be able to qualify for the USA Physics Olympiad by 11th grade, to have the opportunity to take every AP social studies offering before graduating high school) rather than making it sound like your kid is being rushed or pushed for no reason (or because she is somehow better or brighter than her peers).

Compare the following programs, for example:

Typical Unaccelerated Science Program:	9th grade Earth Science, 10th grade Biology, 11th grade Chemistry, 12th grade Physics
Common Science Acceleration Option:	8th grade Earth Science, 9th grade Biology, 10th grade Chemistry, 11th grade Physics, 12th grade AP Biology
Contest-Targeted Science Acceleration:	7th grade Earth Science, 8th grade Biology, 9th grade Chemistry, 10th grade Physics and AP Biology, 11th grade AP Chemistry and AP Physics, 12th grade science competitions and AP Environmental Science
Typical Unaccelerated Social Studies Program (offered in varying order at different schools):	9th grade Global Studies, 10th grade European History, 11th grade American History, 12th grade U.S. Government
Common Social Studies Acceleration Option:	9th grade AP European History and AP World History, 10th grade AP American History and AP Comparative Government, 11th grade AP Economics (macro and micro) and AP U.S. Government and Politics, 12th grade AP Psychology and AP Statistics

★   ★   ★

These are just some sample accelerated four-year plans; yours will depend on how eager your child is to accomplish all the science or social studies courses by the end of junior year—in time for the competitions. Obviously these programs require a lot of work, in many cases doubling up on courses in a single subject. Some students may want to accelerate the plan further, completing all the sciences or history courses before junior year, allowing two years of solid science or social science competition. Any science acceleration should be accompanied by math acceleration, so that the student has a solid calculus background before attempting serious physics. Know the options before your child starts 9th grade and figure out a workable plan to make sure that she gets to take all of the courses that ultimately could be useful for her longer-term dreams.

| SECRET 66 | **If your child accelerates to take high school level courses while in middle school, remember that** |

those course grades will be averaged in to her overall high school GPA—even though she's only in middle school. Taking a high school level science course while still in 7th grade may work for some children, but, truthfully, not for most. When creating your child's four-year plan, be sure to carefully consider whether enrolling your middle schooler in a high school course is the best move for her—you don't want to damage your child's average while she is in 7th grade because of immaturity or lack of study skills. Also, parents of middle schoolers tend to be less informed as to what kinds of grades are needed to get their kid into his choice colleges. In my work, I have seen parents thrilled that their 7th grader is earning a 90 out of 100 in a high school course. But years later, when the kid is a senior and the 90 is averaged in with the kid's overall GPA of 95 or 96, the 90 brings *down* the average. If your accelerated child has aspirations to attend the most-competitive colleges, make sure you fully understand what grades are required to deliver this dream before allowing your child to skip. (Note that much higher grades are required nowadays than a generation ago. Check with the guidance office to see if your high school has a listing of which local kids got admitted where and what their grade point averages were.) Occasionally I have seen teachers artificially lower the grade of a younger student with the rationale "You can't possibly expect him to get a top grade in this class when he's so much younger than the rest of the students."

| SECRET 67 | **Children who accelerate generally require signifi-cant parental commitment to make it work.** If |

your child chooses to accelerate at a younger age, be prepared to help him with studying and homework and possibly advocating for grades. He may find it harder to ask questions in class in front of older kids. Or he may find it harder to get study partners because he's younger. As I mentioned above, if you as a parent have no time to lend this additional support—helping to study, overseeing homework, and meeting with the teacher to smooth over social bumps—and if you don't want to pay for a tutor to perform these tasks, you may be wiser not to let him skip.

Once you've determined which courses your child most wants to take in high school, write down the four-year course plan in list form. (In 9th grade write out a three-year plan, in 10th grade write out a two-year plan, etc.) You may prefer to write it backward, starting with 12th grade to make sure your child gets to take the courses she wants by the time she graduates and in time for any competition deadlines. Then it's time to explore extracurricular opportunities.

Extracurriculars

Look first for school-based activities that seem like they would enhance the already-selected curriculum. If your child is taking Latin, for example, does the school sponsor a classics club where your child might become active? If your child is planning to take additional creative writing and literature courses beyond the English requirement, is there a literary magazine or book club?

Many schools have club fairs or activity fairs in the fall, where your high school student can ask questions and get a sense of the opportunities offered at the high school. Encourage your child to attend meetings of more clubs and activities during the first weeks of school than she ultimately plans to join.

Schools generally do not notify kids of the many options that are available to them outside of school, however. So where can you learn about these opportunities? In part 2 of this book! Once you've finished reading part 1, find the chapter in part 2 that focuses on your particular child's passion.

But first you should encourage your child to take maximum advantage of the extracurricular activities available at school.

Founding a Club

SECRET 68 **Never assume that the menu of clubs offered at your child's public or private high school is limited to what already exists.** Often the best opportunity for your child may be the one that you or he initiates. Active parents can often help their children's school introduce new activities. If your child is interested in starting a club that suits her particular passions, find out what the school's procedures are for establishing new organizations (ask a guidance counselor or check the student handbook if any such guide exists), and figure out whether there is any way that you can help with getting it off the ground. Sometimes budgetary or staffing issues may limit the number of clubs a school can offer. You as a parent may be better able to raise money or help the students hold a fund-raiser or to even temporarily staff the club until a faculty member can be hired.

At one public high school in New York, a group of students showed a strong interest in swing dance, so a parent became active in helping to set up a swing club that taught swing dance and sponsored a swing dance social. At another school, a strong student interest in Russian music led to the formation of the Russian culture club. And other parents that I have worked with have been active in helping schools to form ballet companies, a health professions club, book groups, recycling programs, a fencing team, a features magazine, a film review club, and competitive science teams.

| **SECRET 69** | **An advantage to helping your child start a new club is that the parent initiator's child usually** |

gets to be the leader. Not every student club has to be democratic, with elected leaders. In sports, for example, not every team captain is an elected position—in many schools, captains are appointed by the coach or adult supervisor. Similarly, with many student-run academic and community service clubs, the founders automatically get to lead until they graduate. You make the club, you make the rules. The geology club that your son creates *should* be led by your son, who presumably had the original vision and knows where the best hiking trails are. Likewise, the pie-eating contest fund-raiser that your daughter organized should be run by your daughter. Of course, club organization ultimately depends on school procedures, but most schools are lax in this regard.

| **SECRET 70** | **One reason to form an academic or community service club for your child and her friends is that** |

without a defined group, the activity could not take place. Many team competitions require group participation. Examples include Model Congress, Junior Engineering and Technical Society (JETS) TEAMS competition, *FIRST* Robotics, and Ocean Sciences Bowl. Parents should note, however, that when helping to form a school club, no discrimination can be tolerated and no students should be excluded—not even your kid's competitors.

| SECRET 71 | Not all clubs or teams need to be school based if the school is unable or unwilling to let your child |

start a new club. School-based organizations do not necessarily have more clout on college applications. When the school is unable to offer funding or staffing, consider helping your child start a club outside of school. For example, birding or astronomy clubs meet at a variety of locations for viewing. The same is true for a 4-H club or book club. You don't need the school or the school's facilities.

How to Scout Out Contests and Scholarships That Impress Every College

Start your search for opportunities by checking the many invaluable resources that are located in part 2 and in the appendix of this book. One of my main goals in writing this book was to showcase an inspiring array of these opportunities based on a variety of children's interests.

| SECRET 72 | Check your local community newspaper regularly to find additional opportunities for your child. |

Seek out news articles that announce accomplishments by local high school students. If any of these accomplishments—particularly those of older students—appeal to your child, investigate the details. Clip the articles. Find out how your child can pursue the same track. If the accomplished student is older than your child and has no younger siblings, you might even phone the parents of the achiever directly to inquire. If the student is your child's peer, don't bother trying to get information from the parents—with college admissions being as competitive as they are today, parents are hesitant to share information that might, in some way, result in the competition being even steeper for their child.

A word of caution: If, after assessing the situation, you decide to phone the parents of an older student, don't compare your child to the achiever. Don't boast about your child. Don't imply that your child can duplicate what the achiever achieved. Just congratulate the parent of the achiever and ask how your child might attempt to follow in his or her footsteps. You'll get a much more informative response this way and a more cooperative information provider.

| SECRET 73 | **Another great source of information regarding op-portunities for your child is the local library or a** |

major bookstore, where whole shelves may be devoted to books on student competitions and scholarships. Plan to spend an entire day systematically exploring these books and taking notes while your child is (ideally) still in 7th or 8th grade. Assume that every scholarship and competition that applies to your kid's talents, skills, and background is worth applying to. Some contests offer monetary rewards in addition to recognition. Others offer scholarships to be used years later when your child attends college. Plot out in advance some of the bigger contests and scholarship competitions that your child wants to aim for. Don't overlook ethnic or religious contests—regardless of how dominant your culture is. Look for contests offered for athletes who play your kid's sport and musicians who play your kid's instrument. Check out essay contests that are offered to veterans' kids if you are a veteran or your parents or grandparents were veterans—some scholarships are offered for generations of descendants. Check also for scholarships offered by the company where you work or your spouse works and by organizations and unions of which you're a member. While some contests may be more prestigious than others, the accumulation of contest wins and credentials will help your child to win the most desirable opportunities later on. Go with the attitude that no opportunity is too small.

Top Web Sites for Finding a Wide Range of Opportunities

There is no single Web site that lists every opportunity that might be helpful to your child. But, beginning when your child is in 8th grade, several Web sites should be checked on a regular basis to see listings of opportunities in the arts, humanities, and sciences—and whichever interests your child specifies.

Start with www.FastWeb.com for a listing of current contests, awards, and scholarships and to receive updates of new scholarship and contest possibilities.

Check out www.VolunteerMatch.org for a wide variety of volunteer opportunities within range of the zip code you specify; the nonprofit organization gives volunteers access to 40,000 domestic organizations.

And visit www.house.gov/watt/intern03.htm for government internships and volunteer opportunities in Washington, D.C., Sciserv.org lists many math, science, and engineering summer programs by state.

In addition, check the Johns Hopkins magazine *Imagine* (www.jhu.edu/gifted/imagine/index.html), which features articles and listings of opportunities for middle and high school students based on different interests in each edition, and also visit www.cogito.org, a Johns Hopkins–affiliated "Web site" (launched at the end of 2006) for the world's top math and science students."

Many of my students have pursued excellent opportunities first located on these Web sites.

Designing Your Ideal Four-Year Plan

Once you have selected well-focused summer activities, relevant and necessary school-year courses, competitions in which your child wants to vie, and complementary after-school activities, you are ready to assemble the comprehensive and inspiring four-year plan with your child. This is an activity you should do together so you are both on the same page.

The following ideal four-year plan is meant to provide a sense of what a completed plan—summers and school years combined—can include. In this case, the student is interested in film animation and aspires to win the Ottawa Student Animation Festival, one of the most prestigious international animation festivals with a student category, by her senior year, and to attend film animation programs at NYU, UCLA, or USC for college.

9th Grade

Take a Studio Art I class at high school

Join ASIFA (International Animated Film Association), http://asifa.net

Attend the annual Teen Workshop at the Ottawa International Animation Festival in September

Take computer animation lessons and anatomical drawing classes at a local community college, art school, or adult education program

View classic animated films to familiarize yourself with the art

Practice computer drawing software like Adobe Photoshop or Illustrator

Attend a residential summer program in computer animation, like the New York Film Academy four-week 3-D Animation Workshop at Harvard

Make a thirty-second animated informational spot announcement about some aspect of school procedures or school rules (no opinion pieces or campaign-for-student-office promotions)

Ask to have your animated short aired on school-district TV or local community cable channels

10th Grade

Take Studio Art II at high school

Renew ASIFA membership

Parents begin exploring AP studio art program at your child's high school; support introduction of a program into school if no such program already exists

In September, attend the Teen Workshop at the Ottawa International Animation Festival

Take a more advanced computer animation course at a local college

Make a slightly longer and more advanced animated film about local rules or procedures for your most local government unit

Try to have your film aired on local cable TV or at a local movie theater (gain a local reputation as an animator)

In the summer, attend four-week residential animation program offered by the University of the Arts in Philadelphia

or RISD (Rhode Island School of Design) computer animation Pre-College Program, six weeks

or University of Pennsylvania, Penn Summer Studio in Animation, four weeks

or USC Summer Basic Animation Technique course, 4 credits, three weeks

or Penn State University, Computer Animation course, three and a half weeks, noncredit

or The Art Insitute of Chicago, three weeks, 3 credits

11th Grade

Take Studio Art III or AP Studio Art at high school

Renew ASIFA membership

Parents support creation of AP Art History course at high school (if it does not already exist) for the student to enroll in senior year

Create an animated fiction short that is not a public service announcement

Enter the new film into Ottawa Student Animation Festival; don't wait for senior year to put yourself on the map

Attend Cal State Summer School for the Arts program in animation (InnerSpark) (limited places for out-of-state students), four weeks

or Northwestern University College Prep, Introduction to Computer Graphics Animation, six weeks, 3 credits

or NYU Tisch, Introduction to Animation Techniques, four weeks, 6 credits; includes a two-unit editing course

12th Grade

Take AP Art History course

Renew ASIFA membership

Enter summer-made animated films into Ottawa Student Animation Festival

Enter and attend other international film festivals as well (See festival list: http://asifa.net)

Apply for the top film animation programs for college

The four-year plan above is an ideal program for a high school student interested in a specific field. Note that in addition to completing a full high school program by the time she graduates from high school, she will have created and presented multiple animated films, and the films potentially will have been shown in international film festivals and on local television. The same kind of planning can be applied to any other field that interests your high school student. But to get there, your child will need some carefully choreographed baby steps.

General Scholarship Awards

Top-achieving students eager to make themselves irresistible to colleges should find out the procedures for getting themselves nominated (by their school) for one of the most prestigious academic scholarship awards, *USA Today*'s All-USA First Academic Team. The newspaper names America's top twenty high school students each year (and an additional twenty students to its Second Academic Team, and another twenty to its Third Team). Schools nominate kids—so savvy parents who think their kid deserves to be nominated should make a point of notifying a guidance counselor. Don't wait for the guidance counselor to nominate your child. Not bad to be recognized as one of America's top twenty, forty, or sixty.

Three other national honors are based on standardized test scores: Presidential Scholars names 121 students on the basis of SATs and ACTs; National Merit Scholarship Winners are based on junior-year PSATs. And AP Scholars, Scholars with Honor, and Scholars with Distinction are based on cumulative AP scores. And Educational Testing Service also administers the Toyota Community Scholars Program (one hundred scholarships valued at $10,000 and $20,000) based on community service.

Creating Short-Term Refrigerator Goals

Once you have designed a long-term program with your child, work with her to establish short-term goals. I recommend creating a list of ten such goals two or three times a year (August, January, and June), to be posted on the refrigerator and checked off as they are reached. The list should focus heavily on the child's top area of academic interest and should include other goals as well, including arts and sports to enrich the program. Sample short-term goals might include getting an A-plus in a challenging course, trying out for a new sport, composing a new musical or artwork, creating a new fund-raiser, or aiming for a specific score on a standardized test. (Although colleges today seek "lopsided" kids with expertise in one or two areas over traditionally well-rounded kids, they also want these lopsided kids to be able to converse intelligently, at the least, in multiple areas.)

| SECRET 74 | **The child should be the creator of these short-term goals—so that she is actually working toward her *own* goals, rather than goals imposed by parents, teachers, or** |

others. While the four-year plan, comprised of your child's long-term goals, should be more of a collaborative effort between parent and child, the short-term baby steps to get there should be initiated solely by the child. That said, parents should commit to helping her facilitate these goals, and may even suggest some goals if the child welcomes this guidance, provided the ultimate list of refrigerator goals comes from the child (students are far more motivated when they're trying to fulfill their *own* goals).

Refrigerator goals should not include household chores. Keeping a clean bedroom, for example, should not be a goal. Nor should walking the dog every day for a week. Goals should not be behavioral or social. Acting polite to a sibling for an entire month, for example, should not be a goal. Nor should digging up the courage to ask another student to the prom. Refrigerator goals should be based entirely on the child's academic, athletic, artistic, scientific, career, and community service ambitions.

Note that there should be no punishment for not attaining a goal. And goals and goal-driven stepping stones (such as allowing your star athlete to practice his tennis or your virtuoso to practice violin) should not be treated as privileges to be withdrawn if children don't perform well in other activities. Goals should not be used as bargaining chips for other unrelated expectations. For example, you'll contradict the method if you say to your child, "If you don't get an A in chemistry, I'm not going to drive you to ballet lessons." Or "If you don't clean your room, I'm not going to help you with your conservation fund-raiser." When overseeing refrigerator goals, parents should feel free to discuss logistics and budget—making sure that the child's goals are achievable and affordable.

| SECRET 75 | **To make short-term refrigerator goals most effective, the realization of a goal should be celebrated** |

by the family. The aim is to offer positive incentive and rewards as motivation, rather than fear or punishment. Some celebrate by taking the family out for dinner or dessert when a student's self-prescribed goal is realized. Others prefer gift certificate rewards (for a bookstore, music store, etc.). If the goals are lofty enough, reaching them should be a genuine cause of celebration.

| SECRET 76 | **Do not expect your child to be able to achieve all of his goals, and communicate this to your child** |

clearly. If the goals are all easily achieved, then they're not lofty enough for the refrigerator list. Goals should represent aspirations.

A mother I know, whose child is a very successful Broadway performer, once explained to me her philosophy that a one-to-five ratio was the ratio to strive for at auditions, as well as for other goals in life. The public only sees the one success, she said, not the four rejections, and they don't realize that this kid they see onstage, who seems constantly employed, actually had to face four rejections first.

SECRET 77	**The highest achievers need very caring, supportive parents to carry them through those rejections to**

make it to the next success. In order to raise kids willing to take academic and intellectual risks, they need to know that they don't *fall* in your eyes or in their talent and abilities if they're not selected for a given award or honor.

Sample Refrigerator Goals

Following is a list of fall semester goals for a 9th grader interested in American politics:

1. Immediately enroll online in the U.S. Congressional Award Program.
2. Create a blog focused on politics.
3. Run for class office.
4. Join or create a school Model Congress and participate in debates.
5. In December apply for three-week summer Civic Leadership Institute offered by Johns Hopkins in Baltimore and San Francisco.

   - Also apply to three-week Junior Statesmen, Georgetown, AP U.S. Government and Politics summer course.

6. Speak at a real-life political rally or in support of a candidate.
7. Attend Junior Statesmen State of America two-day congress.
8. Volunteer in the office of a political candidate or cause.
9. Organize an in-school club and campaign in support of a nonpartisan cause that the school can support (pro-environment, anti-drinking-while-driving, pro–English literacy, hurricane relief, etc.).
10. Volunteer for and devote significant time to a community service project that seems interesting. Select one from Volunteermatch.org.

SECRET 78	**One of the best kept Washington secrets is the U.S. Congressional Award Program, which is an in-**

credibly positive motivator for *any* child (minimum age: 13½). Have your child register for this program whether or not she is interested in politics. The program recognizes students for participating in community service (of the student's choice) along with a well-rounded program of athletics and other extracurricular activities. It looks stunningly impressive on a college application, as it's a national award, and relatively few apply. And the program is objective rather than judgmental. Here's how it works: Your kid devotes X amount of hours to community service, sports, and other activities and *automatically* gets the award. Yet it's still impressive to colleges.

After the student completes athletics and other activities and devotes a total of four hundred hours to community service, he is invited to Washington to receive a gold medal before Congress. Along the way, however, he receives benchmark awards that can also be listed on a college application, starting with a bronze certificate for thirty hours of service.

For a student with a passion in the arts, a very different set of refrigerator goals might emerge. Following are sample refrigerator goals created by a student with an interest in fashion.

Sample 9th Grader with Fashion Aspirations (Spring Semester)

1. Design a new fashion and create a prototype that I can model.
2. Go for a professional modeling audition—just for the experience.
3. Attend a professional fashion show.
4. Enroll in a course in fashion photography, weekends outside of school.
5. Take an online course in fashion design/drawing/advertising through the Fashion Institute of Technology.
6. Start a fashion club at school.
7. Write a fashion blog.
8. Apply to the fashion-design summer program at Laboratory Institute of Merchandising in New York City **and** North Carolina State University's one-week Summer Textile Exploration Program.
9. Maintain an A average in a drawing course in high school.
10. Organize a fashion fund-raiser.

Creating a Family Calendar

"My daughter said the school band audition was really difficult last Friday," a woman boasted to the mother of her daughter's classmate the following Monday morning.

"The band solo audition? When did that happen? I thought it wasn't taking place for another two weeks!" the woman exclaimed.

"Oops," the first mother responded. "I thought you knew. We were wondering why your daughter, the top clarinetist in the school, didn't show up. Otherwise, my daughter never would have gotten the solo. I'm sure of it."

The moral here is: Instead of relying on the goodwill of competing parents or the willingness of teachers to inform you about relevant dates and deadlines throughout the school year, do your own homework.

SECRET 79	**Each year, create a calendar early in September (most national school event dates are not determined until September) that includes standardized test dates, local and national contests of interest to your kid, audition dates, summer program application deadlines, in-school performances, and sport meets for the school year.**

If your child is the president of an academic club, let's say debate or math team, you as the parent will likely be expected by other parents to know the dates of all the competitions. In addition to getting this information from your child, you can learn more by speaking with the team's faculty advisor or by taking your search online. Often parents find additional opportunities for their kids' academic clubs by searching the Internet. Many advisors are only aware of contests and events that the club or team has previously participated in because they don't have the time (or directives) to locate additional opportunities. While writing her refrigerator goals, have your child refer to the calendar you create each September to help her keep track of impending due dates and deadlines. Finally, display the calendar near your child's refrigerator goals in a prominent and accessible location—on the refrigerator, perhaps!—so everyone in the family has immediate access to them.

Start Your Child's Résumé Early

SECRET 80	**In addition to creating an annual calendar, start a résumé for your child on the computer when he is**

in 8th grade. This is one of the great secrets to motivating a teenager (and perhaps many adults, too). "Why would an 8th grader need a résumé?" parents may wonder. "And how could a child possibly fill a résumé at such an early age?"

There's nothing as inspiring as seeing one's own credentials (or lack thereof) in writing—at any age. Also, setting up a résumé is the easiest way to keep track of your child's credentials once he starts earning them. Creating a résumé also sends the message that what he does matters and that achievements are cumulative.

SECRET 81

For inspiration, create *two* résumés: an actual, current résumé, and a dream résumé that the student hopes will reflect his achievements by the time he graduates. The sample résumés shown below are dream résumés. Please note that the résumés and the names are fictitious; however (as with the items on the sample summer and academic plans), the major national activities and awards listed are actually available for your child to pursue. While some activities are region-specific or school-specific, most local activities have counterparts in all regions of the country. Parents, working together with their teenagers, should pick and choose elements of different résumés that they would like to see on their own children's résumés, based on their children's interests and passions.

The first is from a girl who is particularly interested in architecture. The second is from a senior who is passionate about literature and writing. **Bold type** indicates actual available opportunities at time of publication.

JESSICA JAY

10 Address Street

E-mail address **Citytown, Illinois** **Phone number**

Architecture and Design Achievements

National Foundation for Advancement in the Arts, silver award, 2009

Presidential Scholar in the Visual Arts, 2009

> One of twenty students selected nationally; Washington, D.C.

Newhouse Architecture Award (for Chicago students)

> One of 155 High School Student Winners, 2007
>> Awarded summer internship in Chicago architecture firm

> Citytown High School Architecture Award, 2009

> Exhibition: Citytown Public Library Architectural Drawing Exhibit,
>> June, 2007; five of my original drawings were displayed

Education

Cornell University, Summer College, Explorations

> Studied architecture, summer 2009; 6 college credits

University of Pennsylvania, College of General Studies

> Studied architecture/Designed off-campus, structure, summer 2008

Duke University, TIP

> Architecture and Art History of Rome and Florence, Italy, two weeks,
>> summer, 2008

Roger Williams University College Summer Architecture, 2007

Discover Architecture Pre-College Program

> Certificate awarded, University of Illinois, summer 2006

School of the Art Institute of Chicago

> Studied architecture design/drawing, weekends 2006–07

> Studied graphic design, weekends, 2005–06

> Citytown High School, full-time student, GPA 3.85;
>> graduating May, 2010

> Founder/President of Citytown High School Architecture Club
>> Led architecture tour for local visitors center
>> Wrote guidebook to Citytown architectural history

> SAT I scores: math 680, verbal 710, writing 710

> SAT II scores: Latin 680, European History 750, English Literature 680

> AP: Art History 5, European History 5, English Literature 5, Biology 3

Community Service and Employment

> Volunteer landscaper and architecture tour guide, Citytown
>> Public Gardens, weekends 2007–08

> Citytown Architects, Inc., handled phones and clerical work,
>> school year 2007–08 and 2008–09

> Volunteer art director, economically underprivileged children's
>> weekend class, fall 2004

KAREEN KAPEL
E-mail address   **Urbanville, North Dakota**   **Phone number**

Mystery Writing and Literature Achievements
Davidson Fellow in Literature, winner
Helen McCloy/MWA Scholarship for Mystery Writing
National award from the Mystery Writers of America, 2008
Wrote and produced whodunit play *Who Did It?* at school
Published in *TeenInk* (magazine for teenagers by teenagers)
Published short story in *Short Stories by Young Authors*, 2007
Blogger: Began a blog on whodunit literature two years ago;
entries updated daily; more than 2,000 subscribers
Harvard Book Award, 2009

Education
TASP (Telluride Association Summer Program), summer 2009
University of St. Andrews, Scotland, Creative Writing Program
Master classes taught by famous Scottish writers, summer 2008
Iowa Young Writers' Studio, Iowa City, Iowa, July, 2007
Specialized in fiction in two-week intensive program
The Jonathan R. Reynolds Young Writers Workshop
Denison University, Granville, Ohio, June 2007
National Latin Exam: bronze medal, 2009; silver medal, 2008
Full-time student at Urbanville Regional High School;
graduation 6/2010 GPA 4.0 unweighted
SAT I: verbal 740, writing 800, math 650
SAT II: English 800, Latin 760, Math I C 670
AP Exams: English Composition 5, English Literature 5,
American History 5, Calculus AB 3, European History 5

Employment and Community Service
Created Mystery Dinner fund-raiser, Urbanville Hospital (2008 and 2009)
Work at Urbanville Public Library shelving books (since 2007)

Memberships
Fiction Editor, *Urbanville Literary Journal* (high school literary magazine)
Drama Critic, *Urbanville News* (high school newspaper; monthly column)
Director, Urbanville Mystery Theatre (high school theater company)
Mystery Writers of America (student member)
The Jane Austen Society of Urbanville, member
Founder and President, Urbanville High School Book Club

Notice in both résumés above that education is the second item, listed after the student's main academic passion. Although these résumés do not conform to traditional résumé writing, they emphasize what the student has *done*, as opposed to what the student has learned. This makes the résumé more powerful in presenting the student as a *doer*.

In assembling a résumé, avoid flowery graphics, fancy lines, large spaces, and hard-to-read fonts. Such résumés look like they're padded to cover up for a lack of impressive credentials. Remember that the people reading the résumés are likely to be age thirty or older and may appreciate a standard typeface of 12 points or larger. Arial or Times New Roman is recommended. Make sure that the wording is easily readable and understandable and doesn't require hours of interpretation.

★   ★   ★

By integrating the four-year summer plan, school course plan, extracurricular activities, out-of-school supplemental programs, and short-term refrigerator goals, you should now have a clear sense of your child's aspirations, motivations, and overall game plan. The next step is to coordinate your child's program with her school. To accomplish this, you'll need to meet with her guidance counselor and teachers before each school year starts or at the very beginning of the school year.

CHAPTER 4

Coordinating the Game Plan with Your Child's School

Inviting the Faculty to Join Your Team

Once you and your child have designed a total program of study that includes long- and short-range goals and strategies, school may seem to take on a more secondary role—a supplement to your child's education. Regardless of how hard your child is working outside of school, however, students who are enrolled in high school still need to remain accountable to their school and earn the best grades they can, even if they're winning the Ottawa Film Festival or starring in the International Chemistry Olympiad. (Grades are still the most important element of the application at most colleges.) For this reason, parents need to work out an acceptable arrangement and collaborative plan with teachers and guidance counselors. I recommend meeting with school faculty members regularly to establish good communication, and inform your child's school at the outset of his out-of-school activities and commitments. This chapter provides tips on how to do this as effectively as possible.

School can provide wonderful reinforcement for your child's knowledge base and aspirations if you work with teachers and counselors as a team. But it also can become a significant hindrance if communications break down and obstacles are thrown in your child's way (e.g., if the teacher gets annoyed that your child needs to miss class for an important event, if the teacher doesn't allow your child to make up missed work, etc.). As your child's advocate, you are responsible for seeing to it that communications flow smoothly. Expect to play a major role in coordinating your child's secondary school education if your kid wants to stand out academically.

You don't need to show the school your four-year plan, but you should let teachers, your kid's guidance counselor, and the principal know that you *have* a plan, along with the general scope of it: "My daughter is pursuing a professional ballet career." Or "My daughter is hoping to qualify for the U.S. Computer Olympiad team." Or "My son is hoping to have a science fiction novel published by the time he graduates." Or "My son is trying out for the U.S. Olympic diving team." Most schools will want to encourage your child and will be enthusiastic, supportive, and even flexible in accommodating your child's plans and dreams. But don't be discouraged if a school official rolls her eyes at the idea of your kid's aspirations. The concept of a four-year plan is foreign to most people. Just work with your plan and believe in it. And understand that not all teachers are necessarily accustomed to involved parents.

| SECRET 82 | **Develop an excellent rapport and an open, comfortable parent-faculty relationship at the high** |

school from the get-go. Even if your daughter is not yet a star and is just beginning to shine in her area of academic passion, even if your son is shy, even if no other parents ever show their faces in school. Arrange to meet with the principal or headmaster. When your child enrolls in high school—before she ever sets foot in the building—make it known to the administration that she has a special interest and talent in a specific subject, and explain to the administration what that interest entails to the best of your knowledge at that time. This will not only help to put your kid on the map, but will also sensitize the faculty members to your child's needs and interests in advance.

"My daughter is a serious gymnast and will need to leave school an hour early every day for practice." Or "My son is a concert pianist, and he'll need to miss school for a two-week national tour he is taking this winter. Of course, he'll make up the assignments." A teacher who is in the loop is less likely to then publicly scold the child for leaving school early or missing school for two weeks.

Be reasonable. If your child has no special needs that you know of, don't create any. If you're asking for your son to miss too much school or exclude himself from too many high school activities, you rightfully may be shown the door and directed toward a private or professional school instead.

To develop excellent rapport with school faculty members, you'll need to sensitize yourself to their needs as well. You may want to join some school committees as a parent volunteer to stay apprised of the issues that teachers are facing. You'll want to ask your child regularly about some of the more interesting lessons so you might praise a teacher who goes out of his way. You might want to write a complimentary note once in a while to be submitted to the file of a teacher who stands out. And you should keep teachers apprised of any major (positive) achievements or events taking place in your child's life.

Keeping Teachers in the Loop

SECRET 83 **Keep your child's activity schedule well organized and make sure to let teachers know as far in advance as possible when that schedule will in some way conflict with a class or lesson.** Most high schools will willingly cooperate when scheduling conflicts arise as a result of another significant academic opportunity. In general, schools like the idea of having an academic, athletic, or artistic star among their students, and will not want to go on the record as having hindered his ambition in any way. Such a student generally is focused, a good influence on peers, and, should he become famous, teachers like the idea of saying that they knew him when! But if you fail to communicate openly with the faculty and administration, the situation can easily disintegrate, to your child's detriment. If you just suddenly pull your kid out of school for a week for a gymnastics meet, for example, individual teachers may resent both you and your child, which may manifest overtly in disciplinary action or subtly in holding her to harsher grading standards.

"That's when I was planning to give a major exam—it's not fair to the other students that she gets to take it a week later," a teacher may say. Or "We'll be doing a very important unit that week. You can't expect me to sit with him to catch him up."

Make it clear to teachers that your child plans to be held accountable for all assignments, both homework and class work. If you know in advance that your daughter will not be in school, arrange for ways as far in advance as possible for her to make up any missed class work. Be up-front about your intention to work with her and/or hire tutors to do so.

SECRET 84 **Update teachers frequently of schedule changes or new achievements.** If you hear that your son is invited to speak at a science conference that you had not expected, notify his teachers immediately so that they may share in the excitement, but also so that they are aware that he may miss class or assignments. Nobody wants to be the teacher who scolds the kid who missed class for a week, only to find that he won the Intel Science Talent Search that week. Notification can be accomplished through notes to school (or by e-mail if an e-mail system is in place). Personally tailor each note to each teacher and clearly label the envelopes. Emphasize to your child that she must hand deliver these notes to the various teachers.

If you want to wow a teacher or two, you could tailor each note with specific information, like "I'm sorry Jessica will be missing your social studies class today. She loved the reading assignment and was especially looking forward to today's discussion on Socratic questioning." Or "I'm sorry Matt will be missing your English lesson on *Our Town* today. The play is a family favorite, and I cried my way through our at-home reading last night." Such a note gives the teacher multiple positive messages: that the family values the teacher, that the family endorses the lesson, and that the parents know details about what's going on in school.

| SECRET 85 | **Never assume that faculty share information with one another—no matter how supportive the teach-** |

ers, no matter how wonderful the school's reputation. It's important to notify each of your child's teachers individually to make sure that they are aware of your child's plans to miss a class, an assignment, or school. If a guidance counselor is willing to notify your child's teachers of intended missed classes or missed work, that can make the teachers' response to these absences smoother. But it's a good idea to be personally accountable for knowing that each teacher is individually notified. Never ask one teacher to notify another.

Create a Team Atmosphere

| SECRET 86 | **Right from the start, make it known that you, as a parent, are a team player, and invite the faculty** |

members to become team players, too. The idea is that you're all working together to see your child's dream come true. Let the faculty know what part you are hoping they will play. "If you could give us the homework assignments in advance, before Jake's concert tour, that would be most helpful." Or "If we could arrange for Sarah to keep a for-credit journal during her tour, rather than having to do the committee book report with her classmates for English, that might be most practical." Make it clear that you want your child to do the same amount of work as the others and that you're not requesting a lighter load. Educators like to be part of a kid's dream, so if your expectations are clearly defined and articulated, many will gladly join.

SECRET 87 — In the course of discussions, *do not say or imply to the school that your child is better than the others*—**just that your child may have some different educational needs that the team should be apprised of.** You're not asking for special favors or dumbed-down homework, just reasonable accommodations so as not to interfere with his larger educational plan.

SECRET 88 — Be especially respectful of teacher and administrative time and labor. Anything you request should require minimal extra teacher work—maybe a few top-of-the-head suggestions for reading assignments or other ideas. Don't expect a teacher to invent an entirely new assignment, curriculum, or lesson plan for your child. Offer to supplement whatever is missed whenever possible by teaching it to your child yourself—even if that requires a tutor—so the teacher knows she is not expected to privately reteach the subject matter missed, and so she is not blamed by any administrative third party if your kid misses material.

SECRET 89 — In general, focus on minimal disruption when making requests of school. Be reasonable. If you want your kid to take supplemental courses in his subject of expertise at a nearby college, don't schedule that course in the middle of the school day. Don't ask for bus transportation for your kid to get to out-of-school programs unless that's routinely provided to other children as well. You might want to drive him yourself. Or figure out public transportation, if that is available, or a taxi ride, if that is affordable. Don't ask the high school to pay the tuition. Work around the school schedule and system, and don't expect administrators to focus on whether your kid arrives safely at that other program. Logistics that veer from the school's program should be handled by you.

SECRET 90 — Invite the teachers and administrators to suggest ways in which *they* think they might be able to

make the workload more reasonable, compact, or relevant. Although you should never ask to have the curriculum simplified or dumbed down for your child, it's reasonable to ask that the administration allow your child's Olympic training to count for the school gym requirement. Or his professional piano tour could count for the school's music requirement. Discuss compacting school requirements (as opposed to individual assignments) with your child's guidance counselor. Or perhaps while your child is away, the teacher could recommend a few books that the child can read that relate to the place where he will be. (Most English teachers will do this gladly.) Always show that you are grateful for their willingness and flexibility. Suggest that you are willing to collaborate with whatever they recommend to see to it that your daughter is able to accomplish the schoolwork while pursuing her larger goal. Make it clear that you understand that they are not one-on-one tutors and that many teachers work with more than hundred students in a single day. Think collaboration.

| SECRET 91 | **If a teacher refuses to make any special accommodations, live with it.** And encourage your child to |

try to work within the system. Affirm the teachers' assignments without being patronizing. Don't argue with teachers about compacting the curriculum unless you think that a teacher is asking something that is unreasonable or unachievable. They are the education experts on the team—even if you hold a doctorate in education or are principal of another school. In their building, they know what's best. Respect that.

| SECRET 92 | **Make sure both you and your child share his victories with teachers.** Teachers should be kept in |

the loop and enjoy hearing good news about their students. Wouldn't you be miffed if the rest of the school knew that your student had just won a U.S. Congressional Award in Washington and nobody had told you—even though you let him miss three days of class *and* took the time to help him catch up?

| SECRET 93 | **Assume that *every teacher* contributed to each of your child's victories in some way, and let each of** |

them know *how* they contributed. Mr. Ramirez let your child miss class. Ms. Hanson let your daughter give her oral presentation first so she could miss school the next day. Ms. O'Toole wrote your son a recommendation.

Mr. Liang let your son hand in his homework in advance. Teachers tend to feel underappreciated—*don't be afraid to appreciate them*, and to let them know that you do. Since you probably don't see your child's teachers on a regular basis, you might write a nice note to each teacher directly and CC each teacher's file in the school office about an achievement in which the teacher might have had some role. Be expansive and generous in the note— even if you're not able to draw a direct tie. Assume that if your daughter won an essay contest that she entered on her own, the English department had a positive influence in teaching her to write well enough to win. If your son wins a chemistry award, assume that his chemistry teachers taught him to love the subject—even if he was tutored through much of the course. We all like to share in good news and feel good about ourselves when we're a part of it. We also tend to exert ourselves more for people who we know appreciate our efforts. Too often teachers are only told of negative news or blamed for student problems. Students can thank their teachers by immediately and enthusiastically sharing the good news and saying thank you directly to their teachers.

| SECRET 94 | **In addition to sharing victories, encourage your child to publicly acknowledge teachers and sup-** |

portive administrators. When interviewed in the media for an academic honor, your daughter should only say positive things about her school. Even if she's upset that her English teacher didn't call on her that day. Even if she feels that the math teacher gave her too much homework the night before. Media interviews should not be viewed as soapboxes to enact changes in the school or vent about unrelated frustrations. Your kid should be a good public relations spokesman for his school, which will pay dividends, as additional teachers will want to become part of your family team. Not only should students not criticize their school in public settings, but they should praise them when appropriate.

★ ★ ★

The next step in creating a game plan that will deliver your child's dreams (and help him win admission into a top college along the way) is familiarizing yourself with the specifics of many of the best opportunities available in your child's particular areas of interest. In the chapters to come, learn about many of these never-talked-about summer programs, Internet courses, internships, jobs, and competitions that spell success.

PART II

THE AMAZING ARRAY
FINDING THE BEST OPPORTUNITIES FOR YOUR KID

Note to the Reader

The remainder of this book is organized so that parents may look up their children's specific interests, educate themselves as to the best opportunities available in those areas, and create a winning high school strategy for establishing an exciting career path and getting into a top college. Subject areas include:

Math (chapter 5)
Science and engineering (chapters 6 and 7)
The arts (chapter 8)
The humanities (chapter 9)
Journalism, media, and advocacy (chapter 10)
Government (chapter 11)
Business (chapter 12)

These chapters are followed by an appendix, which provides forty four-year summer plans listed alphabetically by interest area, for fast and easy reference.

Don't be afraid to explore chapters outside your child's immediate realm of interest. Sometimes by learning about an opportunity in a related field, your child may decide to change or combine fields. If, for example, your politics-passionate kid finds out about an exciting opportunity in business, he might want to combine those interests and become that much more irresistible to colleges that offer business programs. Likewise, if your future engineer is intrigued by a top math program, she may benefit by pursuing both topics, since both skill sets reinforce engineering.

Some parents may prefer to read all of the chapters in part 2 to make sure their kids don't miss out on a single opportunity. I respect that, because I was that way, too. When my sons were in middle school and high school, I had to know *every* top opportunity out there to make sure they didn't miss any.

I emphasize that this book, and the following chapters in particular, should be viewed as a starting point rather than the end of exploration. While I suggest many opportunities, contests, contacts, awards, and so on for parents to pursue, parents need to pick up the phone or e-mail the relevant contacts to pave the way for their children. Parents need to keep track of the deadlines for the various programs, applications, and competitions discussed. And parents need to encourage their children and help make wise decisions about how and where time is spent. A child with a track record of achievement is irresistible to colleges that pride themselves on offering outstanding opportunities.

★　★　★

Over the next year, I am sure that I will learn about more opportunities that I have not mentioned in the chapters that follow—new opportunities that I did not know about (or did not exist) at the time of this writing. As I hear of them, I will add them to my Web site, WhatHighSchoolsDontTellYou.com. Check in now and then, and I invite you to share your own knowledge of opportunities with readers on the site as well.

CHAPTER 5

Mathematics

The Triad—Three Pedigrees for Math Students

I read that schools are much better at teaching math in Russia," a mother complained to other parents at a high school PTA meeting. "Why can't we do what they do?"

"Russia? I heard that the all six members of the Chinese Math Olympiad team walked away with gold medals at the International Math Olympiad in 2006," another pointed out. "Why can't we teach math like China?"

The truth is, it's neither fair nor accurate to judge America's schools based on the top ten or so math students in the world. Some countries earmark their education resources solely for the students they deem most likely to win at the expense of the rest of the nation's children, including some who are completely deprived of an education. The fact that the United States took home two gold medals in the 2006 Olympiad (the world championship math competition for high school students) certainly demonstrates that it is indeed possible to become one of the world's top math contenders with a U.S. education.

What American parents need to know, however, is that in order to be a national or international math contender, a child needs far more math than what is offered in the classroom—even if the child skips ahead into calculus at an early age. The vast majority of our public and private school math classes do not provide enough math training to create international or even national math contenders. Your kid wants to study math at Harvard or MIT someday? He will be at a great disadvantage for getting in and doing well at either of these (or comparable) schools if he hasn't trained for contest math during high school. Even if his high school offers AP Calculus BC (advanced AP Calculus). Contest math isn't covered in the calculus curriculum. So where does he learn it?

SECRET 95

The top math students in the United States all take lessons—either private math lessons, or by participating in the high school math team—outside of the classroom in the same way you would supplement training if your child wanted to become a concert cellist or Olympic swimmer. If your daughter has dreams of making her mark in math, you as her parent need to know the resources that are available to help her acquire world-class math skills. Many of these resources are discussed in this chapter.

The Math Pedigree

SECRET 96

There is a math pedigree in the United States that nobody talks about. Not teachers and not other parents—primarily because most people don't know about it. But if your child aspires to win the Fields Medal someday (math's answer to the Nobel Prize, as Nobel Prizes are not awarded in mathematics), or if you want to seriously be able to claim that your kid is a math whiz, it's important to know what constitutes a *real* math whiz in the eyes of colleges.

The math pedigree has three main tracks: *the contest track*, *the theory-course track*, and *the research track*. A high school student who stands out in any of these three tracks is inarguably a math whiz to colleges. Many serious math contenders choose to combine all three, but a student who distinguishes himself in any one track is regarded just as highly.

The most populated track is the Math Olympiad contest track, which consists of contest-exams known as AMC, AIME, USAMO, MOSP, and IMO, taken in that order, with related contest opportunities along the way, including USA Mathematics Talent Search, MATHCOUNTS, American Regions Math League (ARML), and Mandelbrot.

The second track consists of serious courses in math thinking, usually starting with Number Theory (the study of the properties of numbers, especially integers) and its subset, Combinatorics (the study of collections of objects, counting objects, and quantifying combinations of objects). For high school students, several summer residential math programs situated on college campuses teach these subjects rigorously, with the aim of encouraging original thought. Most prestigious are the Ross Program at Ohio State University (complete the program successfully and you virtually write your ticket into any college—most choose Harvard or MIT), the PROMYS Program at Boston University (a spawn of the Ross Program, with a respectable showing of alums at MIT and Harvard as well as a wider selection of colleges), the Hampshire University program in Massachusetts (much more rural and laid back, but serious math education nevertheless), Mathcamp (serious math taught in a sleepaway camp setting, held in a different U.S. or Canadian city each year), and Stanford University's SUMaC program. For middle school students who want a head start, the programs I'd recommend beginning with are Mathcamp or even the Johns Hopkins Center for Talented Youth (CTY) Number Theory course.

The third track consists of mathematics research, and is pursued by some of the very top math students who most commonly have already gained expertise in both the contest and math-course tracks and are eager to try to tackle some of the world's yet-unsolved math problems. These students seek out math professors from some of the top university math departments (including Harvard, MIT, Caltech, Stanford, and NYU) to mentor them in math research projects. They conduct research in mathematics, write up their findings into journal articles, and submit their work to some of the major math and science research journals and competitions, including the Intel Science Talent Search and the International Science and Engineering Fair, both of which have math categories.

All three tracks reinforce one another, and students who excel at any of these tracks are very much sought after by the top colleges and tech schools. More information on all three tracks is provided in the pages that follow.

The Contest Track

Much of the contest track is school based and school controlled, in the form of extracurricular math teams. (The other two tracks may be pursued outside of school with or without the school's input.) High school math teams administer local and national math contests, sometimes weekly, depending upon how many competitions the individual school participates in.

SECRET 97

In contrast to popular media images of math being dull, math teams generally offer fast-paced, adrenaline-packed competition. In addition, do well enough in some of the school-based contests and a student can earn national recognition.

Some parents may be uncomfortable with the concept of competing in math, arguing that such exams only test a child's speed-math ability under pressure and do not reveal a child's ability to theorize, reason, or think mathematically. And their concern is understood. But parents of math contest winners explain that in order to perform such speed-math, one has to have mastered a greater body of math to apply it quickly. In contrast to what non-math people imagine, the kinds of problems that are asked require considerable thinking and reasoning rather than mere arithmetic. In fact, the purpose of the exams is to encourage students to learn that greater body of math and reasoning skills and apply it rather than to turn children into human calculators. (Many of the competitions allow students to use calculators during the exams.)

American Mathematics Competitions (AMC)

The most significant and prestigious contests are the American Mathematics Competitions' AMC exams and follow-up exams. These are all strictly timed exams. Get a top score in the AMC-12—which is no easy task—and you'll be welcomed into any of the most-competitive colleges. There are three levels: AMC-12 (targeted for 11th and 12th graders), AMC-10 (9th and 10th graders), and AMC-8 (6th to 8th graders). What makes these contests most prestigious is that they start out with hundreds of thousands of entries and eventually are whittled down to the nation's top six students, who are invited to the International Math Olympiads (IMO), in which the world's very top math students put themselves on the map.

Is this only for math-*genius* children? No. The creators of the exam contend: "The contest is intended for everyone from the average student at a typical school who enjoys mathematics to the very best student at the most special school." Everyone can benefit. As discussed above, contest math gives your child additional math training that classroom curricula neglect. So even if your child does not perceive himself to be brilliant at math, he can benefit by participating in the school math team and AMC preliminary rounds.

The creators of the American Math Competitions explain that "the [exams'] problems . . . are chosen so that the solutions illustrate important mathematical principles." Participation in the exams improves one's problem-solving repertoire: "Some problems have quick solutions which seem like 'tricks.' What appears to be a trick the first time it is encountered often becomes a technique for solving other problems. A student's mathematical tool kit for solving problems can be greatly expanded by the acquisition of these techniques."

How significant are these exams? Significant enough that MIT and Yale, among other colleges, have specifically asked applicants on their college admissions applications if they have participated in the contest.

Most students who participate in AMC do so through their school. If your child's school does not have a math team and has no arrangement to proctor the AMC exams, initiate a program in your school or district, thereby creating the opportunity for your child (and others).

Reaching the AIME, USAMO, and MOSP

In 2006, 413,000 students in more than 5,100 schools took the AMC-10 and AMC-12 exams. Of these, 15,000 students qualified to participate in the next round, the American Invitational Mathematics Exam (AIME). Will all colleges grab your kid if she qualifies for the AIME? Not yet. She's still among 15,000 other qualifiers.

Of the students who qualify for AIME, the top four hundred scorers are then invited each year to take the USA Mathematical Olympiad (USAMO) exam. (If your child qualifies for USAMO, you can rightfully say that you have a math whiz on your hands—one of the nation's top four hundred math kids—and colleges want those kids!)

From the five hundred students who take the USAMO, the top twenty-five to thirty scorers are then chosen to attend the Mathematical Olympiad Summer Program (MOSP), a three-week intensive math boot camp at the University of Nebraska. In addition, twenty-five to thirty 9th graders are invited as well. From the older group, an official U.S. Olympic team of six members (and two alternates) is chosen to compete in the International Math Olympiad (IMO).

By the time your child reaches MOSP, she will likely notice a familiar circle of talented math children. (Their names will undoubtedly pop up frequently in other math competitions as well.) Most of the highest scorers end up at the same three or so colleges as well (Harvard, MIT, Caltech, etc.). So if you send your daughter to any of these schools, you can bet this is who she may find sitting nearby in math or physics classes.

Quick Recap of the AMC Qualifying Rounds

1. High school math teams train students for:
2. The **AMC exam**: twenty-five questions, seventy-five minutes; scoring 100 or more on the AMC-12 or 120 or more on the AMC-10 qualifies students for
3. The **AIME exam**; success qualifies the top five hundred scorers for
4. The **USAMO** (six-question, nine-hour, two-day proof/essay) **exam**; success qualifies twenty-five to fifty students (depending on funding) for
5. **MOSP** training, from which six students (and two alternates) are selected for
6. **IMO**, where more than eighty countries compete for medals.

SECRET 98

Regardless of your child's feelings about competition or whether or not he enjoys speed math, the AMC program offers some of the best training for young people interested in mathematics or math-related fields. This is training that most American high schools do not offer through the traditional curriculum but rather only during meetings of the math team. Much of the problem solving written into this exam regimen and required in preparation for these exams is carefully formulated and not part of *any other* American mathematics curriculum. No matter how many years of math your accelerated child skips, no matter how high his average is in math or how well he did in AP Calculus BC, he will miss this most valuable math curriculum if he does not participate in the high school math team and AMC exams and study both before and after the exams (to review errors).

When I first meet with 9th and 10th grade students who profess an interest in math, science, computer science, or engineering, I ask them if they participate in their high school math team. If they do, I know that they are serious and have serious prospects of getting into the colleges with the top programs. If not, I urge them to join if they want to become part of what the top math-science-engineering high school students are doing.

In recent years, the AMC-8 has been scheduled for mid-November. There are two versions of the AMC-10 (each the same level of difficulty) and two versions of the AMC-12. The AMC-10 has been offered twice in February (Contest 10A and 10B), as has the AMC-12 (Contests 12A and 12B)—two separate opportunities to score well on the same level exam, with only the highest score counted. "Do they *really* only count the highest score?" parents ask. The answer is yes.

| SECRET 99 | **Have your child take either the AMC-10 or AMC-12 twice—at both test administrations—even if he or she does well enough to qualify for the AIME the first time around.** |

Eventually the child's best AMC score and AIME score are turned into a combined score, which together determine if he moves on to the next round. Arrange in advance with your kid's math teacher to have him take the AMC exam twice so that there will be enough exams for him at both test administrations.

The next round, the AIME, is only offered once, most recently in March. The USAMO, also a one-time exam, has been offered in April.

USA Mathematical Talent Search (USAMTS)

Despite the AMC's recognition as the official American qualifier for the International Mathematical Olympiad, it does not hold a monopoly on math competitions for high school students. For students who prefer a slower paced yet equally rigorous contest—one that allows them to ponder problems over time and offers practice in writing proofs—the USA Mathematical Talent Search (USAMTS) is an excellent option. Students may do both AMC and USAMTS.

The USAMTS consists of four rounds of five problems each, per year. Students are given a month to think through and solve each problem, and then prove each solution in each round. Participants may use books and other written sources for help, and the tests are taken at home.

Previously run by the National Security Agency (NSA), the nation's largest employer of mathematicians (and therefore having an understandable interest in the nurturing of future mathematicians!), the contest is now administered by the Southern California–based Art of Problem Solving

Foundation, headed by Richard Rusczyk. Although the NSA still funds the competition and grades the exams, the Art of Problem Solving has been designing the contests for USAMTS since 2004. (Rusczyk, a former IMO winner himself, is coauthor with Sandor Lehoczky of the best training books out there, also called *The Art of Problem Solving*. He's also the creator and CEO of an online Olympiad training program that already has trained many of the world's high school math medalists, and which I'll discuss on page 101. He is a key player in leading American mathematics talent.)

SECRET 100 **Parents do not have to wait for their kid's school to recommend her for USAMTS; students may enroll themselves, online.** Performing well in USAMTS provides an alternative route (instead of AMC-12) to the AIME for the U.S. Olympiad. In other words, you can qualify for the AIME through USAMTS. In addition, USAMTS has its own value—independent of the Olympiad—in that it allows participants to hone their skills at math proofs. Proof writing is barely touched upon in American schools beyond intermediate geometry and is not a component of the earlier rounds of AMC and AIME, but it is essential for USAMO and MOSP. For many aspiring mathematicians and scientists, USAMTS is the only opportunity to learn the art of proof writing. (The bulk of higher-level mathematics—beyond high school—consists of conjectures and proofs.)

MATHCOUNTS

SECRET 101 **If it's your child's dream to become a serious contender in mathematics, start preparing him for these competitions in middle school.*** Start with MATHCOUNTS (targeted for 6th, 7th, and 8th graders) to make him a serious national contender by high school.

SECRET 102 **If your child's middle school doesn't have a math team, math club, or Mathletes, create one, and have the group enter MATHCOUNTS.** Prizes for top scorers in MATH-COUNTS are generous (individuals have been known to win $20,000 in a combination of events), and winning nationally certainly puts a kid on the

---

*Some elementary schools have Math Olympiad teams as well.

map for college—even at that early age. In fact, it's not unusual to see the names of previous MATHCOUNTS national winners turn up at the International Mathematical Olympiads a few years later, and some IMO winners claim to have participated in MATHCOUNTS as far back as 3rd grade. In college, some of these same students become Putnam Competition winners and leaders in both science and mathematics.

In addition, MATHCOUNTS surveys have shown that 80 percent of their winning alums score 1400 or above on their combined math-verbal SAT I. The most popular college majors they eventually choose are engineering, computer science, and mathematics. And the most popular college choices have been Harvard, MIT, Princeton, Virginia, Stanford, Yale, Duke, Caltech, Rice, Georgia Institute of Technology, Cornell, University of Pennsylvania, and Brown.

"MATHCOUNTS got my children started," one IMO mother said in a phone interview for this book. "From then on, they were motivated by the excitement of each competition, and that drove them to study math even more." Her children ultimately had their choice of any college, including Caltech, which offered generous merit scholarships.

| SECRET 103 | **Have your child actually sign up for the AMC for the first time during her first year of middle** |

school (if possible) to develop familiarity with the overall feel of the test: the timing, the setting, the pacing. Reassure your child that she shouldn't worry about how she does on the exam, even if she scores a zero—that this first test won't count in your eyes or in the school's. Nothing goes on the school record. This is simply extracurricular enrichment.

American Regions Math League (ARML)

If your child is very successful at his high school math team, winning significant competitions, he can go on to try out for county, regional, or state math teams that compete in the American Regions Math League (ARML) competition, held simultaneously and annually at three locations within the United States (at Penn State University, University of Iowa, and San Jose State University). Tryouts generally consist of a series of math problem sets done at your child's high school during math team meetings. Participants do several rounds (during several meetings) of competition. The top scorers are then invited to move on to larger out-of-school competitions. In the same way that sports offer all-county and all-state and regional U.S. competitions, so does math.

Mandelbrot

The Mandelbrot Competition is a school-based contest, which is both a team and individual competition. If your child's school has a math team that doesn't participate in this competition, encourage her to suggest participation to the faculty advisor. Mandelbrot offers another opportunity for a school and individual student to stand out nationally. According to the Web site, the contest's aim is "to introduce high school students of all ability levels to accessible new topics in mathematics while providing stimulating, challenging problems to stretch the best students in the country." There are two levels of participation: national (for experienced problem solvers) and regional. A math team can elect to participate in either level.

The yearlong contest consists of four eighty-minute rounds. Each round is divided into a forty-minute individual contest and a forty-minute team proof-based contest. Math teams are able to schedule these two portions for two different sessions, according to the team's own schedule. (In other words, the students can take the forty-minute individual test one day and work on the forty-minute team proof-based contest the next.) The Mandelbrot Competition was started by *Art of Problem Solving* authors Richard Rusczyk and Sandor Lehoczky in collaboration with Sam Vandervelde, PhD (a former ARML winner and member of the 1989 IMO team), who still runs the competition.

★   ★   ★

A student who distinguishes herself in any of the high school competitions described above on a national level should have her pick of colleges. Many of the country's top math kids participate in several of the most prestigious competitions, and some participate in all. For those seeking additional challenge, large regional competitions sponsored by college math clubs have sprung up in recent years.

The Harvard-MIT Mathematics Tournament

One of the best-known regional competitions is the Harvard–MIT Mathematics Tournament (HMMT), which takes place annually in February, and alternates between Harvard and MIT each year. The competitions are entirely college-student-run, for math teams of up to eight students each. High school participants may choose to participate either in two fifty-minute (more difficult) subject tests, or the hundred-minute general test; both subject and general exams take place simultaneously. In addition, collaborative events include Guts Round relays that entail groups of three problems to be solved by teams. Students may register without school endorsement, and participants who are not yet in high school may enter if they feel they are ready to compete. For more information, see http://web.mit.edu/hmmt/www/faq.shtml.

Princeton Mathematics Competition

In December 2006, members of the Princeton Math Club introduced the Princeton Math Competition, in which teams of up to ten students compete. The contest allows two teammates to work together to solve problems in any of five areas: algebra, geometry, calculus, number theory, or advanced topics. (When you register the team for the contest, you indicate who will be representing the team in each math topic.) Events include math relays (participants are split into five-member teams; each player gets a different short answer question, the answer for which is dependent on the result from the previous contestant in the line; after twelve minutes, the last person in the relay must give an answer), team contests (team members collaborate to answer ten questions in thirty minutes), and power rounds (one hour test with proofs). Team registration takes place through October, and the actual event takes place in mid-December. More information about the competition is available at: www.math.princeton.edu/~plazonic/TST.

Raising a Future Contest Winner

"How does a child get that far?" I asked parents of international gold medalists at recent IMOs—and one gold medalist himself—while researching this book. Following are some of the secrets they revealed.

SECRET 104 | Parents and teachers need to not only be very involved but also willing to plot out a math training program and schedule—in the same way an Olympic athlete's parents would choreograph training and practice—in order for a child to become

an international math medalist. That's according to Rusczyk of the *Art of Problem Solving*, who attributes much of his own success in winning the USA Mathematical Olympiad to the teachers at his northern Alabama high school and to his parents, who also helped locate opportunities and competitions. "Even if parents can't teach their children," he told me in a phone interview, "parents should be involved in removing obstacles, finding opportunities, and locating resources." The parents of IMO winners that I spoke with for this book—residents of the Midwest, the Deep South, and the Northeast—illustrated this point. They were all heavily involved in overseeing their children's math education: sometimes smoothing over bumps at school or requesting more challenging materials, chauffeuring their children to nearby university courses, and setting up training sessions at the kitchen table. Although some of these parents had math backgrounds themselves, not all did. The common element was their involvement and commitment to their children's math education. Conversely, I have observed that the parents who can't even remember their kids' math teachers' names do not produce the top math students.

| SECRET 105 |

Simple as it may seem, the biggest secret to winning major math contests is serious practice. Surprisingly, few children devote significant time to practicing independently for math competitions—and just how much time winners devote (three to four hours a day, the winners' parents confided to me) is generally kept secret. Unlike ballet competitions, something about math invites most students to just walk in the day of the exam to try their luck. Perhaps they feel that just doing (and mastering) their regular math homework for school is enough to win them a medal. It doesn't work that way. School math teams offer in-school practice, usually once per week for one or two hours. But far more practice than this is needed for a child to reach a nationally competitive level. And even if your kid doesn't aspire to become a top math whiz, imagine how much better she could be in math if she did practice problems just one hour a day.

"In my family, we practice math for four hours a day, in the same way another child who wants to become a famous violinist would practice his instrument," one international gold medalist revealed. "Daily practice—not weekly practice—is required." Another winner's parents said the number of hours in their household was less extreme—two hours a night, using the test books available through AMC, and also *The Art of Problem Solving*. One winner's mother said she did not see her son practice in a regimented way at all, although she admitted that the boy tended to fill every spare moment by exploring math ideas and problems. "Not for the test—just out of curiosity."

Among the very highest ranking students nationally, "the difference between being among the top fifty math students in America and the top five is [not talent but] determination and willingness to work," one medalist said.

SECRET 106 **To get your kids to study, parents of contest winners recommend that parents actually participate in the math study process rather than ordering their kids to hit the books.** If you don't make yourself part of the process, the test books will likely collect dust, even with the most motivated of children and the most interesting textbooks. Again, as with ballet, sports Olympics, or violin students, practice is the key. And supervised practice is most helpful. Even if you never starred in high school math (or got straight Cs, for that matter) and can only offer company, or can only act as the official stopwatch or make refreshments, sit by your child's side and do your own work. Or, if you have some higher math abilities, try taking sample Olympiad exams, too. Your mission as a parent is to provide structure and support in addition to a practice test-taking setting.

Practice Resources for Math Contests

What, exactly, should my child practice? you might be wondering.

Resources include a combination of problem-solving books and, more recently, structured courses that train individual students intensively to compete in math Olympiads, in the same tradition that Olympic athletes train (more on these training courses below). The most important written problem-solving material is offered by AMC itself, which produces booklets of previous tests.

SECRET 107 **Any parent can purchase previous test and answer booklets from AMC by phone or by mail, and AMC now offers CD versions of all levels of the AMC tests and solutions starting with 2001.** You won't find these in bookstores, however. Just as you would purchase an SAT review book for your kid to take practice tests and improve his scores, practice Olympiad exams are most helpful in getting students acquainted with the types of problems and challenges to expect and giving students experience in problem solving. To obtain study materials, fax (402) 472-6087, phone (800) 527-3690, or e-mail amcinfo@unl.edu. Orders are handled at American Mathematics Competitions, ATTN: AMC 10/12 Publications, P.O. Box 81606, Lincoln, NE 68501-160.

| SECRET 108 | **In addition, *The Art of Problem Solving* by Rusczyk and Lehoczky is a must-have for any student who** |

wants to become a serious contender in the Mathematical Olympiad. No, I don't get a commission or any other benefit by telling you this! In my years as an educational strategist I simply have observed that this book seems to cross the desk of every math contest winner who goes on to the international competitions. Don't wait to hear about it from parents of other top math students—if they know about it, they may not want *you* to. And many math team coaches may not even be aware of it. (I first learned about the book from one of my students, who complained that his summer math program roommate had hidden his copy of the book from him, because the roommate wanted to beat him in the upcoming year's national math competitions.)

One of the book's authors, Richard Rusczyk, was in the process of creating a series of additional books at the time of this book's publication. Each will feature a different topic in math, and will target the top 5 percent of the world's math students. Parents may order these books directly through *The Art of Problem Solving* at www.artofproblemsolving.com.

Math Contest Training Classes

Until 2003, no structured Olympiad training existed to help top American math students master the AMC, AIME, or USAMO—until they were among the top sixty or so to be invited to attend MOSP training camp, or unless they were able to privately find and hire someone who could help them. All other students were entirely dependent on school math team training, and if one student had gotten lucky and found a good book of problems, the tendency among the most-competitive students was not to share it.

| SECRET 109 | **Before 2004, it was a dog-eat-dog world when it came to finding training for the top math compe-** |

titions, but since then, Olympiad-targeted training programs have begun to emerge—although they're not well publicized. Among the pioneers was the Art of Problem Solving (a program by the creators of the book by the same name), AwesomeMath, the Stanford University Math Olympiad Problem-Solving Institute, and MathScore.

The Art of Problem Solving Programs

Since 2004, The Art of Problem Solving has successfully trained international medalists through its online series of math courses and discussions specifically tailored for math competitions. Using a "moderated classroom format," the classes are targeted for students interested in competing in AMC-10, AMC-12, AIME, USAMO (via the WOOT—Worldwide Online Olympiad Training—course), and MATHCOUNTS. Instructors include previous IMO winners, and the program's tone is supportive and encourages questions. Each online class has thirty to forty students from all over the world, with several instructors to moderate. In 2006, the online program had 21,000 members.

AwesomeMath.com

SECRET 110 **Two intensive Olympiad training programs are offered by AwesomeMath: a three-week residential summer camp and a year-round online correspondence course.** Neither is heavily publicized; both began in 2006.

The AwesomeMath Summer Program aims to hone middle and high school students' problem-solving skills up to the Olympiad level. It's run by Titu Andreescu, who, for many years, also ran the AMC, MOSP, and U.S. IMO team. If you're of the philosophy that it's better to learn from the master, this could be a good program for your child. (Previously such training was exclusively available to students who had already qualified for MOSP—other serious math students had to find other methods of training.) The residential program is based in Dallas and can accommodate eighty to ninety students each summer.

Your child does not have to attend the camp to take part in the year-round online correspondence course AwesomeMath Year-round (AMY). AMY features eight segments, October through April: Dr. Trig, Let p Be a Prime, Pigeonhole Principle, Concurrency and Collinearity, Always Cauchy-Schwartz, Circles, Mathematical Induction, and Calculating in Two Ways. Each segment is comprised of lectures and problem sets (math homework). Learn more about the program at www.awesomemath.org.

AwesomeMath also offers an online journal called *Mathematical Reflections*, which is targeted for math-interested high school and undergraduate students and uses articles and problems "to expose readers to a variety of interesting topics that are fully accessible to the target audience." For readers interested in publishing their math work, the publication also invites submissions from students and instructors. Visit the Web site at http://reflections.awesomemath.org.

Stanford's Math Olympiad Problem-Solving Institute

Stanford University's Education Program for Gifted Youth (EPGY) offers a math Olympiad training program for students entering grades 8 to 10 (ages thirteen to sixteen). The three-week residential "institute" in Math Olympiad Problem-Solving, targets "those who enjoy finding a solution to a difficult problem, as well as . . . those who simply want to improve their performance on the AMC or similar exams."

MathScore

A Canadian-based company, MathScore is the newest to offer online training for the Math Olympiads. (And in one of the more innovative and accessible programs available even to students who perceive themselves to be of average math ability, in 2007, MathScore introduced an instant-feedback SAT prep course.) Visit their Web site at www.Insightfulmind.com.

Math Circles

SECRET 111 One of the new, unpublicized trends among math parents in the know is the formation of math circles—informal (no grades, no homework, no attendance requirements) gatherings of students to explore mathematics. Such programs have emerged in California, notably in San Diego, UC Davis, UC Irvine, UC Berkeley, San Jose, and Stanford University, and also at the University of Utah, University of Colorado, University of Wyoming, Washington University in St. Louis, Harvard, and Northeastern. Based on the Russian math club model (the word for *club* and *circle* is the same in Russian), the programs aim to bring high-level math to students who seek challenge beyond the high school curriculum. Enrollment procedures vary; at some, students can just show up without formally enrolling. Students attend purely for the joy of learning new math and being challenged. Some math circles assemble teams for national math competitions like ARML that require group participation. To get a sense of the type of problems that math circles focus on, or to participate by computer, see www.mathcircle.org/cgi-bin/mathwiki.pl. (Mathcircle.org is the Web site for jointly run math circles at Harvard, which meets on weekdays; Brookline High, which also meets on weekdays; and Northeastern, which meets on Sundays.)

The Number Theory/Combinatorics Track

For high school students interested in the number theory/combinatorics track—rather than the math contest track—five summer programs are generally recognized by mathematicians as the most outstanding: Ross, PROMYS, Hampshire, Mathcamp, and SUMaC. These are serious summer courses. Ross is the most rigorous and is the most likely to impress the most in-the-know math professors. All impress colleges, however, if the student does well (meaning she completes all the program's problem sets and proofs). And all have helped to produce IMO champions—although producing contest champions isn't their focus, and the intensity differs significantly at each. None advances your kid in the high school math curriculum or offers remediation, either. Instead, all focus on teaching students *how to think*.

The Ross Program

| SECRET 112 | **If your child is passionate about math, you'll need to at least know about the Ross Program at Ohio** |

State—even if he is not inclined to attend, and especially if he dreams of majoring in math someday at a place like Harvard or MIT. This is one of America's best-kept educational secrets. Never mind that Ohio State University is not an Ivy League school—your child will still be accorded the highest prestige for attending. Years ago, one of the program's staffers shrugged and said, "We take the top American high school kids, bring them to Ohio for eight weeks, and they all end up at one of two schools in Cambridge within the next few years." The Ross Program is generally considered the most rigorous number theory program in America, and it's well known throughout the serious mathematics world.

"Arrive at the program inquisitive; leave the program brilliant" is the way one of my clients described the program. Years after attending, a Harvard student remarked that of all the academic courses he had taken—ever—this was the one that contributed most to his thinking.

The eight-week program offers round-the-clock math. No weekend field trips. No movie night or talent show. No TV. Instead, daily problem sets in number theory occupy students' every waking hour. If your child is passionate about math and able to handle this intensity, this could be an exhilarating place to spend a summer. The other students generally include a generous sampling of the who's who of high school math students, who then go on to Harvard or MIT to major in math, computer science, or physics, and then on to doctoral programs to pursue the same.

Don't expect your child's school to tell you about the Ross Program or channel your child toward it, though, unless your child has a math teacher who is among the nation's top-level mathematicians—or has mingled with them—because the program gets minimal publicity, and only those in the know seem be aware of it. The Ross brochure explains that the math it teaches is not available in even the best American high schools, which focus mainly on computation: "This emphasis on computation alone too often produces students who have never practiced thinking for themselves, who have never asked why things work the way they do, who are not prepared to lead the way to future scientific innovation. It is precisely this independence of thought and questioning attitude that the Ross Program strives to nurture."

Program in Mathematics for Young Scientists (PROMYS)

| SECRET 113 |

For Ross "lite"—or at least lighter—the PROMYS program is also a well-kept secret—offering the same overall curriculum as Ross, but without the recreationless intensity. What makes PROMYS less intense than Ross is that it takes place over six weeks compared to Ross's eight. Also, PROMYS offers weekend and evening social activities, and the location is more alluring for venturing off campus (the heart of Boston versus the outskirts of Columbus, Ohio).

However, this also means that students don't complete as much curriculum.

Yet despite the balance of recreational opportunities, PROMYS can boast its share of Intel winners among math researchers (see chapter 7 for more information on the Intel competition). It's a top-notch program, and the curriculum is based on the same Ross problem sets. Graduates are more likely to venture out to other top colleges in addition to Harvard and MIT, although many choose one of those two schools.

The creators of PROMYS are former students of Arnold Ross, the founder of the Ohio program, who continued teaching math to the fullest well into his nineties. In some circles, students of Arnold Ross (and participants in the Ross Program) are known as "Ross-1s." And kids who study under "Ross-1s"—which includes participants in PROMYS—are considered "Ross-2s." (The lower the number, the more prestige.)

The Hampshire College Summer Studies in Mathematics (HCSSiM)

SECRET 114 | **For the student who is passionate about math but requires more down time and sunshine, too, the** six-week number theory program offered at HCSSiM is lower key and less competitive than its urban counterparts—and even less publicized. The first time many students hear about it is late in the spring at ARML (the American Regions Math League) at Penn State, where David Kelly, director of the program, invites participants to apply.

If your child dislikes competition but loves math, this could be an excellent alternative. The setting is Massachusetts farm country, just down the road from Amherst College. Students walk across a pastoral campus to math class each day, taking in sunshine and fresh air en route, and the approach is more collaborative and nonthreatening. For laid-back fun, the program has created its own traditions as well. In the course of daily lessons, for example, lots of attention is paid to the number seventeen, and the program mascot is a yellow pig. Participants celebrate the seventeenth day of each month, and each makes a T-shirt (with a depiction of the mascot), which is supposed to be worn on the seventeenth day of each month forever after. (E-mail reminders are sent out to alums every month on the sixteenth, lest they forget.) It's all in good fun. Weekends include recreational activities and field trips to Tanglewood Music Festival, hiking, and other non-math-related attractions. While a fair number of alums end up at MIT, the spread is wider, including Amherst, other small New England colleges, Yale, and other Ivies.

Mathcamp

Although "camp" is built right into its name, Canada/USA Mathcamp offers a five-week program that includes very serious math instruction for kids ages thirteen to eighteen, in addition to many of the features of a more traditional summer camp—evening activities, weekend field trips, game tournaments, talent shows. The camp changes its location each year. Some years it's in Canada, some years the United States; sometimes East Coast, sometimes West. In 2007, it was held at Colby College in Waterville, Maine. In 2006, it was held at the University of Puget Sound in Tacoma, Washington. With the help of a faculty advisor, students design their own schedule and select the math program most appropriate to their level and interests. Many parents like the fact that the activities are more well rounded and not entirely math focused. Also, it's not uncommon to see kids at Mathcamp one summer, and then Ross or PROMYS the next. I advise math enthusiasts to seek out multiple math experiences to learn a variety of approaches and ways to view concepts.

Stanford University Mathematics Camp (SUMaC)

Stanford University Mathematics Camp (SUMaC) in Palo Alto, California, is a four-week residential program for rising high school juniors and seniors. The SUMaC program explores problems "of historical significance . . . important to the development of mathematics," and that apply to current math and science research. Like the other programs, the overall format is based on problem sets. But a special feature offered by SUMaC is the opportunity for students to experience math research one day per week (Fridays)—albeit in groups of four to five students. (Parents should note that this could be problematic if students want to enter their work into research competitions, most of which prefer projects that were worked on individually. You'd have to seek out fairs that accept group projects, which include the International Science and Engineering Fair, the regional fairs that feed into ISEF, and Siemens, but otherwise comprise the minority of the research fairs.) One of the frustrations that kids who want to do math research commonly have with the programs listed above is that the programs do not really encourage or allow enough time for math research, making entry into science research competitions (many science research contests have math categories) almost impossible when the kids arrive back in school in the fall. SUMaC is one of the few programs that does.

The Math Research Track

The third track in the mathematics pedigree is the research track. Independent math research opportunities are often more difficult to find than science research opportunities, since math is limited to a single department at most major universities. (In contrast, for every university math department, there are usually at least four or more science departments staffed with faculty members conducting research in their respective fields of physics, chemistry, biology, computer science, geology, neuroscience, etc.) That said, math research possibilities do exist. In the math research track, the ultimate goal for students is to contribute to mathematics by making new discoveries or new observations within the field, and then entering this work into research competitions. Making a significant contribution to mathematics usually entails working with a mathematics professor during the summers of high school and pursuing a thorough (and precocious) knowledge of the particular topic within math in order to be able to contribute.

Parents of students interested in this field may try to locate and then directly contact by phone a college professor who is pursuing work on a topic in mathematics that the student finds interesting. That first phone conversation by parents should determine whether a summer internship is possible—with follow-up by the student (sending her résumé and a cover letter) if an internship is deemed possible. Of course, the student will want her résumé to contain an appealing math background, meaning that the summers before freshman and sophomore year should be spent at top math programs (e.g., Ross, PROMYS, etc.), where she should gain familiarity with the process and challenges of theoretical mathematics. These programs will also help her to know if she's really interested in math research and long-term problem solving.

In addition, you'll want to locate some of the major unsolved problems to give your child a sense of what challenges mathematicians face. Find the problems that have baffled mathematicians most at www.claymath.org/millennium, the Web site for the renowned Clay Mathematics Institute.

Parents of math research students should also read chapters 6 and 7 of this book (dedicated to science and engineering), since math research is commonly considered a subset of science research (even if the Nobel Prize doesn't acknowledge it as such). Many of the opportunities available to science research students are also available to math research students. And conducting significant math or science research—significant, meaning publishing a paper or winning a patent—is a surefire way for your daughter to win admission into her choice college.

The Clay Mathematics Institute

The Clay Mathematics Institute, a tax-exempt charitable organization based in Cambridge, Massachusetts, was created "to increase and disseminate mathematical knowledge." The organization also seeks "to educate mathematicians and other scientists about new discoveries in . . . mathematics . . . [and] recognize extraordinary achievements and advances in mathematical research." Most important for ambitious math students is the organization's goal "to encourage gifted students to pursue mathematical careers."

Among its activities, CMI in 2000 classified seven math problems as Millennium Prize problems, and declared that "The first person to solve each problem will be awarded $1,000,000." The seven problems are referred to as P versus NP, the Hodge Conjecture, the Poincaré Conjecture, the Riemann Hypothesis, Yang-Mills and Mass Gap, Navier-Stokes Equation, and the Birch and Swinnerton-Dyer Conjecture. A student wanting to puzzle through any of these—or at least see what the problems are about—can look them up individually on the Internet. (Do a Google search, for example, for "Yang-Mills" or the 2006 excitement over the 2002–03 solution to the Poincaré Conjecture.) Of course, nobody is expecting a high school student to solve these problems. But if you want to tune your child in to what keeps mathematicians up at night and delve right into the challenges of theoretical mathematics, print out either the Clay description or the Wikipedia description: http://en.wikipedia.org/wiki/Millennium_Prize_Problems.

| SECRET 115 | **The Clay Mathematics Institute has become a major player in shaping future mathematicians; however, few parents—aside from the parents of kids who participate—know about it.** The most-competitive colleges know about Clay, however, and

participation (as described below) looks stellar on a college application. (Nevertheless, when mentioning Clay on an application, your child should always describe what the institute is, in case your kid's essay is read by a recent European literature major or an art history major who doesn't know math.) The institute helps to fund some of the top summer math programs, including Ross and PROMYS. In addition, in recent years it has invited up to sixteen high school Junior Fellows to become Clay Scholars. These fellows get to work with "highly distinguished mathematicians on research-oriented programs," according to the institute's literature. The students attend an eight-day seminar in Cambridge, where they are invited to work under the direction of an Academy Scholar (senior research mathematicians, internationally recognized as leaders in their respective fields) and also an Academy Fellow (younger mathematicians, usually at the postdoctoral or graduate student level).

The program was put on hold in 2006 for the 2007 summer season, and the Clay Web site said that "the organization of future sessions is still under consideration," and advised interested students to consider Ross and PROMYS in the meantime. But nominators should check the Clay Research Academy's Web site (www.claymath.org/programs/outreach/academy/about.php) if they think they have a good candidate for 2008 or thereafter.

SECRET 116 | **While most Clay Scholars are nominated by math teachers in-the-know, your child may nominate him or herself (with your assistance).** No need to wait for your child's math teacher to "discover" her if you feel she has special math talent. Participants must be at least sixteen years old and should be *accomplished* mathematicians interested in math research. (This means they must start building up a track record—entering and winning math contests and attending other math programs—years earlier.) Just to give you an idea of the caliber of student: Of the twelve students selected in 2003, four ended up at Harvard; four at MIT; one at Princeton, one at Berkeley, one at Harvey Mudd, and one at College of William and Mary. Of the twelve students selected in 2004, once again, eight went on to Harvard or MIT. In the past, applications for the program became available in the early fall.

SECRET 117 | **The Clay Mathematics Institute does not have a monopoly on math research**. If your child is not selected as a Clay Scholar, he can search online to find universities that are conducting captivating math research. (Once your child has found research that interests him, I recommend that he contact professors who are conducting this research directly via e-mail or phone, as described above.)

| SECRET 118 | **To help your child find stimulating research, check out the Web sites of the math departments of** |

universities and institutes known for their math and science research. If your child is willing to travel to the opportunities—which is optimal—many campuses provide summer housing for summer researchers. More math summer opportunities are listed at: www.artofproblemsolving.com/wiki/index.php/Mathmatics_summer_Programs. In addition, the Johns Hopkins Center for Talented Youth lists opportunities in its magazine *Imagine*, and also at the following Web sites: http://cty.jhu.edu/imagine/linkA.htm and www.cogito.org.

CHAPTER 6

Science and Engineering, Part I

Raising a Science Olympian

A high school valedictorian who was admitted into one of the most-competitive colleges in the country was hoping to pursue a medical career after graduation. As is typical, the college's premedical curriculum included biology, chemistry, and physics courses; the student had aced the sciences during high school, so she felt confident she could compete at the college level as well.

Imagine her surprise when, on the first day of her first physics course, her roommate was able to identify many of their classmates who, as high school students, had been nationally and internationally reputed science superstars. The boy who sat to her left, for example, had won a silver medal in the International Biology Olympiad. The boy to her right had won a gold medal in the International Chemistry Olympiad. There was a girl seated two desks ahead of her who had won the Intel Science Talent Search, and two other Intel winners sat together in the front row, not far from the top scorer at the ARML (math) competition.

The better she got to know the students in her class, the more she realized that they essentially comprised a Who's Who of international college math and science students. And they all seemed to know one another—by medal if not by name. These were students who thrived on competition and came into the school with well-established, well-known track records.

Suddenly this usually confident, well-adjusted, and intelligent high school valedictorian, one of hundreds that the university admitted annually, realized that it would be nearly impossible to earn an A amid this crowd. After sampling another premed-required class, she quit the premed track entirely, realizing that her defeat had happened years before she got to college.

Extreme as this situation may seem, I hear some version of this story often from parents of college freshman. Is it possible for your child to gain admission and then survive as a premed or science major at one of the country's most-competitive colleges if he hasn't made a name for himself at least nationally in high school? Yes. But be aware that it may be an uphill battle; that his qualifications, while seemingly strong to you and perhaps within his school, may look unimpressive in comparison to other kids'— which will make it that much harder to get into the best schools, and that much harder to compete if he does.

| SECRET 119 | **A little-discussed gap exists in the American high-school-to-college math-science curriculum.** The |

traditional science and math curricula at even the top high schools do not fully or adequately prepare students to major in math and science at the most-competitive colleges. In many cases, even coming to college with all As in AP or IB courses isn't enough. At Ivy League schools, Stanford, and the top tech schools, the other math-science majors are often students who have taken math-science courses *at colleges* while still in high school, conducted serious research during their summers, and/or entered (and won) national math-science competitions, and have made themselves stand out in math and science *before* getting to college. What many parents don't realize is that science, like math, has its own pedigree, and students who pursue this pedigree in high school are far more likely to win admission as science majors to the colleges of their dreams—and become successful there.

By now you're likely wondering, *What steps can students take to pursue this pedigree?* This chapter and the next are dedicated to answering that question.

The Two Major Science Tracks

Two major tracks exist for the top science students: the science Olympiad track and the research track. On the research track, students spend summers conducting original research or creating original inventions (in any field of science) with the aim of presenting their work in prestigious national and international high school research competitions like the Intel Science Talent Search, the Siemens Science and Technology Competition, and the International Science and Engineering Fair. Information about how to become involved in and succeed in this track is provided in chapter 7.

On the science Olympiad track, students spend summers accumulating science knowledge and problem-solving skills, and then compete during the school year in regional and national competitions, followed by intensive summer training (for those select few who, based on previous contest scores, are invited to train with the U.S. team) and participation in international science Olympiads (for the handful of students chosen to represent the United States from the summer intensive training programs). This chapter outlines what you need to know about raising a Science Olympian.

Note that some students pursue both tracks to strengthen their background, win a name for themselves, appeal even more to the most desired colleges, and open up more opportunities for themselves.

The Most Prestigious Science Competitions for High Schoolers

While there is no *official* prestige order of science competitions, among the most-competitive colleges success in the following math and science programs and contests adds significant clout to an application, according to what college admissions officers have told me. (Information about all of these competitions and contests is provided in this chapter and in chapter 7.)

1. USA Physics Olympiad, USA Mathematical Olympiad, USA Chemistry Olympiad, USA Biology Olympiad, and USA Computing Olympiad
2. Intel Science Talent Search (the Intel) top forty finalists and top ten winners
3. Siemens Competition in Math, Science, and Technology winners
4. Research Science Institute, Ojai and Socorro participants
5. ARML (math competition) winners
6. Intel International Science and Engineering Fair winners
7. Junior Humanities and Science Symposium national winners

> Earn any of these accolades and you write your own ticket to your first-choice college. (It should be noted that, on rare occasions, some Intel *finalists* have been rejected by some of the most-competitive colleges.)

Essential Coursework for Both Tracks

To excel in (or, in most cases, to even participate in) either science track, students must take a rigorous, accelerated science and math course load, often including college-level science courses *at universities*. (Note that simply taking and scoring top grades in an accelerated science course won't necessarily wow college admissions—or make your kid a shoo-in—even if he takes a few summer courses at Harvard or other prestigious institutions. I've seen kids who have an impressive college grade or two on their records get rejected. However, accumulating a whole bunch of As in college courses while still in high school can be very impressive.)

SECRET 120 **Regardless of which science pedigree your child pursues, math acceleration and a solid math background are prerequisites.** If your child wants to stand out in science in high school or college, encourage her to accelerate in math both in middle school and high school. When she is in 7th or 8th grade, preview her middle school's math curriculum to determine which courses she could most easily skip. (At most schools, there is a lot of repetition in middle school math.) As discussed in chapter 5, acceleration may be accomplished through independent study, private tutoring, and/or summer enrichment courses.

And remember: Make sure to not leave any holes in your child's math education. Whichever method your child uses to accelerate, *she must be accountable for all of the information covered in the classes she skips* and be able to ace whatever exams are required for those classes. Otherwise, this can come back to haunt her years later when she struggles through more advanced courses because she's missing important math concepts and skills.

SECRET 121 **Be selective about skipping your middle school child in science.** In general, the middle school science curriculum is looser and less prescribed than the high school science curriculum, which means that teachers are often allowed to be more creative in their teaching in a positive way. While the high school curriculum usually has to keep pace with the national AP curriculum, which is crammed with material and does not allow much time for deviation, in middle school teachers often feel more free to stray from a curriculum according to their own interests. For the class, this can mean fascinating lessons in subjects as diverse as black holes, genetics, and nanorobots, any of which could spark an interest in a child not previously interested in science. Then again, lack of a curriculum can also mean your child will be getting a dull mishmash of science—with topics dependent on the teacher's whim or which equipment the other classes aren't using that week. Ask parents of older kids (particularly older kids who enjoy science) if their kids found the courses offered stimulating. If the overall opinion is that a course is not stimulating, have your child skip that class if possible. (Sometimes poorly structured classes can do more to turn a child off science than to spark an interest.)

SECRET 122 If accelerating means that when your child is in 8th grade, she will have to walk to a separate high school building or use public transportation to take high school level courses, do not be intimidated. Even if she is shorter or clearly younger looking than the high school kids. Instead, meet with the high school administrators, and make sure that they'll guarantee her safety. Even if they're not proponents of acceleration, they should be able to promise this. Acceleration often is an easy means to educate a precocious learner—rather than making the classroom teacher struggle to cater to a wide variety of levels at the same time. And for a 7th or 8th grader, traveling to a high school can be an exciting adventure. If the high school is far from the middle school and your child needs transportation that the school won't provide, arrange it yourself.

SECRET 123 If the school absolutely refuses to let a child skip, pursue more advanced courses online or summer courses at a program that offers high school or college credit. Don't let her school slow her down. Acceleration is vital for many of the science competitions, and schools that refuse to let kids accelerate push them out of contention.

SECRET 124 Do not listen to "experts" who tell you to wait until your daughter reaches upper grades to have her skip so that she may get adjusted to middle school. Hanging with a class of less skilled math or science students will not help her adjust any better. It's a lot easier for a reasonably adjusted child to accelerate immediately upon arrival in middle school, when parents are more likely to still be able to help with homework questions.

> **SECRET 125**   **In advancing your child, never enroll him in a program that's targeted for older children who are taking the course for remediation.** Such a classroom is not likely to contain a passion for learning but rather a sense of defeat, even if the skill level is the same. Your inquisitive child may be stifled from asking questions in that environment. Such classes may also include children with behavioral problems or other academic issues—the reason they didn't pass the course in the first place—which potentially could be detrimental to learning.

> **SECRET 126**   **If your child is lucky enough to attend a middle school where all of the science courses are stimulating and, hence, won't want to skip any, consider having her double up on high school sciences starting in 9th grade if she wants to qualify for any of the Olympiads or conduct science research.** For example, assuming your child has taken Earth Science in 7th or 8th grade, in 9th grade have her take Biology *and* Chemistry. And in 10th grade have her take Physics *and* AP Biology. By 11th grade, this child is ready to participate in the USA Biology Olympiad or to apply for an internship in a biology or medical lab for the summer. Her 11th grade curriculum should include both AP Chemistry and AP Physics, making her eligible for both the Chemistry Olympiad and the Physics Olympiad by senior year and an internship in a chemistry or physics lab the summer before.

I highly recommend that your child finish calculus before taking AP Physics C, and possibly any physics course. Some schools have students take the courses concurrently; however, AP Physics C presumes a thorough understanding of calculus, so students who haven't previously taken calculus often struggle the entire year—and their grades suffer as well. If your child moves at a faster pace in math in middle school and can complete calculus in 10th grade, she'll be better able to understand AP Physics in 11th grade and avoid the struggling many students experience.

Of course, many variations on this structure work, too. If you know, for example, that your daughter is particularly interested in physics, you may want to have her take AP Physics earlier and calculus even earlier so that she may take part in the first round of the USA Physics Olympiad starting in

11th grade, or start a two-year research project in physics the summer before 11th grade instead of waiting until 12th grade.

My goal here is to let you know what skipping is required at a minimum to help your child to be eligible for the Olympiads and major science research competitions, rather than having you find out belatedly in her senior year that she has missed the opportunities as a result of an inadequate schedule of courses. The usual order of science courses may be fine for the average student, but parents of students who want to compete nationally in the sciences need to explore acceleration options.

The Science Olympiad Track

Just as a student who wants to compete nationally or internationally in the Math Olympiads or even sports Olympics needs to devote significant time to practice and preparation, so do students who would like to become contenders in the national and international science Olympiads. The United States has subject-specific teams in biology, chemistry, physics, and computing. Each of these teams is run separately by different organizations. But the common thread is the big-picture goal of these Olympiads—to inspire students to see the intrinsic value of science and pursue careers in science and engineering. Along the way, the Olympiad competitions spark lots of inquiry, challenge, learning, and excitement.

The first round of the Olympiads generally consist of in-school exams with knowledge and analysis-based questions. First-round exams, which are generally open to all, are administered nationwide, usually in school and by a science teacher. (The Computing Olympiad allows students to take some of the preliminary exams on a home computer.) Each first-round exam is offered on a separate date nationwide, which is announced each year. The vast majority of competitors are eliminated via this first round. But make it to the second round and you're starting to build a nice credential.

Second-round tests vary. In the physics team competition, the second test is another in-school exam. The same is true in biology. In chemistry, lab experiments are required, and participants who make the cutoff are invited to a university or other location with a lab. The Computing Olympiad is taken in school.

When the final group of fifteen to sixty (depending upon the Olympiad) top students nationally is determined, the "winners" are invited to attend an intensive training camp for one to two weeks, at which four to six official U.S. team members are selected to represent the United States internationally.

Just being among the fifteen to sixty students who attend the training camps is an extraordinary achievement and (along with very high grades and very high standardized test scores) can virtually guarantee one's admission into a choice of top universities. As you can imagine, being among that top final team of four to six selected to compete internationally in any one science is *extremely* prestigious. These winners are sent fully funded to contests that are generally held overseas, hosted by different member countries each year.

Obviously, the vast majority of students who participate in the science Olympiads do not win. But the contests are set up so that the experience of *participating* even at the very first level is educationally worthwhile, and participation in these or the Math Olympiad (discussed in chapter 5) can fill in many educational gaps that the regular curriculum neglects.

| SECRET 127 | **Olympiad participants learn a lot of science that is not included in even the best high schools'** |

curriculum—but is invaluable in college science classes. Top high school science students who do not participate in any Olympiads often feel overwhelmed when they get to the most-competitive colleges—largely because they're not as familiar with a lot of the vocabulary and faster problem-solving techniques taught through Olympiad training.

U.S. Science Olympiad Web Sites

To learn more about the science Olympiads, check out their Web sites:

- USA Physics Team, based at University of Maryland: www.aapt .org/Olympiad 2007/
- USA National Chemistry Olympiad, based at U.S. Air Force Academy in Colorado Springs: www.chemistry.org
- USA Biology Olympiad, based at George Mason University: www.cee.org/usabo/index.shtml
- USA Computing Olympiad Team, based at University of Wisconsin: www.usaco.org

- USA Mathematical Olympiad, based at University of Nebraska: www.unl.edu/amc

(Note that each Olympiad is run independently of the others.)

Science Olympiad Basics

To take part in an Olympiad, a student should choose which available individual science Olympiads interest him—biology, chemistry, physics, or computer science—and then enroll at school, usually by informing a teacher of the subject in which he is interested. That teacher then registers the student with the national competition.

SECRET 128 **Don't let your child wait for an announcement at school to find out when to enroll.** At some schools, teachers openly announce that an Olympiad entry round exam will be taking place. "All interested students please let me know by X date." In other schools, science teachers require the entire class to take the exams, or they announce it to all of their AP students. And in other schools, teachers hand-pick the kids they project to be most likely to succeed and inform only them of an upcoming exam. But in the vast majority of schools, no announcements are made. It bears repeating that parents should be aware of all competition deadlines. Don't expect teachers or the school to remind you.

SECRET 129 **At the beginning of the school year, when you devise your own academic calendar (as discussed in chapter 3), make sure to include the Olympiad schedules and deadlines, and arrange with your child's science teachers to have her take the Olympiad exams.** This means notifying the teacher, who may not even be aware that such tests exist. Find out the exam schedules *for yourself* by looking up the Olympiad online—don't wait for an announcement from school.

SECRET 130 **Taking Olympiad exams along with older students is an excellent idea for younger kids.** If you think your middle school–aged child might enjoy these contests as a junior or senior in high school, plan to get her started in 9th grade just for practice and to give her a sense of the pacing, setting, and types of questions to study—even if she gets a zero on the test that first time around. By the time she is in 11th grade, the contest should look familiar and reasonably comfortable, and her chances of success will be far greater than the chances of other 11th graders approaching the contest for the first time. Look over the questions from previous years' contests when your child is in 8th or 9th grade, and ask yourself what materials, study guides, and coursework or tutoring might improve your child's success rate at the contest. (See below for more information on preparing for the Olympiad exams.)

Studying for the Olympiads

SECRET 131 **Parents should note that these tests are not meant to test raw abilities.** Instead, they test the child's ability to master material when given an entire year to study (since the last exam). Make sure that your child utilizes that time wisely—it can make all the difference. Yes, a child needs to be extremely bright to win, but parents of winning kids have told me that their kids' "big secret" simply was studying much more than their peers (sometimes as much as four hours a day for several months). Studying high school course material is not enough to ace the Olympiad exams.

SECRET 132 **Some of the national Olympiad organizers sell strategy books or question-and-answer books with problems from previous Olympiads for a nominal charge.** These books are not promoted or advertised, and winners don't necessarily talk about which books they used to study. But parents of Olympiad winners tell me that their children have leaned heavily on these books. Some of these books are available for sale from the contest organizers. Go the Web site of the Olympiad that interests your child to see contact information and where you might get hold of practice tests.

My advice is to buy just a few books at first (when your child is in 8th or 9th grade), and encourage your child to peruse them. At worst, your kid gets a collection of challenging math and science problems to browse through. At best, she becomes intrigued that her peers were able to master such problems in previous years and vows to study to become an Olympian—and an outstanding young scientist in the process.

SECRET 133
Study with your child for the Olympiads. Invest yourself. Live vicariously a little—regardless of what people may say about "living through your kid." Winners' parents tell me they made Olympic practice a fun family activity. And at a minimum I've never heard of an Olympian being successful without strong parental support for logistics and extra training.

Tips for Specific Olympiads

The Physics Olympiad

SECRET 134
The ranks of the USA Physics Team are largely filled by members of the math Olympiad team and other top math students, so if your kid has physics aspirations, he should also intensively study math starting at an early age (as discussed on page 114). The physics team is generally considered the most prestigious of the teams—if prestige even matters at that stage.

The Chemistry Olympiad

SECRET 135
A warning: Be careful not to *overqualify* your child for the Chemistry Olympiad by enrolling her in more than two college chemistry courses. High school students who have taken more than two college chemistry courses are no longer eligible for the Chemistry Olympiad. (AP Chemistry does not count as a college course.) If your child aspires to become part of the chemistry team, she should, however, try to take the maximum two courses permitted to maintain an edge. Which two? Choose from Introduction to Chemistry, Organic Chemistry Lecture, and Chemistry Lab.

In addition, she should take lots of practice Chemistry Olympiad tests and should memorize key chemistry formulas. When I interviewed a winner's mother for this book she commented that two types of kids do exceptionally well in the USA National Chemistry Olympiad: chemistry professors' children and students with the strongest math backgrounds and study ethic.

The Computing Olympiad

"Shouldn't the Computing Olympiad be the easiest one to join?" parents often ask. "My kid is on the computer day and night. Couldn't that be considered practice?"

What these parents don't understand is that real computer programming is based on a sophisticated knowledge of mathematics, not a general proficiency in e-mail, Web surfing, video games, or even Web design.

Parents should be aware that most college applicants are extremely computer literate nowadays. The ability to type, make charts, do Internet research—general computer literacy—is presumed. The bulk of college applications are filed electronically. And most applicants' computer skills exceed their parents'. This does not make them computer geniuses.

SECRET 136 **What constitutes genuine computer whizzes are the handful of students who make up the USA Computing Olympiad Team.** Encourage your computer-savvy kid to at least try some of the at-home online exams. In the process, he'll gain a lot of computer knowledge that is not taught in high school. Note that students striving to make the USA Computing Olympiad Team are just as likely to be active members of the school's math team as its computer team.

How can your child attain the background and sophisticated knowledge base to be a contender in computer science?

SECRET 137 **Start early and ensure that your child accelerates in math as well as computer science.** There's no reason, for example, that a middle school student could not take some of the introductory programming courses (names of the courses vary by school, but are usually something like Computer Science 1, Computer Science 2, Introduction to Programming, Intermediate Programming) that lead to AP Computer Science, so that by the time she is in 9th grade, she could take AP Computer Science. When should your child start learning how to program? When she shows interest.

SECRET 138 **For very young children who show an interest in programming, introduce them to Usborne Books' books on computer science for ages ten and up.** For years this company was one of the few that took it upon itself to explain complex computer science to elementary-school students using a comic-book format of colorful pictures along with text. Titles have included *101 Things to Do on the Internet* and *101 Things to Do with Your Computer*, both by Gillian Doherty. Usborne also offers *Build Your Own Web Site* as well as a *Computer Dictionary* and *Computer Graphics*. You'd be surprised at what very young children can do. If your child is already in high school and wants to enhance her computer knowledge, start with an Usborne book and she'll quickly advance to more age-appropriate literature.

SECRET 139	**Seek programs outside of school to enrich your child's computer science curriculum.** As high

school course offerings tend to be limited, I recommend calling local colleges to investigate what's available in your area. Also check out some of the talent search course offerings (through the programs described in chapter 2) and local computer (weekend) schools that offer programs for teens. Among the talent search programs, for example, the Johns Hopkins CTY offers students in grades 7 and up three-week courses that include Fundamentals of Computer Science, Theory of Computation, and Data Structures and Algorithms. Duke TIP offers grades 9 and up Computer Programming 1 and Java Programming. In addition to the talent searches and local privately run computer schools, consider sending your child to an intensive computer camp. The largest chains of computer camps with a combined total of more than a hundred university locations are run by iD Tech Camps, www.internaldrive.com, and Cybercamps, http://cybercamps.com/index.aspx. If your child wants to learn serious programming, avoid regular camps that happen to offer a computer class or two—these are not nearly as serious.

SECRET 140	**Find out while your child is still in 8th grade if her high school will be offering AP Com-**

puter Science, and if not, help to initiate AP Computer Science and the courses that lead up to it. To do this, you'll have to propose the new course or courses before the group (board of education) or individual (financial officer) responsible for the school budget. You'll want to write up a proposal for the new courses, including how many children you expect to benefit from the new courses, how many faculty members would be required, nearby districts or schools that offer the course successfully, a general description of the proposed curriculum (borrowing from other schools' descriptions), any additional equipment that might be required, and any additional facilities that might be required.

By the time your child is ready for that curriculum, the course should be available. You may even want to start her taking computer courses at the local high school while she is in middle school. *What's the rush?* some parents may wonder. The idea is to get as much computer programming knowledge as possible at as young an age as possible, so she may qualify for some of the national computer competitions when she gets to high school. Students that "stay on level" for computer courses in high school offer no competition to the top Computing Olympiad competitors—even if they get top grades in their high school computer courses. Accelerating means maximizing the number of years your child gets to participate in the Olympiad during high school and perfect his skills, so that by junior or senior year he is a real contender.

SECRET 141   **If your child's high school does not have a computer club or computer team, initiate one as soon as possible, preferably before he enters high school.** Some national competitions, including the American Computer Science League, require students to be part of a computer team in order to participate. (More than two hundred schools in the United States, Canada, and a few from Japan and Europe participate in ACSL. After the in-school rounds, winning school teams are invited to a national competition, held in a different location each year. To find out more about having a school team participate in ACSL, locate the organization on the Internet: www.acsl.org.)

The science Olympiad track is the more populated track for science kids, probably because, unlike the research track, participation in the earliest rounds doesn't require devoting an entire summer to working in a lab or any other long-term commitment. (Of course, for those who aspire to win, studying is required.) But for those whose aspirations include inventing, conducting original research, and discovering cures to diseases, the research track will likely be much more rewarding.

For a child to be successful in science research, an investment of time—and a lot more legwork—is required on the part of the parents. Chapter 7 will provide you with the information you need to help your child embark on (and excel at) this exciting track.

Science and Engineering, Part II

Launching Inventors and Explorers on the Research Track

Make sure he does research the summer before 11th and again before 12th grade," the highly educated, foreign-born mother whispered to another parent before a PTA meeting at their local high school.

"Research?" the American-born mother asked. "He was planning to take summer courses at a college."

"No, no," the other mother said. "You have it wrong. In my country, they tell us that when you come to America, if you want your children to do science or medicine, you have your children do research internships in a professional laboratory in the summers before 11th and 12th grades."

"They tell you *that*?" the American-born mother asked. "Before you get here, you know *that*?"

"That's the American science pedigree," the other parent said, proud to offer advice to the American-born mother on the American education system. The foreign-born parent and her friend who was seated next to her both nodded with authority.

"There's no pedigree in America. Americans don't believe in pedigrees," the American-born responded.

"Here, nobody shares information," the foreign-born mother laughed. "But *there* they told me: Research the summer before 11th grade."

Over time, the American-born mother learned that the foreign-born women were right.

| SECRET 142 | **For a student interested in science research who wants to get into a top college as a "science kid,"** |

it's important to conduct research during the summers before 11th and 12th grades. Do you want your child to really wow a college? Encourage him to try to earn a patent or publish a paper in a professional journal. Even if he doesn't win a single research competition, a patent or published paper will open the doors to the college of his choice. Of course, if he wins any of the top national science research contests, the doors will open as well.

Contrary to what outsiders might imagine, the science research track is a very exciting route to pursue. It's not about looking up old science and summarizing it—it's about creating new science. Students start with questions that science and engineering haven't yet answered, and they set out to find their own original solutions. (Sometimes the search for knowledge takes place in a lab, sometimes out in the field, or on a computer, or through dives in the ocean, or at an astronomical observatory.) The students then conduct their experiments, write up their findings into journal-style articles, and enter these papers into science research competitions; finalists in these competitions are invited to present their research at science fairs, using poster board displays. Note that these are not the elementary-school-style science fairs where kids whip up projects the night before based on book research and make a pretty display to illustrate some already-known textbook science phenomenon. And if your image of research consists of sitting in a quiet library reading text after text or collecting Internet sources and putting the combined texts into one's own words, it's time to clear away the cobwebs. What science research competitions are *really* about is encouraging students to conduct original experiments on phenomena that pique their interest. (Is time travel possible? Can the healing behavior of insects be useful to humans in curing disease? Do other planets in our galaxy support life? Can human memory be enhanced by computer chips?) Research students' experiments are generally supervised by a scientist and take place in a lab, observatory, or field station as part of either a formal research program or through independent arrangements made with a lab.

This chapter tells you how to help your kid find the best research opportunities—both formal lab programs and independent research—and how to help her gain the right credentials in the years before 11th grade, so that she will have the opportunity to work in a very selective lab by the summer before 11th grade.

SECRET 143

Start by familiarizing yourself with the research and invention competitions that are "big players" (and their criteria) when your child is in 8th or 9th grade. Look them up online. Your child needs something to aspire to, and you need to learn about the criteria years before your child enters.

The most prestigious contests include the Intel Science Talent Search; the Siemens Competition in Math, Science and Technology; the International Science and Engineering Fair; the Junior Science and Humanities Symposium; the First Step to the Nobel Prize in Physics; the First Step to the Nobel Prize in Chemistry; the National Gallery for America's Young Inventors; American Academy of Neurology Competition; and the Davidson Institute scholarships. In addition, there is a small selection of research programs that are prestigious enough to impress colleges just as much or even more than winning the big science competitions. Among these most prestigious programs are the Research Science Institute (RSI) at MIT and Boston-area facilities, Ojai, Socorro, Minority Introduction to Engineering and Science Program (MITES), MIT Women's Technology Program, various states' Governors' Schools, and the Center for Astrophysics, Space Physics and Engineering Research (CASPER). Information about many of these contests and programs is included in this chapter.

SECRET 144

Begin taking your child to regional science fairs, preferably when he is in 8th grade, or in 9th grade. This is an essential outing—an eye-opener—even if you and he have to miss a day of work and school. (Most high school fairs take place on school days.) He needs to see the top of the mountain before he'll agree to climb. Either ask your child's science teacher for specific dates or look for the particular fair online. To find the nearest regional feeder fair for the International Science and Engineering Fair, for example, go to www.sciserv.org. Look there for "Find a Fair." Specify your state (or nation), and the listing will show you the nearest regional fair locations and dates.

When you visit the fairs, focus first on what high school juniors and seniors with interests similar to your child's are able to accomplish. Ask some of the more approachable student presenters where they conducted their research, and take notes. Some of their choice research facilities might interest your child as well in the future. At the poster board sessions (where students display their science findings on posters and stand by them ready to answer questions), interview some presenters, but explain that you're not a judge—just a visitor. Ask a presenter, for example, how much she liked the lab where she worked. Ask if she has any advice for your child in finding research. Seniors probably will be the most helpful, since they are finished with high school competitions and have nothing to lose by sharing secrets with a novice.

Also check out the poster boards themselves. Get ideas for what constitutes a good visual presentation and what constitutes a weak one. Encourage your child to walk around independently at the fair if that is permitted. Let her show you poster boards of projects that particularly interest her.

Research Basics

First-time visitors to science fairs can sometimes be heard muttering in disbelief, "This isn't high school research. Somebody must have done the project for the kid." Depending upon the high school contest, the projects can be pretty impressive and even intimidating. Otherwise-jaded adults are commonly either shocked or enchanted by what serious and dedicated high school students produce.

| SECRET 145 | **Judges tend to prefer previous winners. For that reason, an earlier start tends to be a major ad-** |

vantage in national science competitions. It's not uncommon for serious science enthusiasts to enter the ring in 9th or 10th grade—having pursued research starting the summer after 8th grade. And many contest applications ask what other science competitions the child has won previously. The more time she has devoted to research, the more likely she is to have won other contests, and this makes her a better candidate for winning yet-to-be-judged contests. Note that the summer before junior year is the last possible start date if a student hopes to win a major competition in high school.

The summers before junior and senior year can be devoted to similar or to two completely unrelated projects. What counts is that the student gets initial research experience before junior year and then is able, during her junior year, to gain experience presenting her findings.

What Does Science Research Entail?

During each year that the student participates in research, he needs to do all of the following:

1. Conduct science experiments or investigations on a finite project or create an engineering project during the summer—usually in a professional lab.
2. Keep lab notes.
3. Write up the research into a science journal–style article.
4. Create an appealing poster board to exhibit the research.
5. Enter the project into multiple science research competitions.

SECRET 146

Note that if your child is interested in entering her work in competitions, she only needs to create one project per year. She is then free to enter the same project in multiple competitions—even competitions offered by different or competing companies. Newcomers commonly assume that the child must create a new project for each competition, and that task sounds overwhelming—because it would be. They worry that entering the same project into multiple competitions is cheating—but it's not. All of the competitions let you reenter the same project within a given year. But the student must create a new project each year—your child can't enter last year's project again in next year's competition. And your child can't enter a project as a team project in one competition and then call the identical project an individual project for the next competition. Either it's a team collaboration or an individual project.

SECRET 147

The vast majority of science research contest winners conduct their research at professional laboratories or field research stations (during the summer)—not at school. To connect with lab opportunities, students generally apply to a formal summer research program or make their own inquiries directly to lab scientists. More information on how to secure these opportunities can be found below.

Once a project is started in a lab, some students are able to continue their projects at school during the school year if they are able to find a teacher who can help in the specific field of the project and if the school has the necessary facilities and supplies—although this is very, very rare. This is not a poor reflection on the schools, however. Imagine, for example, that your daughter's research fascination is with the language of beluga whales. Her high school probably won't have a tank full of belugas for her to listen to, nor is it likely to have underwater recording devices or a biology teacher with expertise in whale communication—no matter how prestigious the high school. For that reason, many students prefer to work in labs that are within easy commuting distance from home so they may continue their research during the school year. But sometimes better opportunities are found afar. If you're able to swing the logistics, go with the best opportunity—the one that interests your child most—rather than the most convenient.

SECRET 148 **Very few students conduct their research at home.** Similar to the above, most people simply don't have the kind of high-tech, specialized equipment necessary for students' projects. (That said, every once in a while a winning project will have stemmed from home-based research. Homegrown winning projects have included observing backyard ant communities, determining the local threat of disease-bearing mosquitoes, creating a new kind of microscope, and measuring the effects of invasive plants on local gardens. But these projects are the minority. And for a decent percentage of supposedly homegrown projects, at least one parent is able to act as a supervising scientist or engineer.)

SECRET 149 **The summers leading up to freshman and sophomore years of high school are the most important summers for acquiring the extra knowledge (beyond the high school curriculum) that may be required for internships.** Do not expect that the lab where your son wants to conduct research on Parkinson's will teach him basic biology, nor that the lab where your daughter wants to examine local water pollutants will teach her basic chemistry. Students will need to master these (and other) subjects *before* applying for a summer research internship. In fact, to secure an internship at a lab, your child generally will be required to present a résumé that demonstrates an ample track record of science courses, experiences, and knowledge to be able to contribute to the particular lab's work in a meaningful way. Building up such a résumé requires time and planning starting at the very beginning of high school.

SECRET 150 **Encourage your child to take serious summer and school-year enrichment courses to build science**

credentials as soon as possible in middle school and early high school. Acceleration (skipping) is most beneficial to students who want to participate in the big science competitions. A child who has more science under his belt by the time he applies to labs is more likely to get the internships he chooses. Understand that these summer courses have to come to an abrupt end by the summers before your child's junior and senior year in order to appropriate those summers for pursuing research. Your child is on a tight summer schedule.

What if your "late-bloomer" isn't interested in science until the end of his junior year of high school? He can still major in science in college, but he's too late to win any major high school research competitions. Some local science fairs may be more accessible and willing to accept a total novice. But, in general, he'll need years of track record to win any of the major competitions. For that reason, have your child participate in science fairs at as young an age as possible. While she may not have good odds at winning during the early years of high school, participation will give her experience in formulating her own scientific ideas, presenting those ideas to strangers, assembling an entire project, designing a poster board display, and writing a research paper.

If some local competitions exclude younger high school students, find other local competitions that welcome them—they do exist. If your child's science teacher doesn't know of any, ask students from neighboring schools or districts which contests their schools participate in.

SECRET 151	**Do not base your search of contests and opportunities entirely on what your child's school science**

teachers tell you. In some schools, science teachers are required to play the role of gatekeepers and are charged with restricting the number of children who may participate from that school. (For some fairs, the school must pay per child participating, so schools are hesitant to allow too many participants. Other fairs have maximum limits on the number of students who may participate from each school, and preference may then be given to upperclassmen.) Some schools make up arbitrary rules about who may participate as a means of encouraging students to enroll in additional years of science research courses in order to "earn" entry (see below for more information about high school research courses). This may help fill undersubscribed courses at school, but it doesn't help the aspiring scientist. Go online and seek out other competitions that are relevant to your child's subject area.

Google "science contest" or "astronomy competition," for example, or visit www.cogito.org. And don't assume that your child is dependent on the school to enter a competition.

In-School Research Programs

Thousands of American high schools—both public and private—offer science research programs, and the number has been increasing steadily. Years ago, the most exclusive prep and public schools kept away from contests in general, as if the schools were too elite to compete with the riffraff. Gradually, however, the number of elite schools entering the top science research contests has increased. Most recently, semifinalists in the Intel Science Talent Search have included students from such prestigious institutions as Phillips Exeter, Chapin, Sidwell, Durham Academy, and Phillips Andover.

Does your child's school have a science research program? If not, you may want to consider initiating one if your 8th or 9th grader has a serious interest in science or social science research. Although in-school programs don't *provide* research projects for students, they help facilitate research for high school students. They introduce the subject of research and teach lab techniques, journal-article-writing skills, and presentation skills. The better research programs also help students find out-of-school summer internships according to the students' own interests.

If you want to push for a science research program, know what kind you're seeking. Three basic types exist: (1) research techniques, (2) invention and discovery, and (3) a combination of the two. Techniques programs structure science research as a four-year sequence whereby students are required to take introductory courses in 9th and 10th grades that teach general laboratory techniques, basic statistics and data gathering, science paper writing, oral presentation skills, and poster board design. The aim is to give the students the skills needed so that when an internship is eventually secured (the summers before 11th and/or 12th grades in these programs), the students are able to contribute to a professional laboratory environment. As a highlight, the younger students are generally taken to science fairs to see older kids compete.

The biggest drawback to this type of program is that the intro students are rarely encouraged to conduct their own original science research during those first two years. If any research takes place in these courses, it is generally as part of a group or with the entire class. Thus the student walks away from the course with nothing to claim as his or her own—no original research—and nothing to enter into contests. This works for some students but turns off many others. They miss the delight of making their own independent discoveries—the whole purpose of science research. Two years, or even a year, feels too long to go without conducting original research if the student is genuinely interested in research. Another drawback is that when research is only conducted as a class project, the individual doesn't get to focus on the area of research that most interests him. The computer science enthusiast gets stuck for months learning chemistry lab techniques. Or the chemistry enthusiast is assigned to build a new wind-powered device.

The second approach is to offer 9th and 10th graders a course that focuses on invention and discovery. (Proponents of this approach contend that individual lab techniques are often nontransferable from lab to lab anyway, and that there may be no reason for a student interested in computer research, for example, to learn about how to use pipettes or how to focus a particular microscope or telescope.) In this second, more engineering-oriented curriculum, students are asked to search science magazines and journals to find scientific problems that intrigue them. Students then invent devices to address those problems, build prototypes at home or in school, and present these engineering projects at science fairs, most of which offer an engineering category. This kind of program is generally more engrossing and inspiring. Students learn about presenting at competitions through immersion—by actually getting to participate. In some cases, high school students have been able to patent their inventions.

The third approach, combining the first two, is probably the best to push for in a school that doesn't already offer science research. You want your child to be able to invent and focus solely on his own scientific interests, but at the same time you want to get him the best instruction on how to write a journal paper and present his work. In the ideal situation, English teachers and journal-article experts would be brought in to discuss how to write a winning journal paper, art teachers would discuss designing poster board displays, and teachers of public speaking would show students how to present their scientific findings before an audience.

Regardless of which style course your child's high school offers for 9th and 10th graders, by 11th and 12th grades most high school science research programs focus on supporting students after they return from summer internships (guiding them in filling out forms, writing science research papers, creating poster boards, and practicing public presentation skills). At some schools, these upper-class courses meet regularly as a group. In other schools, students meet independently with in-school research advisors. The group course can be nice if the teacher knows how to build a collaborative spirit among students who otherwise may feel strong rivalry.

Maximizing Summers

For children who aspire to invent a new solution, help find a cure, or contribute new information to science while still in high school, all four summers of high school—and even the summer before 8th grade—should be planned in advance if possible. The following is a generic winning strategy successfully used by many of my science-bent students. (In addition, check the appendix for listings of field-specific summer plans, e.g., medicine, engineering, forensic science.)

The five-summer program for the research kid should consist of the following:

Summer before 8th grade: Enriching, stimulating math or science courses

Summer 1: Enriching, stimulating math or science courses

Summer 2: Combination of science enrichment courses and part-time research project

Summer 3: Research project with paper

Summer 4: Research project with paper

In contrast, the Olympiad kid would pursue the following kinds of summers:

Summer before 8th grade: Enriching math and science courses

Summer 1: Enriching math and science courses, Olympiad online course

Summer 2: Enriching math and science courses, Olympiad online course, study for Olympiad

Summer 3: College math and science courses with credit, Olympiad online course, study for Olympiad

Summer 4: College math and science courses with credit, Olympiad online course, study for Olympiad

The Process of Finding Research

"Quit your day job when your son reaches senior year," the mother of an older science student advised only half tongue in cheek. "If your son wants to do Intel and Siemens, the paperwork alone is a full-time job for parents. And that's before you get to college applications."

SECRET 152

In contrast to what newcomer science parents commonly assume, it's not the school's responsibility to find the child a winning research project or set her up with a lab—it's the parents'. Some science teachers help out in directing students toward lab programs or individual scientists. But ultimately, even though a student's parents may not be scientists, they are the ones who are expected to play the largest role in helping to secure research opportunities for their children. Parents help to make lab arrangements. The lab scientists then ideally help the student to formulate an original research project.

Schools may not tell you any of this because they are not supposed to give parents assignments. You're supposed to figure this out—and most parents don't.

From their child's high school research teachers, parents should expect: (1) encouragement for the child, (2) initial suggestions as to where the child might find a suitable lab, (3) willingness to help proofread the child's resulting journal-style paper after it's written and provide suggestions on how to strengthen the research project and paper, (4) advice on suitable competitions to enter, (5) willingness to write references for contests and colleges that require teacher recommendations, and (6) advice on how to create an appealing poster board and how to present one's research orally. This only applies to schools with research programs. If your child's school doesn't have a research program, your child probably should ask a supportive science teacher to help out with the above tasks, but it's likely that the support will be choppy, since the world of high school research requires its own specific expertise.

If your child's school has a research program, do not expect his research teacher to: (1) come up with a project idea for your child, (2) match your child up with the perfect mentor or research lab willing to take in your child, or (3) supervise your child's research.

This puts enormous pressure on parents, as you want to help your kid secure the lab that will give her the best odds of becoming a serious contender in the major competitions. You know that if your kid comes away a winner of a major competition, she can have her pick of colleges. But if you're like many parents whose children are interested in science research, you have never been in a real science laboratory yourself. Surely you know some practicing doctors and dentists and maybe engineers. But you may not have contacts with any research scientists to guide your kid through a real science research investigation.

| SECRET 153 | **Family connections generally are not a good way to select a laboratory for your child, anyway.** Although |

utilizing a parent connection may at first seem like the easiest route to giving your child access to a lab, it's not always the best route to take. If your daughter is fascinated by genetics, for example, instead of sending her to your cousin the physicist's lab—rationalizing that even a geneticist needs a physics background—seek out an actual genetics research opportunity. Your child's lab work should emerge from her specific interests, not from connections.

Information on how to find and make contact with scientists, institutions, and suitable research labs can be found below.

Go with Your Child's Dream

A parent phoned me for advice, explaining that his son loved meteorology, would watch the Weather Channel at every opportunity, and eagerly wanted to pursue science research in weather-related phenomena like tornadoes, hurricanes, and El Niño. But his school earth science teacher tried to discourage him, telling him that there would be no future (money) in meteorology, that the best paying career he could hope for would be as an earth science teacher or a TV forecaster. Discouraged, the father wanted me to recommend a "better field of science."

"Hmph," I told him, "if your son's true interest is meteorology, stick with meteorology. In a time when global warming dominates the news, the sky's the limit (forgive the pun) when it comes to careers in meteorology. The boy could someday become a top environmental attorney and earn $500,000+ a year. He could become a medical expert who specializes in air-quality breathing disorders or an astronaut who explores weather on other planets. Or he could become head of FEMA or a weather disaster relief organization. Or he could become an architect or developer who creates indoor environments—indoor ski areas that have become popular in other countries, for example—on a national scale. The opportunities stretch as far as the imagination." Don't belittle any science that captivates your child based on other people's limited vision.

Finding a Winning Project

Once your child has settled on a field of interest, and before your child enters competitions, she'll need a specific project she can believe in. The pressure to find the perfect project is enormous, particularly as senior year approaches, and sometimes more so for parents than kids—since the task of finding the right lab is often left to the parents. Since some of the most prestigious contests like the Intel Science Talent Search only permit students to enter during their senior year of high school, many top science students find themselves scrambling around in the early part of junior year to find a winning project, with "killer applications" (discussed later in this chapter) for that summer before senior year.

SECRET 154

To be most helpful to your child, start by having him *dream big*. The first step is for your child to state the area of science that most fascinates him, then narrow down the options with a subtopic. For example: "I am most interested in <u>meteorology</u> and would love to research <u>harnessing lightning</u>." Or "I prefer <u>astronomy</u>, and I want to study <u>binary stars</u>." Or "I would like to work in a <u>marine biology</u> lab and want to find out about the <u>mating habits</u> of <u>electric eels</u>."

Is it important to have your child focus on her *exact* interest for her long-term research project? Yes. When conducting research or working on a long-term project, if she doesn't see and feel the excitement of the project, she is much more likely to abandon it in the long run or devote considerably less energy and creativity to it, affecting the quality of the outcome and the way she feels about the time spent. If the greater purpose of the project is to interest her in a new field, a bad assignment could have the opposite effect.

SECRET 155

There is no "best" field in which to enter a project. "Doesn't my child have a better chance of winning a contest if he enters in one field over another?" parents often ask when their child is deciding on a topic.

Say the kid who won the big competition in your region last year did a physics project. The year before it was also a physics project. Second place both years, it turns out, was medicine. Should your kid do a physics-related project? Would that give him better odds than a medicine-related one?

No. If your kid likes medicine, have her pursue medicine. The more enthusiastic and energetic your child is about her research, the more likely she will be to devote her all and win. At a minimum, she'll learn to love science. Remember, you want your kid to come away from her research experience loving science—the real prize—and being a lot better able to excel in science in college. That's more important than trying to predict the judges' decision.

Parents should also note that it's not unusual for a child to change interests over the course of high school. The kid who is passionate about meteorology and conducts research in weather in 9th grade may want to venture over to a completely different science, let's say materials science, in 10th grade, and then a tissue engineering project in 11th and 12th grades. There's nothing wrong with that.

| SECRET 156 | **In helping your child choose a topic, encourage her to read science fiction to stretch her imagi-** |

nation. Discuss with her some of the more interesting fictional technology, and explore with her the idea of bringing that fictitious technology to the real world. Would she like to research time travel, for example? Life on other planets, inventing a *Star Trek*–style Holodeck, interpreting the language of whales, using exotic plants to create new medicine, or freezing humans to revive them in the future? These are all topics in science fiction that scientists are currently researching. Your child should choose a project that piques her interest and addresses her most burning questions.

In addition, you might encourage her to read some *real* science in publications, including *Science News* magazine online, www.sciencenews.org, and *Scientific American*, to learn about ongoing research and explore topics that interest her.

If your child is drawing a blank, the following exercise can help her brainstorm and identify her interests.

Directions for the child: If you could pursue any kind of research at all, what would you find most rewarding?

1. I would help find the cure for cancer.
2. I would provide an innovative design for a new World Trade Center, or the City of New Orleans, or some other major construction project.
3. I would solve a problem that has baffled mathematicians.
4. I would design a robot that _____.
5. I would design an international food distribution system to feed the hungry.
6. I would research cloning as a potential cure for diseases.
7. I would research cryogenics as a method of saving lives.
8. I would go on a pharmaceutical expedition to a jungle in Brazil.
9. I would find a genetic way to prevent birth defects.
10. I would find cures using stem cell technology.
11. I would invent artificial body parts (hearts, lungs, etc.) and have them patented.
12. I would create a time machine.
13. I would create a transporter system.
14. I would design my own *Star Trek*–style Holodeck.
15. I would create nanorobots.
16. I would create a better earthquake or tsunami warning system.
17. I would figure out an alternative to oil.
18. I would create a noninvasive surgical machine to mend body parts.
19. I would help design a biological weapons inspection and detection system.
20. I would design prostheses (robotic arms, legs, etc.).
21. I would study insects and figure out how to help people regrow body parts.
22. I would design protective, solar-protected, bulletproof clothing.
23. I would create a computer chip implant to enhance memory.
24. I would create a language translator computer chip that could be implanted.

SECRET 157 **Parents need to be supportive of (and, ideally, enthusiastic about) the general topic selected by the child, because any project ultimately becomes a family commitment—no matter how independent the child may be.** Parental tasks range from chauffeuring, running errands for supplies (sometimes long distance depending on how exotic the needed supplies are and how little the particular lab can supply), helping a child to create a poster board to ultimately display his findings, helping to edit a complex technical paper (even if you don't know science, you can help with grammar and spelling), and accompanying your child to competitions. You're also the cheering squad when the experiment goes awry. (Don't expect lab scientists to try to cheer your son up when he has to start over because someone inadvertently turned on the darkroom lights or dumped out the murky petri dish solution.)

SECRET 158	**Try to avoid having your kid do a project that sounds similar to any other kid's project from his**

school. If his school has a designated research advisor, have your child tell the advisor as early in the year as possible what project he is working on to help claim the topic and have the teacher act as a clearinghouse so that no other student is conducting the same or similar research. At science fairs, projects are generally displayed side by side with others in the same category. It's better not to compete head-to-head with a kid from his own school.

SECRET 159	**In a very competitive, secretive school where no teacher acts as a clearinghouse, warn your child to**

not even discuss his project idea with other students, lest they try to pirate the idea—which has been known to happen in many science competitions. In a more open school, however, students may be required to discuss their project ideas in a group or course before embarking on research. This could eliminate plagiarizing. Once the idea is out in the open and everyone is aware of whose idea it was, it becomes harder for another student to copy without getting caught. If you have any say in the system, push for an open exchange of ideas.

SECRET 160	**Do not let your kid invite "friends" to help with research.** Otherwise they may decide that they de-

serve credit, too, and therefore disqualify a project that was supposed to be done independently. I have seen high school friendships broken up over this issue and potential contest wins and science credentials forfeited.

Once your child has a sense of what she would like to accomplish, it is time for you to go online with her and seek out scientists and institutions that are conducting that kind of research.

Making Contact with a Lab

Although organized programs can sometimes be beneficial (specific programs are discussed later in this chapter), your child doesn't need an organized or formal summer program to create a winning project. Many of the top winners do not come directly from organized programs.

| SECRET 161 | **If your child desires a specific internship, as a general rule it's better to go directly to the person** |

who supervises that internship or conducts that research than to the personnel office of the company, laboratory, university, or organization. If your son, for example, wants to investigate body part regeneration of sea stars and a researcher off the coast of Maine is exploring that topic, contact that researcher directly—not the personnel office of that university.* Likewise, if your daughter wants to discover an anatomical role of the appendix, contact a scientist who is conducting that research rather than the personnel office of the hospital. As a general rule, go directly to that person—not that person's administrator.

| SECRET 162 | **At a university, do not go to the department chair and ask what's available within the department.** |

Chances are the well-intending chairman or chairwoman will tell you that they'll get back to you if something comes up. And you'll never hear from them again—because few scientists announce lab openings through their department chairs.

Instead, help your child to focus his interest more specifically, and go directly to the professor who is researching that topic. If your child is interested in, say, zoology, without specifying what kind of zoology, do not go to the head of a university zoology department to ask which professors are seeking interns. None is seeking an intern when approached that way. Instead, help your child to further define his interests—is it dolphins, tarantulas, or zebras? Then, again, go directly to the professor who is studying that topic. No professors are interested in kids who have given their topic so

---

*While many high school students participate in organized university research programs, many others spend their summers working directly under a specific professor, independent of any formal program.

little thought that they wouldn't even know which animal interests them. Much more appealing to the exotic snakes expert, for example, is the kid who is fascinated by venomous snakes rather than the kid who could just as easily be satisfied to study a goldfish. The same applies in every field.

| SECRET 163 | **Don't be afraid to explore opportunities at think tanks, government research facilities, private labo-** |

ratories, hospitals, zoos, aquariums, botanical gardens, and industrial research departments. Working in such environments can provide your child with cutting-edge resources and invaluable guidance, depending on his interests—however, doing so may require parents to make additional logistical arrangements. If your child finds a job at a think tank or hospital, for example, and no summer student housing is offered, you might phone a college near that opportunity to ask if your child can reside on campus while working nearby.

| SECRET 164 | **Don't look for an ad seeking an intern.** When you search online for opportunities for your child, |

don't look for the "Employment" or "Personnel" button on the Web page. Again: If a search shows that Dr. Anita Jones is conducting interesting scorpion research, simply contact Dr. Jones and ask how a high school student might work as an intern in her lab. She might tell you outright that she won't take a high school student under any circumstances—or that she has no budget for such. But it is also very likely she will ask you to forward a résumé to her.

Seeking Out Independent University Research Opportunities Online

1. Start your computer search by going to the Web site of a university.
2. Go to the department that interests your child (i.e., geology, robotics, bioengineering).
3. Go to "Faculty."
4. Read up on each faculty member's ongoing research in his or her bio.
5. Contact faculty members whose research interests coincide with

your child's *demonstrated* (meaning, your child should have at least the basic course background of high school biology, chemistry, or whatever the research subject entails) interests.

6. Be prepared to send a résumé.

| SECRET 165 | **Always have your child's résumé updated on the computer and ready to e-mail.** The résumé should |

highlight activities that are relevant to the internship your child is seeking. If he's applying for scorpion research, the résumé should feature scorpion-related activities. Don't just send the previous résumé that he used when applying for an internship in rainbow research. Tailor the résumé. Highlight relevant activities **in bold**, even if that doesn't conform to standard résumé-writing guidelines.

| SECRET 166 | **Contrary to popular assumption, it's okay for parents to make the first contact to inquire about** |

application procedures. "Shouldn't students do this on their own?" parents ask. "Nobody ever did this for me." Theoretically, yes. And some students will take the initiative. But the reality is that the majority of high school kids—even the brightest of the bright—will not feel comfortable enough to make the initial inquiry. (And, in all fairness, most parents never had to seek an internship in a cutting-edge lab when they were in high school.) So if a parent doesn't do it, it often doesn't happen. Researchers who support the idea of helping the younger generation generally won't respond negatively to an initial parent inquiry. (Note that, when contacting a lab for your child, you should not apologize for your call by saying that your child is immature or shy. Do not demean your child.)

| SECRET 167 | **When seeking a summer internship for your child, don't mention Intel, Siemens, or other competi-** |

tions. Research scientists feel, as all parents do, that children should not learn to do research just for the prospect of winning a competition. They want the child to be genuinely interested in the process and not overly motivated by the endgame of winning. They want students to love research for its own intrinsic value. Keep in mind that the mere mention of awards can put unfair pressure on a scientist, who doesn't want to be blamed if your kid doesn't win a competition after interning at his lab. Also, competition results can often seem arbitrary to scientist-mentors, and rightfully so. (The judges may pick the kid who made a stride in curing diabetes, for example, over the kid who helped cure epilepsy.)

Instead, indicate that your son wants an internship in which he could conduct original research and be able to write his own research paper or journal article based on the work he does in the lab by the end of the summer. Buzzwords to use include *original* and *his own*. Some scientists will tell you that in their specific field it's impossible to complete any meaningful research within a single summer—that the child may be required to promise a second or third summer in the lab. If your daughter is entering her sophomore or junior year and feels very passionately about the subject, this could be fine. Be appreciative for the opportunity, and hope that she sustains her interest over a few years.

Interviewing at a Lab

Expect scientists to be noncommittal about offering a summer research internship until they meet your kid and are convinced that he could make a constructive contribution. After a scientist reviews a student's résumé, the next step generally is to have her in for an interview.

SECRET 168	**Before the interview, have your kid read up.**

Search the Internet or science-related libraries to find relevant articles (not necessarily difficult journal articles—*Scientific American* articles and other pieces written for lay audiences can be helpful). He should have enough mastery of the subject to speak intelligently at an interview. He should also have a basic familiarity with published articles written by the scientist who will be interviewing him.

SECRET 169	**As a rule, labs are only interested in people with cooperative personalities, flexibility, maturity, and**

independence. Instruct your child to behave this way in the interview *and for the duration of the internship*—even if it requires a crash course in growing up taught by Mom or Dad. If your child wants to conduct real-world research, he must act like an adult.

Labs tend to have close-knit working environments, and workers view themselves as a team. Your daughter should go into the interview alone (carrying an extra copy of her résumé and any props—inventions or papers—that might seem relevant). And remind her to smile—even if she's nervous. If you want to chauffeur your kid to the interview, drop off your young researcher at the front door and drive away. Arrange to meet again at a campus bookstore or nearby coffee shop. Don't hover. And don't set a time limit on her interview. Tell her to take her time and not rush the person interviewing her.

Owning the Project

SECRET 170 | **When your child is planning to conduct research in a professional lab, make sure that he develops an independent project for which no other student will want to share credit.** While other researches at the lab may assist in the research, your child should be the sole author of any paper that's to be submitted to high school contests. (It's fine for your child to be a coauthor of any professionally published paper, though.) Not all laboratory scientists are tuned in to the rules of the major science competitions, and since you won't have emphasized that your child plans to enter a competition, they may want to assign your child to work alongside a peer. (This is unacceptable in most competitions, unless the student wants to enter the contest in a "group project" category.) It's better for your child to clarify up front, *before* any research actually starts, that he wants to work on a project or a piece of the project that he can call his own. Make sure he establishes what that portion will be. (For example, if the lab was studying the effect of hot beverages in enhancing sleep, your child might handle all the floral teas, while another student might explore milk products.) Make sure that there are lines, so that everyone in the lab (mentor and peer) will be very clear about it and not try to claim credit for his work. I have seen families arguing at the end of the summer over whose child did more of the work on a group project and whose child therefore deserves to claim the project as her own in a contest that doesn't accept group projects. As a rule, once a project is entered into *any* contest as a group project, nobody is entitled to call the project her own project again. Settle at the outset.

| **SECRET 171** | **Labs are not supervised in the same way summer programs are, so you and your kid should go into** |

it understanding that he won't have the constant attention of supervisors. "The professor was gone the entire summer," a father complained. "The only people around to offer my son guidance were a graduate student and a postdoc. We were horrified. The professor just showed up at the beginning, helped get him set up, made sure he understood the work, and then told him to ask the grad student and postdoc if he had any further questions."

This is a very common complaint among panicking parents of high school students who are newcomers to laboratory research and who worry that their kid's work will be overlooked if they don't advocate for their kid. Many of the principal investigators (PIs—the lead scientists who run the labs) take summer vacations, write, go on lecturing tours, or conduct field research during the summer and do not report to the laboratory frequently. They leave contact information at the lab, but they are not to be called unless there's a crisis.

And that's not necessarily a bad thing, when it comes to your kid.

| **SECRET 172** | **Working with a grad student or post-doc can be just as productive as, or sometimes even more** |

helpful than, working with a full professor. Often a grad student who is closer in age to your child will have a better idea of what needs to be explained and how to make the information understandable. In some labs, the PI's job consists more of administrative duties and grant writing, and the postdocs and grad students are the ones who really know the equipment.

| **SECRET 173** | **That said, letters of reference for contests and college are generally valued more if written by the** |

principal investigator. If the PI is too busy, your child might suggest ghost-writing a recommendation and having the PI sign it.

Formal Summer Research Programs

Formal residential research programs are structured science "camps" that generally provide room, board, supervised social activities, a set realistic schedule, and a lab experience. The greatest advantage to a formal research program is that the research is contained. Research programs keep students on a strict schedule and see to it that a contest-quality paper is completed before the end of the summer. The student comes home with a written paper and maybe even a completed poster board. The word *contest* doesn't scare the administrators of the formal programs—since many of the programs are created specifically to prepare students for competitions. Some programs rehearse the students on giving presentations. When the student returns home from a summer of research, little or no work is required on the part of the parents or school research teacher.

This can alleviate an enormous burden from the parents. Less structured research often leaves the student scrambling to write the paper when he returns home at the end of the summer or, worse, when he's back at school in the fall.

The major disadvantage is that many formal research programs charge tuition—sometimes several thousand dollars for a summer. (Independently arranged internships, in contrast, sometimes result in the student earning a summer stipend instead of paying the equivalent of expensive camp tuition.) And research options are limited to the work being done by professors and PIs affiliated with the program. At some programs, the research field is randomly assigned—not necessarily according to students' interests—to make sure that every participating student has a project and every participating professor is assigned a student. I know of a student, for example, who was primarily interested in chemistry but was assigned to work at an entomology (insects) field station, and another student who was interested in astronomy but was assigned to a biology lab.

The summer science program application process is usually similar to applying to college—students fill out written applications and submit transcripts and standardized test scores. And the research is of the same high quality that it would be if the student made her own research arrangements at a lab—since college professors run the research part of the formal programs.

| SECRET 174 | For a first research venture before 9th, 10th, or even 11th grade, some of the formal programs can |

be ideal (from the parental perspective)—provided the kid gets a project he likes—since program projects do not require as much guidance from family members or teachers unfamiliar with the area of research. Nonscientist parents are off the hook. But after the first project, the student should be more attuned to finding a lab that matches his or her interests most accurately—rather than limiting himself to programs.

SECRET 175

For rising seniors, beware of programs that assign projects randomly. By senior year, a student shouldn't be as dependent on an organized social schedule or heavy dorm supervision. As a general rule, it's better to find the lab that's conducting the research your child wants rather than hope for interesting research to be part of an organized program. If your senior—or even junior—wants to participate in a structured program, she should investigate which labs within the university participate and then state to the program administrators in advance what topics and labs she would like to work in to help guarantee that she gets her topic of interest. Parents can do the legwork of researching different opportunities within programs online. Have your daughter mention this preference on her application for the program. This will not only help her land a project most in line with her interests, but it will also help the lab scientist to want to accept her more readily.

SECRET 176

Science judges prefer research that answers original questions that students have formulated over questions that were assigned to them. In research programs, students are sometimes handed questions that the scientist needs answered. Note that in some contests, students are supposed to have come up with the idea for their project themselves, based on their own curiosity. One of the most common questions that contest judges ask students is "How did you come up with the idea for this project?" Answering "It was assigned to me" is not impressive. Nor is "My mentor gave me this project." A better answer is something along the lines of: "I was working in this laboratory, reading all these journal articles, and helping to conduct their ongoing research, when I suddenly realized that nobody had tried a certain approach that I wanted to try."

SECRET 177

If your child insists on applying for a research "program," and is not admitted, a little known option is to have your child apply directly to the professor who is conducting the desired research _at the same university_. For some students, that's a viable back door into the program. Often it's the _program_ (which can only accommodate a limited number of students) that rejected the child rather than the professor. A program might reject a student because of a low grade bringing down his overall grade point average, thus making another applicant for the same space look more appealing. Whereas a PI might not care about the grade if it's in an unrelated subject, especially if the student has special skills or enthusiasm to offer the lab to which he is applying.

Say your child wants to study computer science, and a college lists more than forty professors in the computer science department. Meanwhile, your child applies to one of the college's summer research programs with the hope of pursuing research in the lab of Dr. X and is not admitted. Have your child contact Dr. X directly, or go online to see who else in the department is conducting interesting research, and have your child contact *that* scientist directly. Or you as a parent may contact that scientist directly and ask how your child might go about applying independently. Assuming your child has some background in related topics, the scientist may be willing to offer your child a separate internship for the summer. You would then separately arrange with the university to have your child reside on campus—possibly in the same dorm as the summer program kids.

Highly Selective Summer Research Programs

SECRET 178 **While your child should never feel dependent on getting into a structured program in order to conduct research and win major competitions, parents should be aware that some of the most selective programs do have higher-than-average success rates.** But perhaps one of the reasons is that they tend to draw top students, they get first pick of these students, and they select students that they deem likely to win. Because admissions is so competitive, they are able to require of their applicants the highest GPAs and PSAT/SAT scores, and they prefer candidates who have already won national recognition or demonstrated outstanding talent.

The Research Science Institute (RSI)

One of the biggest names in structured science research programs is the Research Science Institute (RSI). The six-week summer program offers rising seniors the opportunity to conduct original research at the Massachusetts Institute of Technology (MIT) and other research institutions in the Boston area. A student who gets into RSI becomes very desirable to the most-competitive colleges, and often ends up at Harvard or MIT.

For science-impassioned students, this program is in many ways the ultimate high school experience, since they get to explore projects of their choice using some of the best resources and under the guidance of some of the world's greatest scientists. Tuition is free; however, admission is extremely competitive. More than one thousand apply; only seventy-five get picked. (The program is jointly sponsored by MIT and the Center for Excellence in Education, which also sponsors the USA Biology Olympiad team.)

While RSI graduates tend to fare disproportionately well in the Intel Science Talent Search (STS), the most valued credentials for admission into both RSI and STS are similar: a passion for and record of achievement in math or science, additional expertise in other areas outside the passion (most play a musical instrument or a sport or are very involved in extracurricular and community activities), leadership, excellence on standardized tests, advanced coursework, participation in math and science fairs, and straight-A grades in a rigorous curriculum. The same credentials will get your kid into her choice of top colleges.

The PreCollege Research Abroad Program (PRAP)

PRAP, initiated by faculty members of Stuyvesant High School in New York City in 1993, is not as well known as RSI, but has produced impressive results. PRAP arranges for high school students to conduct cutting-edge research in science, mathematics, or engineering at the Russian Academy of Science in Puschino, Russia's premiere research facility, with more than five thousand scientists. Most of the work relates to the life sciences—ranging from agriculture to biomedicine and genetics—but the facility is also home to the Moscow Physics Institute's radiotelescope. Students rank in order of preference the general area of science that they would like to pursue during the one-month summer stay, then PRAP matches them up with senior scientists. The program is conducted in English and includes two presentations per student per summer, with feedback from scientists and program coordinators, targeted preparation for the Intel Science Talent Search and other contests, lessons in journal-article writing, and cultural excursions to Moscow and St. Petersburg. Up to twenty-five students in grades 10 to 12 may participate.

Program administrator Eduard Mandell boasts that the program has an excellent record in U.S. competitions: On average, 30 percent of its students have been named Intel semifinalists; 5 percent finalists; and thirty-two students have been published in prominent journals, with alumni landing in Ivies and other most competitive colleges. Participants earn 9 college credits through the program. Although the application deadline is officially in March, admissions are rolling—first come, first served—and most of the program's spaces fill up by the end of December.

The Simons Program

The Simons Program, another program that has launched many successful science competition winners, is named for its founder, SUNY Stony Brook mathematics professor Jim Simons, who started it in 1984. The program is small and very selective. About 140 students apply each year, and 25 to 30 are admitted—with a maximum of 3 per high school. In the beginning, the Long Island program took only local kids. But as its reputation grew, it drew applications from as far away as Texas and New England (including prep schools like Choate and Phillips Andover). Among the most recent applicants are high school students who have published in journals or who already hold patents. Simons students work one-on-one with scientists on individual projects. And the seven-week program is funded by the university, so there is no tuition.

The Garcia Program

Another highly competitive program offered through SUNY Stony Brook is the Garcia Program. This program is attended by about 120 applicants each year from all over the United States. Recent participants have come from California, Texas, Minnesota, Florida, New Jersey, and Connecticut. (The lab fee is $1,000 for the seven weeks.) The program trains students in lab techniques and oversees the students' projects from formulating an idea right through final papers.

★   ★   ★

The top qualities that both the Simons and Garcia programs seek in admitting students are genuine interest in the subject, passion for science, and enthusiasm. Note that the programs only accept rising 11th and 12th graders.

Stony Brook claims to account for, on average, 10 percent of the Intel STS semifinalists each year. And in 2006, four of the forty Intel finalists had conducted research at Stony Brook, according to Simons Program director Karen Kernan.

One of Stony Brook's greatest lures is the opportunity to work in the Materials Science Laboratory of the legendary Dr. Miriam Rafailovich, who runs the Garcia Program; some Simons students also work in her lab.

For seven weeks each summer, her polymers lab allows high school students to work on group (two students working together) and individual projects. She has produced many winners over the years.

If your child wants to conduct research at Stony Brook but is not accepted into Simons or Garcia, encourage her to apply directly to the professor and laboratory of interest. Many high school students conduct research at Stony Brook without going through a "name" program—the university even arranges dorm stays for student researchers who are not affiliated with structured programs. And some of these students are among the major award winners.

Michigan State High School Honors Science-Math Engineering Program

This program claims to be the "oldest continuously-run high school research program in the country." One of the special features of the seven-week program is that students may choose from thirty different general topics—participants rank them in order of preference upon arrival—and the program has produced many award winners at Intel, Siemens, and ISEF. Anywhere from one hundred to two hundred qualified rising juniors and seniors apply each year, but the program only accommodates twenty to twenty-four. Admission is based on previous coursework, recommendations, an essay, demonstration of out-of-school science reading, and enthusiasm. The program seeks to bring in kids from all over the country. Cost in 2006 was $2,600, including room and board; some scholarships are available. Kids leave the program with finished papers and experience at presenting their work.

For Students Interested in Astronomy

A few summer programs in astronomy are so selective that students who participate can virtually choose any college they want. No other specific field of science offers quite the same degree of prestigious program.

The Summer Science Programs (SSP) at Ojai, California, and Socorro, New Mexico are considered among the nation's most prestigious astronomy programs, but both receive little publicity. Described as six-week residential enrichment programs "in which gifted high school students complete a challenging, hands-on research project in celestial mechanics," the SSP uses "college-level astronomy, calculus and physics." At night, teams of three participants take telescopic observations of asteroids, measure them, and "write software to convert their measurements into a mathematical description of the asteroid's orbit." The Ojai and Socorro programs are jointly sponsored by several prestigious institutions, among them Stanford, Harvey Mudd, and Caltech, top colleges for kids interested in science and astronomy.

Each campus houses thirty-six students, mostly rising seniors, but some exceptional juniors as well, and teaches the same curriculum. Candidates are their high schools' top math and science students. The programs also want to see evidence of good character, so they take seriously the two required recommendations—one from a math teacher and one from a science teacher. They seek a diverse group of students who will benefit from the program and be highly motivated to conduct the work involved—and show math and science interest outside the classroom as well.

Students who want to conduct independent astronomy research over and above the program's curriculum are preferred—so students who want to enter contests independently can benefit from both programs. But the programs don't push students to do projects to enter into competition. Ojai and Socorro, in fact, deemphasize competitions. Most of the time, students cooperate in teams, working on homework together. Many of their students end up going to college at MIT or Caltech.

One more very small program (two students each summer) worth looking into for top students who are heavily interested in astronomy is run by CASPER (Center for Astrophysics, Space Physics and Engineering Research) offered jointly by Baylor University, www.baylor.edu/casper, and Texas State Technical College.

Major Research Contests

There are many local and regional math, science, and engineering research competitions in the United States, and, as mentioned above, in order to win the top research competitions, a student needs to begin establishing a track record in those local contests years before. (Winning regional contests makes students more appealing candidates in national and international competitions, which ask on their applications which other contests the applicants have already won.) For more information on what opportunities are offered locally, parents should check with their children's high school math and science departments. In addition, check Web sites such as www .FastWeb.com (which lists competitions in all subjects), Intel International Science and Engineering Fair's Web site, www.sciserv.org/isef (click on "Find a Fair"), Johns Hopkins' www.cogito.org, and Google "high school, science competition" (substitute "science" with a specific math or science subject that interests your child).

Intel Science Talent Search (STS)

"My son just won the Intel Science Talent Search!" a father excitedly announced to his office in March.

"Intel?" another parent asked. "But Intel was announced months ago!"

"My son gets to go to Intel ISEF!"

Just for the record, Intel ISEF is *not* Intel STS. And being an "Intel winner" refers to STS, not ISEF. The more prestigious research competition is the Intel Science Talent Search. Both competitions are sponsored by Intel, but when people refer to "the Intel competition," they mean the Intel Science Talent Search, which started in 1942 (as the Westinghouse), is run by Science Service, and is sometimes referred to as the "Junior Nobel Prize."

Of course, Intel ISEF is also prestigious. About 1,500 top science students—some from other countries—get to attend each year. Not bad to be among the world's top 1,500 research students. In comparison, only forty American finalists attend Intel STS.

Each year, about 1,700 high school seniors enter the Science Talent Search (STS) by submitting science journal–style papers based on their own original research, along with lengthy applications that require multiple essays. (Sample topics of required essays: What ideas, devices or creations have particularly attracted your attention, and what have you done to pursue them? What have you done outside your school curriculum that demonstrates initiative? Have you ever pursued an idea or experiment that was new to everyone? How do you accommodate unforeseen circumstances in your work?) The deadline is mid-November. Of the 1,700 students, 300 are named semifinalists. And of the 300 semifinalists, 40 are named finalists. These 40 are then invited to Washington, D.C., to present their research (using poster boards) to the contest judges and to the public. They compete in science knowledge—each student is called individually into rooms of two to three judges, who grill them in science (some questions related to the projects, and some not)—to compete for the ten "winner" positions.

In recent years, each of the 300 semifinalists was awarded prize money of $1,000 for themselves and an additional $1,000 for their school. The 40 finalists were each awarded $5,000 undergraduate scholarships, a state-of-the-art notebook computer, plus a one-week trip to Washington, D.C., to compete for the top ten slots. The first place winner was given a $100,000 undergraduate scholarship, the second place winner a $75,000 scholarship, third place a $50,000 scholarship, fourth through sixth place $25,000 scholarships, and seventh through tenth place $20,000 scholarships. Locate the contest information at www.sciserv.org/index.htm.

| SECRET 179 | To get a better sense of what credentials are expected to enter (and win) a national science |

competition, check out the Intel Science Talent Search (STS) application—regardless of whether your child plans to enter that competition. Find the application form at www.sciserv.org/sts/intfrm.pdf. You may even want to design your child's four-year high school game plan around this particular application, since the same kinds of activities and experiences that are valued by STS are also valued by colleges, research programs, other competitions, and most parents. Look at Entry Page 2 in particular to get a sense of the diversity of activities that the Intel STS looks for in students. (Unlike other competitions, Intel Science Talent Search is based largely on "the person," in addition to its focus on "the project." So while a winning research project and paper are essential toward winning Intel STS, so is a solid track record showing strong background experiences. The application asks applicants to specify music, sports, engineering clubs, 4-H or Scouts membership, and school publication and leadership involvement. Students with such involvements tend to fare better.)

Old-Timer's Hints

A former Intel Science Talent Search judge told a small group of adminis-trators and science teachers in a district that was setting up its research program years ago that in his day, the judging procedure for the Intel STS consisted of a point system, in which the information provided by the stu-dent on the application counted for a total of 50 points out of 100, and the student's research and science paper counted for the remaining 50 points. In other words, he said, the project itself only counted for half of the points it took to win the competition. The rest relied entirely on the ap-plication, a very lengthy, multiple-page document, in which each question and section was assigned a specific number of points. One question asked the applicant to list any relatives who were scientists, mathematicians, or engineers, for example. And another asked applicants to describe the per-son who influenced them most.

In the activities listing, he said the child was awarded one point for be-ing a *current* member of Boy or Girl Scouts or the 4-H club. Another point was awarded for being a *past* member of Boy or Girl Scouts or 4-H. Two points were awarded for both past and present participation in school publications; two points were awarded for both past and present participation in a sport; another two for music; and so on. The system even awarded a point if the child was a firstborn in her family, following the popular notion that firstborns are the most likely to succeed in every endeavor.

Nowadays, however, the system is different. (A spokeswoman at the talent search confirmed to me in a phone interview that being a first-born is no longer seen as a predictor of success—although the family position question remains on the application "just to find out more about the ap-plicant.") Still, I always advise parents to familiarize themselves with the application years in advance (as per Secret 179 above) to make sure that their children are, from an early age, aware of some of the criteria on which they may eventually be judged—if not by STS, then by other con-tests and college admissions offices.

Siemens

Another top research contest is the Siemens Competition in Math, Science and Technology, run by the Siemens Foundation, a foundation of the international electronics company, in partnership with the College Board. This competition, begun in 1999, gives out comparable prize money to the Intel Science Talent Search. Students have even been known to win first place prizes from both (each worth $100,000, for a total of $200,000). But the two competitions, though both research based, are very different. While Intel looks at the "whole person"—in attempt to "discover" future leaders of science—by asking the applicants about their background and activities, Siemens is more of a one-shot deal: successful participants don't necessarily have to have a long-term future commitment to science research. Entries are judged solely on the work submitted, and the application is a much faster process. In the Siemens Competition, events take place earlier in the school year—the research paper is due at the very beginning of October; semifinalists and regional finalists are announced by the end of October—allowing high school seniors to mention any positive results in their Early Decision applications to college. But this also means that juniors need to be ready for that early-senior deadline. In Siemens, about one thousand projects (1,200 to 1,300 students contributing individual and team projects) are entered each year. Participants can work individually or as part of a team with one or two other students.

In the individual competition, the student must be a high school senior and must have worked on the project alone. The first round is a "blind reading" of papers by research scientists. From those papers, three hundred students are invited to present their work at one of six regional fairs. At each regional fair, competitors are expected to present a poster display of their project, deliver a twelve-minute oral presentation, and participate in a twelve-minute question-and-answer session with judges. Each of the three hundred regional finalists' high schools is given $2,000 "to be used to support science, mathematics and technology programs in their schools." From each group of regional finalists, one individual and one team are named winners and receive $3,000 scholarships per person. The other regional finalists (individuals and team members) receive $1,000 each. The six regional winner individuals and six regional winner teams then get to compete in Washington, D.C., at the National Competition, where the Number 1 National Winner individual is awarded $100,000 and the Number 1 National Winner team of two or three gets to split an award of $100,000 in scholarships. The second-place individual wins $50,000 and the second-place team splits another $50,000. Third place wins $40,000; team splits $40,000. Fourth place wins $30,000; team splits $30,000. Fifth place wins $20,000; team splits $20,000. And sixth place is $10,000, with sixth-place team splitting $10,000.

| SECRET 180 | **The Siemens Competition no longer requires that teams include at least one high school senior, open-** |

ing up the opportunity to younger high school students. (In earlier years, younger students could only submit a project if they teamed up with a senior.) Many teachers still don't know this, and, as a result, may discourage younger kids from entering based on outdated information. Don't let your kid be discouraged.

Students and parents can learn more about the competition and download applications at www.siemens-foundation.org/students.htm.

Intel International Science and Engineering Fair (ISEF)

As I mentioned above, when people refer to "the Intel competition," they are not referring to the Intel ISEF but to the Intel STS. Still, offering more than $3 million in scholarships and prizes each year, including a $50,000 top prize, the International Science and Engineering Fair is one of the world's most significant science research contests. Billed as "the world's largest pre-college science competition," hundreds of winners of local ISEF-affiliated science fairs are invited to attend each year. Because of its large size and tendency to take place at large urban convention centers—a different city each year—the fair has a convention-like atmosphere, with students attending from more than forty nations. Unlike the Intel and Siemens competitions, nobody walks away with $100,000, but many more awards are given out—by government agencies, the U.S. military, and private corporations—occupying a day and a half of awards ceremonies. Among the most coveted awards are the Seaborg SIYSS Awards, which honor three high school seniors with all-expense-paid trips to Sweden "to attend the Stockholm International Youth Science Seminar during the Nobel Prize Ceremonies in December."

The ISEF application is elaborate, with lots of forms to fill out—some have to be completed *before* the student starts research (a peculiar request, since at that point the student doesn't know what he'll find), helping the student to focus his research, making sure that the young scientists don't put themselves (or any vertebrates) in harm's way in the course of their experiments, and so on. An application can be obtained at www.sciserv .org/isef.

Beware: While ISEF claims to be one of the only major fairs to welcome students in grades 9 through 12, many of the local feeder fairs weed out the younger grades from competing locally, only accepting kids in older grades, and in effect barring 9th graders from winning the chance to attend the international competition. The initial local rounds include more than 65,000 students at more than five hundred regional Intel ISEF–affiliated fairs around the world. Regional fairs are held in forty-six states, Washington, D.C., and more than forty countries and territories. Winners of those fairs then are selected to go on to ISEF. The program is administered by the Science Service (which also runs the the Intel).

Junior Science and Humanities Symposium (JSHS)

Somehow the word *humanities* doesn't seem to belong in the title of a major national competition in which students conduct an original research investigation in the sciences, engineering, or mathematics. But the Junior Science and Humanities Symposium aims to reinforce the philosophy that "a good science education includes an appreciation of the humanities." The competition is sponsored by the departments of the Army, Navy and Air Force, and is administered by the Academy of Applied Science, a nonprofit institute.

To become involved, applicants must write a science research paper and an abstract. Participation is free.

SECRET 181 | **While most of the nominations for the Junior Science and Humanities Symposium are handled through participating high schools, parents do not have to wait for their high school to nominate their kids for the regional symposia.** Parents can nominate their own kid directly—even if their kid's high school does not participate.

Once your child's entry is ready, you can contact the symposium to make arrangements for your child to submit a paper in your region directly in the fall, months in advance of the regional symposia, which generally take place in February, March, or April. (For a list of regional fairs and dates, check the Web site: www.jshs.org/regions.html.)

Submitting a paper to JSHS does not guarantee that your child will get to present at the fair. Papers are first read by a panel of professors, and then only some students are invited to present. But everyone who submits a paper may attend.

JSHS involves more than 12,000 high school students throughout the United States, Puerto Rico, and the Department of Defense Schools in Europe and Japan through forty-eight university-held regional symposia, some of which are multistate. Instead of standing by poster boards—as at most of the other fairs—students give formal presentations to an audience of peers and teachers.

At each regional fair, five finalists win an expense-paid trip to the National JSHS, which takes place in May in a different location each year, alternating among army, navy, and air force locations. First and second place finalists at regional symposia get to present their work at the National JSHS; the remaining three get to come and watch. And $4,500 in undergraduate scholarships are split among the first ($2,000), second ($1,500), and third ($1,000) place regional finalists. At the nationals, six $16,000 scholarships are awarded, six $6,000 scholarships are awarded, and six $2,000 scholarships are awarded. In addition, trips to the London International Youth Science Forum are awarded to each of the six first place finalists.

FIRST *Robotics Competition*

If participating in those robot battles you see on TV sounds like your kid's idea of excitement, she won't have to wait until college or engineering school to participate in robot design competitions. The *FIRST* Robotics Competition claims to be the largest engineering-only activity for high school students, involving more than 30,000 kids through 1,300 teams and thirty-seven regional events. The contest boasts teams from most states, plus Brazil, Canada, Ecuador, Israel, Mexico, and the United Kingdom. Contests are described as "high-tech spectator sporting events, the result of lots of focused brainstorming, real-world teamwork, dedicated mentoring, project timelines, and deadlines." Regional events take place in March, and the international championship takes place at the Georgia Dome in Atlanta in April, when major universities (largely state schools) award $8 million in scholarships. In addition, twenty-five nonmonetary awards are given out to twenty-five teams. Most prestigious is the Chairman's Award for the team that best represents a model for other teams to emulate.

Parents should note: Participation comes with a heavy price tag. "The registration fee for a team's initial event of the season is $6,000. Subsequent regional events are $4,000 [per team] each, and the Championship is $5,000 [per team]." And the average annual team budget, including transportation to competitions, is a total of $15,000. For this reason, most teams seek local corporate funding and enlist lots of teammates to chip in.

SECRET 182   **If your kid's high school is unable or unwilling to fund his team, you can start a home-school or community team.** Because this is a cooperative "sport" in which all team members may contribute, teams average twenty-five kids, but some have ten and some have more than a hundred. If you can recruit a hundred kids to participate at, let's say, a community center or after-school program, the $15,000 fee comes down to $150 per child. While the cost may still sound high, the competition provides months of engaging engineering challenge to teenage participants and, for the very involved kid, can act as the equivalent of an intensive college course in engineering. Watch the 2007 kickoff event that took place in New Hampshire in January of 2007 at http://robotics.nasa.gov/events/2007_kickoff.php. Or visit the organization's Web site, www.usfirst.org. (For younger kids, there's a *FIRST* Lego League for ages 9 to 14.)

National Gallery for America's Young Inventors

For student inventors and engineers who prefer to work independently, the Christopher Columbus Fellowship Foundation's National Gallery for America's Young Inventors selects up to six young inventors in grades kindergarten through 12 for their annual award. To qualify, the young inventors' work must already have been nationally recognized by other competitions—so this is a contest to steer your kid toward after she is successful in other contests—and the student must also either be a patent holder or have a product on the national market. Winners (mostly high school students) are inducted into the national gallery, and each receives a sextant, compass, and $5,000 savings bond. You may nominate your own kid (or he can nominate himself). Obtain a nomination form at www.pafinc.com; the deadline is in January. The top tech colleges and most-competitive liberal arts universities are very impressed with high school students who hold patents, so this is an excellent credential to add to your child's application if invention is his passion.

A Final Note on Patents and Publishing

How do you get your kid a patent or published journal paper? parents ask, as if they're expecting me to devise some magical formula. If there were an easy answer, I'm sure the prestige level of these two tasks would be diminished. Many professors and grad students struggle to come up with original ideas worth patenting and worth publishing in journals, so there's certainly no easy access for high school students. That said, the short answer is to try to help your child find a laboratory that is conducting cutting-edge research and will allow your child to have his own piece of the research. Advise your child to be alert to discrepancies in experiments—sometimes those frustrating variations are the sparks of new ideas and inventions, and observations of unpredicted reactions in experiments often spark journal articles. Teach your child to think creatively. And try to connect your child with a lab where journal articles are produced regularly, and from which patents emerge frequently. Patents tend to be expensive, and you'll want a lab that might be willing to help foot the bill.

CHAPTER 8

The Arts

Spotlighting the Creative Applicant

At a high school graduation ceremony, a quiet girl who had been a yearbook photographer for four years was congratulated for winning the Arts Recognition and Talent Search from the National Foundation for Advancement in the Arts. In addition, they announced that she had been one of twenty students nationally to be named a Presidential Scholar in the arts. For her photography, she was offered admission into Cornell.

A collective gasp rose from the audience, followed by polite applause. The girl beamed. Then the audience began buzzing.

"Did you know *she* was getting this award?" "How did *she* get it?" "Certainly there are plenty of equally talented kids in the school: the concertmaster, the painter, the ballerina, the boy whose short story was published, the budding actress. How did they pick *her*?" parents asked, barely disguising their envy.

The moral here is: Don't wait until graduation to become motivated by someone else's kid winning a prestigious arts award. If any of the credentials discussed in this chapter seem relevant to your kid's interests and skill level, start pursuing them now. Look them up on the Internet, and get your kid an application.

| SECRET 183 | **Some of the most prestigious awards in the arts take years of training and planning.** Just how does |

a high school student become one of the top high school artists in America? Lessons, practice, hard work, and tailored preparation—starting early, and over years of high school. As with the other subject areas in this book, winning national awards is not the result of a last-minute effort; winners tend to have elaborate and impressive track records. (In the case of the yearbook photographer, the girl's out-of-school credentials might have included Scholastic's National Photography Portfolio Gold Award, first place in the Photo Imaging Education Association's International Student-Teacher Photo Exhibit and Competition, Visual Arts Scholastic Event, Drexel University High School Contest Exhibition, International Open Amateur Photography Contest, and the NAACP ACT-SO Competition.) Nor can a child do it on his or her own. If a child is to apply for a Presidential Scholar or other extremely competitive award, it's the *parents'* job to initiate the application—the child fills it out. Few teachers will do this for your child. And fewer still will inform you that these opportunities exist. In addition to initiating the application, parents need to make themselves aware of the different judging criteria for each art form in order to help their children submit applications that demonstrate winning credentials. Earning these credentials starts with the right training (finding the right instructors outside of school is also the parents' responsibility) as well as knowledgeable people who can offer advice on creating an impressive portfolio. Many school art teachers are able to do this or can recommend someone to help.

The credentials discussed in this chapter will dazzle all colleges—not just art schools or conservatories—that have programs and facilities to accommodate the particular art. Long-term dedication to an art alone can be impressive to colleges as well, depending upon how developed the student's talent is and also how the student uses the talent to better his high school. Does the artist lend her talent to illustrate the school newspaper or yearbook? Does he contribute art to campus exhibits? Does the musician play in the school orchestra? The student's level of involvement in school activities and organizations is often viewed as a predictor of how the student will use her talent to contribute to college life.

| SECRET 184 | **In the arts, compared to other subjects, it's more understood—even by arts teachers—that success** |

requires serious training outside of school. And for some arts—particularly music and dance—out-of-school lessons need to start *years* before secondary school. A child doesn't become a concert flutist by relying solely on the high school orchestra or any other in-school flute lessons, unless the child attends a conservatory high school like Interlochen in Michigan, LaGuardia in New York, Carver Center in Maryland, Perry-Mansfield in Steamboat Springs,

New Orleans Center for Creative Arts, or Idyllwild in California. But even in those specialized schools, each student is expected to audition to get in, thereby demonstrating that he has had years of solid training before applying.

| SECRET 185 | **When seeking training for your child, unless she is mentored by someone really famous or someone** |

whose technique seems to click with her 100 percent, you can provide a secret edge by exposing her to multiple teachers, experiences, and skill sets. In most arts, it's better to expose your child to a repertoire of techniques and approaches rather than only developing familiarity with one—even if your child ends up rejecting all but one technique, and even if your kid's instructor insists that he is the only one for your child. (An exception might be in some of the more physical arts—playing an instrument or dance—where mastering a certain stance or position may require a student to stay with a single teacher.) When one technique doesn't work for a particular challenge, another approach should be readily available. The same applies to acquiring skills: The dancer who wants to specialize in jazz should also get background in ballet and modern to enrich his versatility and increase his opportunities.

| SECRET 186 | **When looking for arts instruction for your child, if he is serious about the art, scout out opportunities** |

that will treat your child's artistic expression seriously. By high school, your artist child should be taking lessons at a top quality art school or college with a knowledgeable artist rather than at a neighborhood teen program. Your serious young musician should be studying at a conservatory or college with a professional musician rather than with a neighbor who teaches a variety of instruments on the side (unless the neighbor is a professional musician). Your young dancer should be studying at the best available conservatory or dance-company-endorsed or -affiliated school of dance rather than at the local children's after-school program that displays trophies in the window. And your theater-loving child, in addition to performing in school productions, should be performing in local community shows and summer stock at a minimum—and taking serious voice and/or dance training as well.

If all this sounds expensive, it's the parents' job to seek out scholarships and funding. Some arts programs offer discounts (and sometimes full tuition) to students who demonstrate talent and dedication. (For example, the Ballet School of Chapel Hill and other nationally known dance companies have been known to offer boys lessons for free. And New York Tech, a public school in New York City, features free dance lessons for boys and girls who reside within the city.)

In addition to providing top instruction, parents should seek out workshops, summer stock, local exhibit space, contests, and festivals that offer showcase opportunities while the child is still in high school.

| SECRET 187 | **Exhibiting one's work publicly and performing for an audience can make all the difference in a col-** |

lege application. Exhibits and performances provide valuable documentation and credentials that prove to the admissions committee that your child is good enough at his art to showcase his work publicly.

| SECRET 188 | **When your artist child is applying to a liberal arts college, sometimes it is better for him to be able to** |

list successful auditions, performances, and art competitions that document his talent rather than show the college admissions officers his actual work. To the untrained eye or ear, the actual work may not appear impressive. A student's winning status in a contest may validate the child's abilities, however, which the committee member—who might have been a chemistry or linguistics major—may not "get" or like. It's often much more impressive—and convenient—to let contests and performances vouch for your kid instead.

National Arts Awards to Strive For

There are several national awards that can help to put your child on the map within his particular art. Here are a few of the most impressive.

| SECRET 189 | **The Presidential Scholar in the Arts award is one of the most prestigious high school arts awards** |

in the country. Sponsored by the National Foundation for Advancement in the Arts (NFAA), winners and honored participants share $525,000 in scholarship awards for their work in dance, film and video, jazz, music, theater, photography, visual arts, voice, and writing. Students must be high school seniors to enter, and twenty individual prizes range from $250 to $10,000. The deadline is in October, and the awards are announced December 1. Apply at: www.artsawards.org. In addition, the NFAA compiles a list of participants for its Scholarship List Service (SLS)—"to offer col-

leges, universities, and professional schools the authorized names of high
school seniors who register for NFAA's Arts Recognition and Talent
Search," helping participants to find college placement at top arts colleges.
The list of more than thirty participating colleges includes USC, North-
western, NYU's Tisch School, North Carolina School of the Arts, Oberlin
Conservatory, and Rhode Island School of Design (RISD).

| SECRET 190 | **One of the opportunities mentioned most often by Presidential Scholar winners are the Scholastic** |

Art & Writing Awards, administered by the Alliance for Young Artists &
Writers, a nonprofit organization supported by charitable contributions "to
provide guidance and support for the next generation of artists and writers."
In 2007, the awards, which began in 1923, marked their eighty-fourth year.
How prestigious is this award? Past national winners have included Truman
Capote, Red Grooms, Bernard Malamud, Joyce Carol Oates, Robert Red-
ford, and Andy Warhol.

The competition starts with regional contests that annually draw about
250,000 entries in both fine arts and writing. Of that number, about 190,000
entries are art projects submitted by students in 7th through 12th grades. Seniors who participate are required to submit entire portfolios, and from that
pool seven senior artists are awarded $10,000 apiece as Gold Portfolio winners.
Up to seven additional students receive Notable Achievement awards of
$1,000. One thousand artists (including these winners) are then honored at
the winners' celebration event at Carnegie Hall—in addition, 400 writing student winners are invited to the Carnegie Hall event, too—and all 1,400 students are eligible to access some of the $1.5 million in financial aid and
scholarships provided by more than eighty participating art institutes, universities, and colleges. (Winners don't have to show up at Carnegie Hall to receive
scholarships.) Most scholarships are tied to specific sponsoring institutions, so
depending on which college your child chooses, scholarships may be generous. All of the major art schools and many university art programs participate,
including RISD, Savannah, Pratt, Carnegie Mellon, and Parsons.

Fine arts categories include art portfolio, animation, ceramics and glass,
computer art, design, digital imagery, drawing, mixed media, painting, photography, photography portfolio, printmaking, sculpture, and video and film.
Students in grades 7 through 12 are eligible to compete. To enter, find
the registration information at www.scholastic.com/artandwritingawards/
enter.htm.

| SECRET 191 | **For more information about which awards and other credentials the country's top art, music, and** |

dance students have earned, go the Web site of the National Foundation for Advancement in the Arts (NFAA) Arts Recognition and Talent Search (another extremely prestigious contest). At www.artsawards.org, you'll find bios of national winners of this talent search, listing their credentials in dance, film and video, jazz, music, photography, theater, visual arts, voice, and writing. This can be an excellent way to learn about opportunities.

Fine Arts

| SECRET 192 | **If AP Studio Art and AP Art History are offered in your young artist's high school, he should take** |

both courses to demonstrate interest and gain depth of knowledge. The most-competitive colleges prefer students who utilize the most challenging resources available at high school. If your child is considering majoring in art, AP Studio Art and AP Art History are well-respected courses. Don't let your child shy away from them if he is presenting himself as a prospective art major, presuming that his college would automatically prefer to see a course like AP Physics.

| SECRET 193 | **Students who attend private art schools or university art "institutes" after school, weekends, or** |

during the summer, tend to have significantly stronger portfolios and applications. That's the word from the admissions office of UCLA, the art program that claims to be the nation's most competitive, since it only accepts 10 percent of its applicants.

Kavin Buck, artist and director of enrollment management and outreach for UCLA's School of the Arts and Architecture, says that students who attend private programs (RISD's summer program, Cornell's Summer College, or Interlochen, for example) or institutes (UCLA Summer Art Institute and BU Visual Arts Summer Institute, for example) after school, weekends, or summers, learn how to *talk* about their work, and this becomes extremely helpful in writing their application essays and in interviews. (Regular high school art programs do not teach students how to discuss their work.) In addition, high school students who attend private programs and institutes sometimes get the opportunity to work with accomplished artists and can cite these experiences on the application. And for those students who work with college faculty members, "a lot of time, the faculty remembers them and is helpful in the admissions process."

Among the most rigorous summer art programs mentioned most frequently among admissions officers are the Art Institute of Chicago, Parsons (New York), Otis College (Los Angeles), Kansas City Art Institute, and Rhode Island School of Design. In addition, university institutes cited as most rigorous include Michigan School of Art, Tisch (NYU), and UCLA. The art *programs* are generally affiliated with art schools, whereas the *institutes* are generally affiliated with a large university.

| SECRET 194 | **One benefit to a university art institute is that high school students can often get transferable** |

college credit for their work. If they're attending the institute in the summer, they can also take courses to fill other college requirements (language, English composition, etc.) alongside their art courses to get this work out of the way before college. Such courses could include basic English composition requirements, but may also include introductory science classes that are sometimes easier at a university than in an AP class in high school.

| SECRET 195 | **The most important single factor in a college art school or art program application is the student's** |

ability to draw well from observation. That's the word from an admissions officer at the Rhode Island School of Design. Next in importance are personal style and creativity, coupled with good grades in high school in every subject.

To demonstrate ability to draw from observation, RISD's college application requires three drawings: a bicycle, an interior/exterior space, and free choice. In addition, the portfolio itself usually contains twelve to twenty pieces of the student's best work (more information about portfolios below).

| SECRET 196 | **Submitting a drawing of a bicycle as part of the portfolio to any other college art program is the** |

telltale sign that the student is also applying to RISD. No other art programs require bicycle drawings. And admissions officers of the other colleges all know that RISD does. So if your child doesn't want all the other schools to know exactly where he is applying, omit the bicycle drawing from the portfolio when applying to other colleges or art programs.

A Fine Arts Student's Four-Summer Plan

A fine arts student's summers should be designed around serious summer art activities that contribute to his or her portfolio. Following is just one four-summer plan for a painter. (A more elaborate list of options is offered in the appendix.) Hundreds of opportunities exist for high school art students, and not all entail travel or residential expenses. This is just a sampling of what can be accomplished and what kind of credentials your child can accumulate in four summers through some of the most highly reputed programs, without taking budget into account.

Four-Summer Plan: The summer before 9th grade, the student could study painting at Interlochen Arts Camp for six weeks. Then the following summer he could take a four-week painting class at North Carolina School of the Arts and a one-week painting course at Kansas City Art Institute's Summer Studio Intensives. In the summer before junior year, he could travel to Italy in July with the Knowledge Exchange Institute (KEI) to study Venetian art history with a studio course in painting, and that would be followed by a two-week session at the Art Institute of Chicago. The summer before senior year could be spent at UCLA Design Summer Institute, a four-week program that provides portfolio assistance, helping the student to be ready for college applications and interviews in the fall.

Does a student need to attend all of these programs to get into college? No. A fine arts student needs to have plenty of time to create, and unless the art form specifically requires use of an art studio, much of the work can be done at home.

A high school student who pursues such a four-summer plan—or any portion of it—will have experienced some of the most highly reputed art training by high school graduation and (assuming that grades and test scores are in the right range) should be able to stand out in any college or art school applicant pool.

The Portfolio

In order to apply to college specifically for art, your child will need to assemble a collection of his artworks. This collection is called a portfolio. No, it's not necessarily a collection of large paintings made to fit in that giant-size black portfolio case you've probably seen artists carrying. Nowadays most schools prefer small, slide-style or even electronic portfolios, which are much less cumbersome. But each art school or art college has slightly different specifications for how they would like to see their applicants' art. Always check ahead; colleges rarely want to see (and be responsible for) originals.

| SECRET 197 | **While your artist child is in 8th or 9th grade, familiarize yourself with how portfolios look in general and what they ideally should contain.** Help your child determine a |

strategy for assembling a solid collection over the high school years. While senior-year work is likely to represent the best example of your child's abilities and technique, it's wise to know in advance what types of samples will be expected so these requirements can inform the work going forward.

| SECRET 198 | **Although the image of artists is often one of laid-back free expression, pursuing the arts is no excuse for a student (or his parents) to become lax about organization.** |

Colleges are much more impressed with applicants who are organized and structured in terms of portfolio, application, and résumé and can provide tangible evidence of their artistic achievements. And "don't go too crazy with packaging," an admissions officer advises. "Slides on a clear plastic slide sheet in an envelope will do; prints in an envelope as well. Pages should be 8½ by 11 or smaller, since they will be stored in a file folder in the admissions office." And some colleges prefer digital images.

Less Is More When It Comes to Packaging Your Child's Portfolio

A young painter assembling his portfolio last minute for an art program was told by a well-intending teacher to place his work in a loose-leaf binder and decorate the binder to make it look more appealing.

"Use interesting designs and patterns. Whatever appeals to you. The portfolio should show that you're bursting with passion for art," the teacher told him.

Sounded like good advice at the time. The boy then proceeded to paint bright cheery stars and planets—cliché "boy decor"—on the binder cover. In contrast, other students handed in unadorned slides and individual sheets, which came across as more sophisticated and professional. The implied statement was "Judge my work on its merits, not by my decorative packaging." The boy with the decorated portfolio was not admitted into his first-choice art school.

It is also important to ensure that all photographs or slides are of high, professional quality; amateurish "snapshot" photos of your child's art work will not do.

SECRET 199 Parents should find out from parents of older students and art teachers which local studios provide the best photography of works that need to be represented in photos or slides. If you own a good camera and good lighting equipment, you may be able to set up the photo shoot in your own home. But be very fussy if your child plans to do all of the photography at home. Fuzzy or blurred photographic images are not acceptable. (Nor are artworks themselves that are torn, damaged, or unfinished.) When photographing, watch out for flash-bulb reflection, shadows from incorrect lighting, or poor photography such as partial views, miniature views (each work should occupy the bulk of the slide), or slanted photos (lines should line up).

In overseeing your child's fine arts portfolio, make sure he also avoids the following pitfalls: (1) putting multiple works onto a single photo or slide, (2) forgetting to identify each work, (3) lacking a descriptive sheet explaining each work, and (4) submitting originals—always submit copies, and don't expect them back.

SECRET 200 Variety is good in a portfolio, but don't sacrifice quality. *Only include your best works*, admissions officers recommend. Art schools are more impressed with portfolios that contain all best-quality works in limited categories than those that show variety, weaker works included. "Most students will have completed ten pieces for every one that is included in the final portfolio," Kavin Buck of UCLA advises.

SECRET 201 If you're not sure what a specific art program or college is looking for in your child's portfolio after

checking the school's Web site, phone the college admissions office directly and ask. Students should expect to prepare multiple portfolios depending on the colleges to which they apply, as portfolio requirements differ at different universities and art programs. However, "most art programs will want to see works that fall into three distinct categories: observational art, personal art or a home exam," notes Kavin Buck. For details on these classifications and more advice on creating a portfolio, check out Buck's article on the Artschools.com Web site, www.artschools.com/articles/portfolio.

| SECRET 202 | **College isn't the only time an art student will need a portfolio—some of the more competitive** |

high school summer art programs, competitions, high school conservatories, and internships that can be impressive to colleges may require one as well. So the student's portfolio, like a résumé, should constantly evolve as the student accumulates more works to show.

National Portfolio Day

| SECRET 203 | **For one-on-one advice on an individual student's portfolio, the National Portfolio Day Association** |

sponsors events throughout America in which students can actually bring their portfolios to obtain specific suggestions from professionals. It's not a contest—just free consultations. And students are encouraged to seek many opinions and speak with many professionals during these events. The organization's calendar of events is available online at www.npda.org/tips.html.

Drama

| SECRET 204 | **Start building your child's résumé early.** For many college drama program applications, students are |

expected to include a theatrical résumé, listing the name and date of each production in which they have participated, their role or crew assignment, and the name of the producing organization (i.e., the high school, community theater, college, etc. that staged the production). Obviously, for a student to supply this information, he or she needs to have *had* some prior credentials and experience. Note that many applications require an academic track record as well, including transcript; grade point average; class rank; PSAT, SAT, and/or ACT scores; and school profile sheet (provided by your child's school).

The applicant is also asked to have her drama teacher or coach write comments on his or her talents, experience, personal characteristics, leadership skills, and so on. This assumes that the applicant *has* a drama teacher and that she has taken part in school productions and theater courses—yet another reason to start early.

Students who accrue credentials in 9th and 10th grades gain a strong edge in auditions for college theater programs senior year.

Auditioning for High School Productions

SECRET 205 **When it comes to college applications, *starring* in school shows is better than being a good soldier and playing small parts, regardless of what the school drama teacher may say.** Although high school teachers may rationalize that somebody has to play those small roles, and occasionally the small-role player can steal the show, lead roles or substantial character roles tend to be viewed as more significant experiences (requiring greater talent and commitment of time) to colleges. Bigger, more challenging roles also make better success stories in college application essays. Landing the starring role or a major role is often a matter of experience and time devoted to practice. (More below on how a student can gain this experience.)

SECRET 206 **Don't be daunted if the first time your drama-oriented child auditions for a school production, she gets a small role.** A small first role means less pressure (to memorize lines and perform for peers the first time around). When she is first granted the role, she might let the teacher know that she is pleased to have landed a part (and you should affirm to your child that you as a parent are pleased as well), and that next year she is hoping for a more challenging role. You want her to sound grateful, but you don't want her permanently typecast as the kid who will always be satisfied with a small role.

SECRET 207 **One way for your kid to gain an edge when auditioning for school productions is to familiarize**

himself with the lines and music ahead of time (unless his school is a conservatory where all the kids know to come prepared). A high school was holding auditions for the school's annual musical—this year, *Oklahoma*. As aspiring actors were called one at a time to read, sing, and dance for the role of Curly, the other students eagerly waited for a boy we'll call Rodney to have his turn. Rodney had requested the last audition and, as a result, all the other drama students, who were permitted to leave after their own auditions and normally would have left, waited to see him try out. Student after student got up to read lines, and each sang "Oh, What a Beautiful Morning." But the teacher barely seemed to pay attention.

To look at Rodney, nobody would see him as the traditional hero character. He wasn't particularly tall, nor was he the type to turn heads in the street. But Rodney was known to always give a dazzling performance.

By the time it was Rodney's turn, the audience of competitors was psyched. And sure enough, when Rodney stepped onstage, something magical happened. He knew the lines like he invented them himself. He knew the music as if he had sung it every morning looking out at the cornfield. Unlike the other kids, he didn't seem nervous, fidgety, or distracted. Instead he was comfortable in his hide, as if he were asked to play himself. He *was* Curly. Of course, the year before, he *was* Tevya. And the year before that, he *was* Henry Higgins.

"It's not fair," one of the younger boys muttered to a friend. "It was a done deal before the auditions even started. He knew he'd get the part. He always gets the part."

Sheer luck? No. Favoritism? Only inasmuch as a drama teacher is bound to favor a child who comes to auditions well prepared and ready to convince the audience that the part was made for him. This same scenario happens repeatedly at high schools across America. This year it's *Oklahoma*, but last year it was *Fiddler*, *My Fair Lady*, or *Music Man*. Parents complain to me that the same kid always gets the lead, and it's impossible for their kid to break in.

Drama teachers will tell you that most kids come to auditions unprepared. They stumble through scripts, squeak through songs, and step out of character. Give your kid an advantage by helping him prepare for a role or roles in advance.

| SECRET 208 | If your child knows she would like to audition for a school production, try to find out in advance |

what the play will be, and get a copy of the script, DVD, and CD (if it's a

musical). Play the CD as background music during car rides and other op-
portune moments in the weeks leading up to the audition. Practice the
lines with your daughter (in an organized way, little by little) to free her
from having to read the script at the audition. This will give her an enormous edge.

SECRET 209	**Record practice sessions at home.** Then your son can play back his part as background music during

spare time, while he sleeps, or even while doing other homework. It will
give him time to "live with the part" and hear his part often enough for him
to memorize it with minimal effort. This is especially helpful if you're unable to practice regularly with him. (Make sure the recording is error free.)

SECRET 210	**If your child is given a choice of audition order, last is often best.** Last is often the performance

that is most remembered. In addition, last gives your child time to observe
mistakes other students make so that she can avoid those same pitfalls.

Summer Programs

Where does a middle or high schooler get top acting experience? Summer drama programs vary enormously in quality and mission. Some are
merely sleepaway camps in which drama is offered as an activity amid
swimming and arts and crafts. Others provide serious drama education in a
camp setting. And still others offer college-level (college credit) drama
courses on a college campus—taught by college faculty—or summer stock
experiences, theater tours, or theater-related internships. The more serious
and advanced programs carry more clout when it's time to apply to college.

Quality college-level summer drama programs are abundant. Among the
more competitive options for high school students are North Carolina
School of the Arts (NCSA Summer Session Drama), NYU Tisch (Drama,
Dramatic Writing, Film, and Photography in New York, and also a 6-credit
abroad program called Drama in Paris and a 6-credit course called Drama in
Dublin), Carnegie Mellon (Pre-College Drama), Harvard (Summer Secondary School Drama Program), Idyllwild Arts (Academy Summer Drama),
UC Berkeley (Actors Workshop), Sarah Lawrence (Create & Invent Theatre Intensive), UCLA (Acting and Performing Institute), Northwestern

(National High School Institute Theatre Arts Program and two-week Musical Theatre Extension Program), and Yale's Acting in Film Workshop.

If you're starting your kid with a summer camp or summer program instead of a summer college program, ask in advance what guarantee, if any, your child has of getting either a part or a fair shot at a part in the camp/program's production. If your child is seriously interested in drama, you don't want her to waste away at a camp where she's taught by someone of questionable experience who gives her a nothing part. Ask in advance, for example, *Does seniority require that all major parts be given to previous campers who've already "paid their dues"? How many summers does paying one's dues entail? Does the program base casting on age—do only older campers automatically get lead roles? Do they typecast roles, potentially excluding your teenager?* Also find out which productions are scheduled so you might prepare your child for the audition before she arrives at the program.

| SECRET 211 | When investigating summer training, never assume that the higher the tuition, the more impressive |

the theater program. Think about it this way: In the most professional situations, the student is *paid* to perform.

Which programs impress colleges *most* depends a lot on how professional the program is and what your kid gets to do at the program. Starring in a theater production on a professional tour, on Broadway, or in Hollywood is clearly more impressive than singing in the camp play after color war, for example. Also, look at who is teaching the program—is it a high school CIT? Or a world-famous theater director?

Preparing for Out-of-School Auditions

Parents can play a major role in helping a child who is interested in drama prepare for out-of-school auditions and college auditions. The most obvious parental role is being an enthusiastic audience during home practice (or reading the other parts so the kid can practice his lines in context). Parents can also research scripts to find audition monologues that showcase their children's talents.

| SECRET 212 | Drama auditioners generally prefer to hear lines from actual plays that they're familiar with rather |

than monologues that are written specifically for auditions and published in monologue anthology books. In other words, they'd rather hear a monologue from Shakespeare's *Romeo and Juliet* than from Mary Smith's *Monologues for Teenagers*. Also, keep an eye on suitability of monologues—kids often select monologues written for much older actors or heavy in dialects; both are turnoffs at college and professional auditions.

SECRET 213

When your kid goes on a professional audition, encourage him to dress and appear as much like the character as possible. This secret came from the mother of a very successful Broadway child star whom I first met when we were seated together in a waiting room outside the audition room where our sons were competing for a role in a big new Broadway musical. The auditions were down to the final three. She whipped out a blow dryer from her handbag to slick her son's bangs straight up and then emptied a can of hairspray to keep his locks in place to match the cartoon figure that the character was supposedly based on.

"Don't you think that's a bit much?" I asked as I watched this mother fuss.

"No," she said, with a knowing smile. "Not all casting agents have a good imagination. You want to leave as little to their imagination as possible. Show them how you could look the part *perfectly*."

And she was on to something: While the third mother and I sat smugly in the waiting room, proud that we weren't fidgeting with our sons' hair in the final seconds before the auditions, the blow-dry boy landed the starring role. No question, he looked the part.

Applying to College Drama Programs

Admission into many college drama programs is extremely competitive. Among the most difficult to get into for an undergraduate, for example, are Juilliard (out of one thousand applicants each year, they accept twenty-five, a meager 2.5 percent odds—more difficult than Harvard or Wharton), Carnegie Mellon, NYU Tisch, SUNY Purchase, and Michigan.

SECRET 214

Parents should familiarize themselves with the requirements of desired programs years before the child starts preparing for auditions. To audition for Juilliard's drama program, for example, applicants are required to perform by memory two monologues, one contemporary and one classical, each about two minutes long. But applicants are also advised to prepare two additional (different) monologues—one contemporary and one classical—in case they are called back for another round of auditions. The monologues should be excerpts from actual plays (as mentioned above), and students may be required to discuss the context and answer questions about the whole play.

In contrast to Juilliard's requirements, Michigan's Department of Theatre & Drama encourages modern pieces. Michigan wants two memorized contrasting monologues (less than four minutes total), incorporating some physical movement; they advise students to avoid age-inappropriateness, "excessively stylized pieces, dialects, extreme physicality and props."

Ideally, by senior year, a student will have accrued a comfortable repertoire of monologues so that the audition memorization isn't last minute and clumsy. If your daughter is planning to pursue multiple auditions, help her locate monologues that satisfy the standards of several programs.

| SECRET 215 | **When it comes time to write college application essays, the drama student should focus on a single** |

incident or two that caused him to grow as an actor—rather than simply listing names of drama programs and directors. For example: *The time we performed* Singin' in the Rain *in an outdoor theater and real rain fell right as I sang the theme song*, or *The week I slept on a bench to get in character for* Waiting for Godot, or *Learning how to fly for the musical* Peter Pan, *or The time the famous director Jane Jones critiqued my performance.*

Finding a Talent Agent

While colleges won't care if your kid has an agent, landing significant roles in professional productions *will* wow most top colleges (assuming the student's grades and test scores are in a suitable range)—and having a talent agent increases the likelihood of landing these roles.

| SECRET 216 | **Many talent agents are surprisingly accessible.** Parents whose teenagers want to model or act are |

led to believe that only insiders can find agents, and few people know how to become insiders. In reality, information about reputable agents is just a click away.

SECRET 217   The Association of Talent Agents (ATA) Web site lists talent agents and what they're looking for: www.agentassociation.com/frontdoor/actors_agent_search.cfm. At the site, you can look up the name of any child star, find out who his agent is, and obtain contact information (including phone numbers) for that agent. Or you could just go through the alphabetical listing of agents and look for the (Y) that designates "works with youth."

According to an ATA administrator, the best way to find a suitable talent agent for your child is as follows:

1. Go to the ATA Web site to the list of member talent agencies.
2. Call agencies with (Y) designation. (Note that parents should call— not kids.)
3. Ask the agency for its "new submission and new client policy." Some agencies may tell you that they're not interested, others may be eager; some only take referrals from an industry person, and some take walk-ins. Each is different.

SECRET 218   For those agencies that express a potential interest, be prepared to send a photo—not necessarily a professional photo—and a performance résumé if you want your kid to be taken seriously. The business is very competitive, and children with no prior performing experience will not be given a second look—unless they have some rare or unusual appearance or talent that is needed. This means your child should build up credentials (school plays, outside drama lessons, and outside productions) long before you start searching for an agent.

(Note that at each professional audition to which your child goes— once he has an agent—your child is expected to bring along a professional photo that's 8½ by 11, with his performance résumé, including contact information—name, parents' phone, e-mail—on the back. For safety reasons, the ATA recommends against including your child's address on any résumé or photo. If the talent agent wants to get in touch with you, she should phone you, the parent.)

SECRET 219   An intriguing means of finding your kid an agent is offered by a company called commercialkids.com. This company provides lists of legitimate licensed agents that work with kids (ages zero to eighteen, and slightly older young adults who can pass for kids) and charges $14.95 per list (with names and addresses) or, more inter-estingly, $19.95 for preprinted labels already addressed to agents. (The idea is for parents to send their kid's photo and résumé to all the agents on the list simultaneously.) Customers specify a category—e.g., children's agents, children's casting directors, children's managers, children's modeling agents, music agents, dance agents, TV, stage, and so on. Twenty-one categories for children are updated daily. Lists and labels in each category range from only thirty-five children's New York modeling agencies, to 220 New York cast-ing directors, to about 325 to 340 Los Angeles casting directors. Parents can contact the company via their Web site or by phoning (877) 570-9662.

| SECRET 220 | **Legitimate talent agents do not charge for their services—they make a percentage off the child's** |

performances once they've agreed to represent her. Parents should be wary of businesses that call themselves talent agencies but that charge money to assemble a portfolio, arrange a photo shoot, or offer training.

| SECRET 221 | **When having your child audition for agents, be prepared to console your child for rejection—** |

that's part of the business. If twenty agents say they're not interested, and one is, remember that your child only needs *one* agent, after all.

Music and Dance

Musicians and dancers often begin training long before they enter high school. It's not unusual to hear of a top-level violinist who started as a Suzuki student at the age of three or four. And to develop the body and skill of a ballerina, one can't suddenly pick up dance for the first time at age six-teen. Years of preparation are required to make the high school performer stand out. If your child wants to present herself as a prospective music or dance major to the most-competitive colleges, she needs to demonstrate professional experience and ability—not just proficiency. To use music as a secondary asset (let's say, she is intending to major in English literature), she still needs to demonstrate ability—not just interest.

As with the other interests discussed in the book, throughout the process of training a future professional dancer or musician, parents need to be involved—even if they themselves are not musicians or dancers. Their job is to familiarize themselves with who's who among teachers and performers in the particular art, be encouraging, arrange the logistics (lessons, practice space, transportation), and then scout out the best opportunities for their children—even once the child has reached high school.

In both fields, no matter whom your kid studied with or which summer program your kid attended, what ultimately counts is your child's performance—how he or she sounds or dances at a live audition or on a tape.

Finding the Best Private Training for Your Child

For high school musicians and dancers who want to seriously pursue their art, there are lots of outstanding instructional programs. Because performing music and dance is similar to being an athlete, the performer needs to stay in shape and therefore needs to take lessons and practice year round. This cannot be relegated merely to summer programs, although summer programs are also required to maintain and improve the year-round learning.

SECRET 222 **If you're not sure how seriously your child feels toward a musical instrument (and your child isn't either), err on the side of serious training.** You can always "dumb down" the program, but it's much harder to make up for lost time if you discover later that your child is serious about her passion.

SECRET 223 **When seeking instrument lessons for your child, place more emphasis on how well he will be taught than by the reputation or fame of the overall training.** The top consideration should be whom your child will study with and how that teacher will work with your child. Note that within individual instrumental music programs, quality can vary by instrument. One prestigious program might have a great viola teacher, and a lesser known program might have the best bassoon teacher. While the most prestigious programs (translation: best funded, most publicized) tend to attract top-notch teachers, if the teachers for your kid's instruments aren't top-notch, it's generally better to forego the prestige and opt for the program with better training.

That said, don't completely ignore prestige.

| SECRET 224 | **Although prestige should not be your top priority, well-known programs can add weight to a college** |

application, particularly if the reader is not a good judge of the art but is familiar with the names of the most highly reputed programs.

"I took dance lessons at Miss Abby's Ballet School," a student mentioned at a group interview for a competitive liberal arts college.

"Well, I studied at Alvin Ailey," another student boasted, raising eyebrows.

For the remainder of the session, the Alvin Ailey student was treated like a superstar, and every effort was made to appease and recruit her. Nobody saw either student dance, but the assumption was that the kid with the name program was more accomplished.

Not every applicant will be given the opportunity to perform or demonstrate her abilities and talents. When no performance opportunity is provided, a name program often will win more admission points for the student.

| SECRET 225 | **When you explore a music or dance program, ask who, specifically, your child's teacher would be.** Do |

students choose their teachers? Is there a lottery? Are students just assigned? Do students change their teachers over the course of years at the conservatory?

At the beginning of an arts camp program, the campers were gathered at an introductory assembly awaiting the announcement of which child would study with which teacher. A student named Sarah leaned over to her best friend, Grace, and said, "I'm so excited. Mrs. James has agreed to be my voice teacher. I can't wait until they announce it!"

"How did you get Mrs. James to teach you?" Grace asked. "I thought we weren't allowed to request teachers."

"My parents said there was no harm in asking anyway," Sarah said. "So they did, and Mrs. James said yes!"

The moral here is that if you or your child has a specific preference, voice it with the program or instructor before teachers are assigned. Kids are generally not aware of their options. But savvy parents can do some investigation and quietly request this teacher or that after their children have been admitted—even in programs that claim not to honor requests.

| SECRET 226 | **Don't assume that all the teachers within a given program will be equally good at teaching your** |

child—or even that the most sought-after teachers will work the best with your kids. Within a large conservatory or dance program, you're bound to have variation, and different personalities respond well with different kids. If you know in advance that your child learns better with a particular approach, state that preference after he is admitted into the program. (If you state such a preference beforehand, he may sound too fussy and risk not being admitted.)

| SECRET 227 | **In seeking a teacher or coach who will run with your child in a serious way, look carefully at the** |

results of some of the teacher's older or previous students. To what level has this teacher taken her students? Have past students reached professional level? Where did they go to college? Is the teacher part of a relay system in which she brings the student to a certain point, at which another coach must take over to bring them to professional level?

You should also observe the instructor's interactions with other kids. Does he respect the kids he works with, and would his style work for your child? (His fame will be much less important if he has no rapport with your kid.)

| SECRET 228 | **In choosing a teacher, time allotment may be an important factor.** Try to get a sense of how much |

attention he will be able to afford your child. Find out if the instructor is handling other superstar kids who may monopolize his attention and affections. Ask the teacher directly. In response, the teacher may boast about his other students to you to win you over and to give your child confidence that she has come to the right place. But beyond that initial boasting, you might want to specify that you're seeking a teacher who will really believe in the capabilities of your child and will dedicate himself to bringing out those talents.

That said, encourage your performer child to be flexible and able to work with a variety of personalities. Performers often have to collaborate with difficult or eccentric personalities: a panicked director, a conductor who yells, a performer who freezes onstage, and one who forgets the staging. The more flexible and affable your child is, the more opportunities he or she will be given and be able to handle in the future.

Music Credentials

| SECRET 229 | **To impress colleges, the serious musician should combine in-school musical participation with out-** |

of-school achievements. Compared with some of the other arts, classical music is more closely tied in with a child's school and has a tighter in-school structure—and if your child wants to stand out musically, she should take advantage of the opportunities that are offered through her school at the county, regional, and state level. There are also numerous out-of-school opportunities in which a young musician may shine, and parents can be extremely helpful in scouting out these programs and contests for their kids. (See below for specifics about many of these opportunities.)

School-Affiliated Music Credentials

| SECRET 230 | **There's a music contest hierarchy in the nation's public and private schools.** Top high school musi- |

cians are invited to participate in county, district, or city music festivals—a nice credential, but not enough to wow most admissions officers. Many of those students may then audition for state music festivals—each state has its own organization and event. Some states invite auditions from students in grades 9 through 12; others only allow juniors and seniors. Most states hold music festivals annually, but some, like Washington and Oregon, only hold festivals in alternating years. Participating in a state festival can impress many colleges—particularly if the student comes from a heavily populated state where music is competitive. Performing a solo or being named a concertmaster in a state performance is especially impressive.

In the Eastern and Northwestern conferences, all-state performers are then eligible to audition for honors ensembles. The Eastern Conference (Maryland to Maine, including Washington, D.C.) accepts 650 students each year in concert band (150 students), symphony orchestra (150), jazz ensemble (20), and mixed choir (300 to 325). The Northwestn Conference (Alaska, Idaho, Montana, Oregon, Washington State, and Wyoming) has a mixed choir (300), women's choir (175), concert band (150), symphony orchestra (150), jazz band (20), and jazz choir (24).

In other states, including the Southern Division Conference (Virginia to

Florida, including Louisiana and Mississippi) and North Central Conference (Indiana, Iowa, Illinois, Michigan, Minnesota, Nebraska, North Dakota, Ohio, and South Dakota), the all-state ensemble is as far as your child can go. And the same is true in California and other western and southwestern states where there is no regional conference. The Music Educators National Conference is held only on even years, and the regional conferences are held only on odd years. (So if you're living in a state that only allows juniors and seniors to participate, and junior year falls on an odd year, don't wait until senior year to have your child audition.)

The process of selecting audition pieces differs from state to state. The National Association for Music Education (MENC, whose initials don't coincide with the name of the organization, as the initials are based on a previous name: Music Educators National Conference) advises that parents check for lists of acceptable audition pieces with their child's high school music teacher. Different works of varying difficulty are acceptable tryout pieces in different states.

SECRET 231 To qualify to be named All-USA High School Musicians in band, orchestra, or choir, your child does not have to wait for a nomination, nor does your child have to qualify for all-state. The competition is handled separately, and students may apply online at www.menc.org. Note that USA Musicians is not a performance group, but rather a national honor given to one hundred young musicians.

Being outstanding at a musical instrument can sometimes translate into scholarship money. And receiving merit-based scholarship money is viewed by some colleges as an added credential on the application.

SECRET 232 The National Association for Music Education (MENC) Web site warns that applying for music scholarships requires advance planning, preferably starting in sophomore or junior year of high school. High school music teachers may not tell your child this, because they may think that the early focus could make their high school music program too competitive—yet by March or April of senior year, MENC scholarships have already been awarded. To prepare for MENC auditions, the organization also recommends determining audition repertoire months *or even years* in advance: "Decide on an opening piece that shows off your strengths. A difficult selection played well can show off your skills." MENC provides an online listing of music-related (not necessarily

MENC-sponsored) scholarships for college at www.menc.org/information/
infoserv/Scholar.html.

MENC's advice for preparation for all kinds of classical music auditions:
Make sure the kid is dressed for an interview; have him arrive early to warm
up; and have him bring musical scores, extra strings or reeds (for instrumentalists), and a résumé. The parent should make sure in advance that the child
knows that during the audition she should make eye contact with the audition committee, keep going if she makes mistakes, and never make excuses.

Working with Your Child's High School Music Department

The accomplished trumpet player was told that she would not be al-
lowed to audition for the big trumpet solo because she was a 9th grader.
"Ninth graders don't play solos," the high school band conductor said.
"Only seniors play solos."

"But my skills are so much better than any senior!" the girl protested.

"You *do* play well, but no exceptions!"

The girl felt so frustrated that she wanted to quit band.

If your kid finds himself in a similar situation, encourage him to cooperate with the high school and demonstrate good team spirit; this will ultimately serve him best in the long run. But never rely on your child's high
school alone to showcase his talents. Schools have lots of politics, personalities, and arbitrary rules to deal with, and not every opportunity is based on
merit—some opportunities are based on giving seniors chances to shine or
giving everyone a turn.

SECRET 233	**If you feel that your kid's talent is not being prop-erly recognized at school, focus on out-of-school**

opportunities. If you observe that your child is being overlooked, speak directly with the teacher in charge. If you oppose the school's performance
policies because only upperclassmen are allowed to solo, involve yourself in
a parent organization that can make changes—don't argue with the teacher.
And don't be too fast to demand changes without exploring the music/the-
ater teacher's perspectives. I have seen many parents who vehemently opposed "senior privileges" when their kids were freshmen but who changed

their views 180 degrees when their kids reached senior year. You may find that, philosophically, it's better to give each kid a solo or a chance to perform at some point during high school—even if they're not the best artists—because once they reach college, everything will be merit based and these kids will never again have an opportunity to perform. But in the meantime, make sure that any school-related obstacles don't stifle your child's musical advancement.

SECRET 234   **Remember, schools don't have the monopoly on student success in music.** In researching out-of-school opportunities for your child, note that teachers who offer private instrument or voice lessons often know about local out-of-school orchestras, bands, opera companies, and other ensembles that can help your child form an impressive track record. Enroll your kid in a community orchestra. Or form a quartet or other ensemble where she can shine. Have her perform a solo tour at day care centers and senior centers. Lots of people would appreciate seeing her perform. Transcend school.

In addition, books and Web sites list top out-of-school competitions. (Check www.Violinist.com, for example, which lists upcoming international violin competitions. For piano competitions, check www.afn.org/~afn39483/index.html, which lists 650 contests from fifty-eight countries.) Winning any national contest could impress a college admissions committee. Contests range from simple songwriting challenges (like those listed at http://musicians.about.com/od/contests), to weighty national contests like the Davidson (www.ditdservices.org) and Sphinx (www.sphinxmusic.org/applicants/general.html), to major national and international piano competitions like the Van Cliburn, Busoni, Chopin, Franz Liszt, or Hamamatsu Piano competitions, violin competitions, and other instrument- and ensemble-based contests.

SECRET 235   **Parents can ease the way for their young performers by becoming an ally to the high school's music program.** Remember that high school teachers are required to be diplomats in order to meet the needs of students who range from virtuosos with perfect pitch to tone-deaf novices. If you're the parent of a serious musician, become an ally to the music department—be a team player, even if instinct tells you to lobby for your daughter to have the big solo in every production. At many high schools, parents—even big-time professional parents—run bake sales as fund-raisers for the music department during intermission. They arrange for the purchase of a bouquet for the teacher and soloists for curtain calls. They help make costumes or paint scenery. Involved parents generally get to have more say in the goings-on of the department as long as they remain team players and respect the fact that the music teacher is in charge.

Out-of-School Music and Dance Programs

What follows is just a sampling of music and dance programs that offer top-quality instruction. Many more exciting opportunities exist in both fields.

| SECRET 236 | **Students can apply directly to most programs without having to be "discovered" or nominated** |

by a third party before applying. Too often young students don't apply for opportunities, buying into the notion that they first have to be discovered by someone with clout.

Interlochen: Interlochen Arts Camp attracts two thousand young artists and one thousand faculty and staff to its Michigan campus each summer. The camp claims to bring together "the world's best and brightest students" (3rd to 12th grades) and "world-class instructors" for more than four hundred presentations in dance, theater, creative writing, visual arts, motion picture arts and music.

Dancers in grades 6 to 12 attend one or two three-week sessions that feature six hours of intensive ballet or modern dance training each day. For instrumentalists, singers, and composers, Interlochen offers Advanced Horn Institute, Advanced String Quartet, Advanced Vocal, Advanced Choral, Classical Guitar, Composition, Ensemble Program: Strings (World Youth Symphony Orchestra, Interlochen Philharmonic, and chamber music), Ensemble Program: Winds and Percussion (World Youth Symphony Orchestra, World Youth Wind Symphony, Interlochen Philharmonic, Interlochen Symphony Band, and chamber music), Harp, Jazz, Organ, and Piano.

Programs Geared Toward Music Students

Tanglewood: The Boston University Tanglewood Institute offers summer programs for high school students who want to study music intensively and perform at the world-renowned Tanglewood Festival in the Berkshire Mountains of Massachusetts. Among the Young Artists Program (ages fifteen to eighteen) offerings are orchestra (six weeks), vocal (six weeks), composition (six weeks), harp (six weeks), piano (three or six weeks), and wind ensemble (four weeks) classes. In addition, for students who want to commit less time, two-week Institute Workshops (ages fifteen plus) are offered in flute, oboe, clarinet, trumpet, horn, trombone, tuba/euphonium, double bass, string quartet, and percussion.

Auditions are required for all participants, except composers who "submit three [musical] scores in lieu of an audition." In addition to learning to compose music, composition students get to have their music performed by real ensembles and recorded. And they get to meet with some of the world's leading composers. Admission to all other Tanglewood programs is by live audition or recording. Applications are available at www.bu.edu/cfa/music/auditions/index.htm.

Northwestern University School of Music: The National High School Music Institute five-week summer program in Evanston, Illinois, features classes (modeled after first-year conservatory studies) and more than twenty-four ensembles for 180 serious musicians. The curriculum includes performing, field trips to performances, master classes, and sessions on audition preparation and applying to top music schools.

UCLA's World Music Summer Institute and Music Academy: In 2006, the Department of Ethnomusicology launched a one-week program in which participants "immerse themselves in one of three performance traditions: Music of African Americans, Music of Korea or Music of Mexico" and earn 2 credits. For another 2 credits, experienced high school musicians may apply for UCLA's one-week Summer Music Academy to participate in band, symphony orchestra, or collaborative performance (piano) classes.

Programs Geared Toward Dance Students

Summer Dance Intensive: Extraordinary Dance: Colorado College offers three weeks of dance for ages fourteen and up with at least two years' dance experience. Participants get six hours of daily technique work (ballet, yoga/acrobalance, modern dance, hip-hop, and jazz), supplemented by forty-five minutes of lecture and discussion, and an evening elective on experimental or uncommon dance forms.

Alvin Ailey Junior Division Summer Intensive Program: For boys and girls twelve to fifteen with at least two years of ballet training, the Junior Division Summer Intensive Program offers ballet supplemented by modern and jazz classes. The program builds up to a performance in the Ailey Citigroup Theater. This is a very prestigious program. And participation in it, along with top grades and standardized test scores, will wow any college that offers a dance program or access to a dance program. Apply by video or audition. For ages sixteen to twenty-five, a seven-week Professional Division is offered.

School of American Ballet: This is one of the most prestigious high school ballet programs in the United States, and is a top credential for college. (The residential program is based at Lincoln Center in New York City.) Admission is by audition only for boys and girls ages twelve to eighteen. "Videotapes or DVDs are accepted only for students living outside the continental United States." But students need not travel to New York to audition. National auditions are conducted in twenty-two cities.

Sarah Lawrence Summer Dance: For grades 10, 11, and 12, this two-week course teaches "technical and creative components of dance in a supportive and noncompetitive environment." Topics covered include contemporary dance, improvisation and choreography, and technique.

UCLA Summer Dance-Theater Intensive: Introduced in 2006, this one-week program taught by the university's dance faculty leads to 2 college credits. The program features "daily movement technique classes ranging from Contemporary Modern/Post-Modern dance, to Brazilian Capoeira and Hip-Hop, as well as an Improvisation/Composition class."

Recording Your Child's Performance

SECRET 237

If you're making a DVD or CD of your child's performance for applications to colleges and other programs, use the best professional facilities available. Gone are the days when your child could sing into a tape recorder in your living room. An instrumentalist who plays beautifully but submits a shoddy home recording impresses nobody. To locate a professional recording studio, speak to your child's music teacher. If you live in a rural or remote area and no studio can be located nearby, have your child make a recording in a school music room with good acoustics. If your child plays a solo during a school performance, try to record that as well so the admissions officers have some context in which to appreciate your child's musicianship. Don't wait until senior year to start recording concerts. Samplings are preferred over hours of complete material because you want to focus the listeners or viewers on the highlights that will impress them most. If the application instructions tell you to limit your recording to a specified amount of time, stay within that limit.

Creative Writing

The promising young writer's poem was rejected by the high school literary magazine editor, who was worried that publishing it would help the girl get into the college to which both of them had planned to apply. Frustrated, the girl's mother submitted the poem to a professional publication, which published it immediately. When the girl applied to college the following year, she discussed the publication of her poem in her application essay—not mentioning the high school magazine's rejection of the piece—and was admitted to her first-choice college.

SECRET 238

Your child's writing need not be limited to high school publications, and what's rejected from a high school publication may be appreciated in a more knowledgeable environment. Parents can seek out-of-school venues for their kid's creative writing, including op-ed pages of daily newspapers, where you'll occasionally see a poem published, or special-interest magazines if your child's poem or short piece relates to that special interest. Many local weeklies will also gladly publish student-written news articles about school-related news. (If your child would like to submit articles to weeklies, advise her to focus only on the positive and give credit to all those involved in the activity being written about—this should not be investigative journalism.)

A few books provide excellent sources of information on publishing your child's article, poetry, or book. *The Writer's Market* (Writer's Digest Books, 2007) doesn't specifically focus on children's writing, but it can still be used to find the right periodical or literary agent for your child's work if you feel that the work is of high quality. The *Children's Writer's & Illustrator's Market* (Writer's Digest Books, 2007) can also be helpful.

To publish a poem or article, go directly to publications (rather than first seeking out a literary agent). Parents may speak directly to the editor in charge of the particular column or section to inquire about how to submit a piece. Each publication has different procedures. Some allow you to submit to multiple publications at a time. Others require that you submit the piece only to them.

Susquehanna University offers high school creative writers the chance to publish in its literary journal, the *Apprentice Writer*. Because literary journals for high school students are rare, publishing in this one, with a circulation of 11,000, is very prestigious, and it can be extremely appealing to colleges. But note that when mentioning the *Apprentice Writer* (as with any publication) on an application, the student should describe the journal. If the application is read by an officer whose major was unrelated to literature—anthropology or biology, for example—he might not know of the *Apprentice Writer*.

Other places that specifically publish works by teens include *Positive Teens* magazine, www.positiveteensmag.com and *Merlyn's Pen*, www .merlynspen.org.

| SECRET 239 | **In addition to being published and winning the Presidential Scholar Award, the two other honors** |

that stand out as most prestigious for high school literary writers are the Davidson Fellows Award and the Scholastic Art & Writing Awards. To apply for a Davidson in literature, your child needs to submit "a 60- to 75-page portfolio of prodigious work containing three of the following four genres: fiction, nonfiction, poetry, drama/screenplay." He must also submit "a 500-word reflective essay about the works in the portfolio."

Preparing the required writing samples may take years of work—thus it's advantageous to start thinking about assembling a portfolio when your child is in the earlier years of high school. Like most of the most prestigious college application credentials, this is not an overnight activity whipped up for a college application.

What does the talented writer receive for winning? Scholarships of $50,000, $25,000, or $10,000, a most impressive college application credential that establishes the winner as one of the nation's top young writers, and an awards reception in Washington, D.C., at the Library of Congress.

The Scholastic Art & Writing Awards, discussed in the Fine Arts section at the beginning of the chapter, are open to students in grades 7 through 12 and feature five $10,000 Portfolio Gold writing awards, plus up to seven (total writing and arts) $1,000 Notable Achievement Portfolio Silver scholarships for seniors for their writing portfolios (rather than a single work). Past jurors have included Robert Frost and William Saroyan. Writing categories include dramatic script, general writing, humor, journalism, nonfiction, novel, personal essay/memoir, poetry, science fiction/fantasy, short story, and short short story. In 2006, 1,700 manuscripts went on to the nationals (selected from 62,000 submitted regionally). Of those, 400 (grades 7 to 12) received recognition at Carnegie Hall (in addition to 1,000 fine artists). All of the recognized students then became eligible for access to the $1.5 million in financial aid and scholarships provided by more than eighty art institutes and colleges.

Helping Your Child Hone His or Her Craft

Before seeking out venues for your fiction writer or poet to publish or be recognized, first encourage her to focus on writing and polishing her work. If, for example, your daughter's goal is to write and publish a novel by high school graduation, you might include in her game plan a top-quality summer writing program (see below). Or, if sending your daughter to a retreat isn't in the budget (usually upward of $100 per day), create your own summer writer's retreat at home. If you decide to take this route, in addition to creating an overall conducive work setting, work with your child to set deadlines—and possibly offer rewards or additional incentives for meeting those deadlines. (Parents who are aghast at the notion of rewarding a young writer for meeting deadlines should note that, although everyone would agree that the true reward is meeting the writing goal, sometimes mini-incentives can be very helpful in coaxing adults and kids alike to meet our goals.)

| SECRET 240 | **All writing deadlines should be self-imposed.** You may suggest deadlines (e.g., a certain number of |

pages a day), but, ultimately, the child should decide what deadlines to impose upon herself. She might spend the first few days of her retreat outlining a novel. In helping her reach her long-term goal, include in the schedule a full hour daily for lunch. (She is not allowed to touch her writing during that time. An hour later, she should be rarin' to go again.) In addition, write into the schedule at least an hour for exercise or other nonwriting-related activity at the end of the day or first thing in the morning. And evenings should be free. Her work day (assuming she starts work by 10:00 a.m. daily) should end promptly at 5:00 p.m. and she should not work on weekends. These limitations are important to keep her from burning out, but also to foster creativity and allow her to feel like she's on a summer schedule. You want her to return to school in the fall feeling like she's enjoyed various summer activities, but also that she has been extremely productive.

If your child sets a goal of writing five pages a day, she should have twenty-five pages written by the first weekend, one hundred pages written by the end of a month, and two hundred by the end of two months, with time to spare for a family trip at the end. When she returns to school in the fall—let's say as the author of a two hundred–page science fiction novel—she now has more clout to participate in a school-related writing activity like the school literary magazine to enhance her writing credentials as she proceeds through high school. School publications are good activities to have on a college application. But a two hundred–page novel will make her stand out—even if she doesn't have a publisher yet.

Summer Writing Programs

| SECRET 241 | **Pay attention to the literary form that interests your child, and tailor his training around that** |

form. Watch out for summer programs that will have your child write a sampling of pieces—short stories, essays, poetry, and screenplays—if your child wants to focus on a single genre. Being asked to devote time to poetry when your son wants to write science fiction, for example, can be frustrating and counterproductive. (Of course, if your child is unsure and would like to sample various writing forms, don't send him to a narrowly focused program that will only give him one experience.)

There are many prestigious writing programs for high schoolers. Among the most intriguing: Duke TIP offers a two-week summer creative writing retreat at Georgia O'Keefe's former residence at Ghost Ranch, New Mexico, situated between Santa Fe and Taos on 21,000 acres. The program is called **A Writer's Art: Creative Writing**, and it's targeted for students entering grades 10 to 12.

For young writers who want feedback and the chance to meet other young writers, check out the the **New England Young Writers' Conference at Bread Loaf**, held each May at Middlebury College in Vermont. The participation fee in 2007 was $220, and that included dorm living, writing workshops, dining, and recreational activities for the weekend. The annual deadline for applying and submitting writing samples is in mid-November. Contact: neywc@middlebury.edu.

Columbia University offers an annual for-credit Fiction Writing Workshop as part of its Summer High School Institute. Included in the program is short story writing, fantasy writing, science fiction writing, novel writing, word games, journal writing, and discussion of professional and student writing. An anthology of student works is published at the end.

Summer at Stanford features a five-unit fiction writing course that focuses on narrative and imaginative writing. Participants read and discuss one another's work, and produce two complete stories; discuss published stories; and write critiques of other students' stories.

For the student with general writing interest who does not want to specialize in any one particular genre or form—or who wants to gain a solid background in multiple forms—outstanding programs are offered at the **Iowa Young Writers' Studio** (students who have completed grades 10, 11, or 12) and **Interlochen** (grades 6 to 9).

Four-summer plans tailored to your child's particular writing interests can be found in the appendix. In general, students should pursue only one formal program per summer, and spend the remainder writing. "A writer is someone who writes," my father used to say. What he meant was that for the student who wants to pursue creative writing, no number of writing courses and seminars will make up for not having actually *produced* anything. Prospective writers should (before summer starts) block out a specific length of time for summer writing. Otherwise they risk coming away from their four-year plans with knowledge about a particular writing form (or forms) but no original, publishable works to call their own.

CHAPTER 9

The Humanities

The Scholar Every College Wants

N ot every student who is interested by the arts or sciences wants to actually create new art or science. For some students, what's more interesting is to study the history or role of the arts and sciences in society—not as an insider but as an interpreter. These students are most fascinated by the subjects that comprise the humanities: language (modern and classical); linguistics; literature; history; jurisprudence; philosophy; archeology; comparative religion; ethics; the history, criticism, and theory of the arts; and some topics in the social sciences.

Unlike the arts and sciences, the humanities offer fewer established pedigrees and hands-on opportunities. Nevertheless, exciting opportunities do exist if you know where to find them. And colleges have many seats to fill in humanities subjects. At top liberal arts universities like Princeton, more than half the bachelor's degree majors are offered in humanities—versus art, science, math, and engineering combined. To help create a top humanities student, the first step is to focus on helping her polish her essay-writing skills. Most humanities subjects are writing intensive, and students' grades are based largely on their essays (as opposed to short-answer tests).

If your child's high school doesn't provide the kind of focused essay-writing instruction your child will need, have him take a writing course at a local college. Most have expository- or essay-writing classes. The theme of the course—King Arthur, film as literature, American political movements—doesn't matter, as long as it interests your child. The point is to gain essay-writing skills. Find one that meets one evening per week. Or sign your child up for an online essay-writing course through Stanford's Education

Program for Gifted Youth (EPGY) program, where students are divided into virtual classrooms based on age and standardized test scores, and classes meet online once a week. There are long and short essay assignments. Contact EPGY at http://epgy.stanford.edu/courses/english.

SECRET 242	**The most tangible way to start working toward a humanities pedigree for your child is to inquire**

about the Telluride Association Summer Programs (TASP), the humanities' answer to science's Research Science Institute and the arts' Presidential Scholar, Davidson, or Scholastic awards. Although the program's information can be found on the Internet, TASP—a not-for-profit summer enrichment program for rising seniors—is not widely publicized and in more competitive communities is kept hush-hush.

When your child is still in 8th grade, download a sample application for TASP from the program's Web site (www.tellurideassociation.org/tasp1 .html). The application can serve as a framework or end goal for designing a productive three- or four-year plan for your child as he approaches high school. It will give you a sense of what qualities colleges seek in a humanities student—what makes them stand out—as well as give you a heads up regarding what credentials your child needs to qualify for TASP or its equivalent by her junior year of high school. (While there's no *one* profile that the program is seeking, using TASP as a reference point to help your child organize her secondary school schedule can provide a very well directed high school career for the aspiring humanities kid.)

SECRET 243	**Although invitations to apply to TASP are sent out to high school juniors who score in the 99.5 per-**

centile (top half of 1 percent) on the SATs, students may nominate themselves (and apply) for TASP without an invitation. The program receives a total of about 950 applications each year, which get whittled down to 120 to 150 applicants who are invited in for interviews, and then 88 students are ultimately chosen to participate. So the odds of admission are less than one in ten for an applicant to get to participate.

Participants attend seminars with up to eighteen students at Cornell University (Ithaca, New York), University of Michigan (Ann Arbor), University of Texas (Austin), or Washington University (St. Louis) for three hours per day, five days per week, for six weeks. Led by college professors, the classes are taught like upper-level college humanities courses, consisting largely of discussions rather than lectures. Students do extensive reading and writing, but no grades are assigned—nor is college credit awarded. The Telluride Association emphasizes that it seeks students from all kinds of educational backgrounds who demonstrate intellectual curiosity and motivation.

What makes TASP so prestigious, in part, is the lack of tuition. TASP is free; every student attends on a full housing, dining, and tuition scholarship—regardless of income.

"Where do TASPers end up in college?" I asked a staff member by phone for this book.

"A lot go to Cornell. Some Michigan," she said. "But aside from those schools, the biggest draws are Harvard, Yale, Swarthmore, and Berkeley."

Despite its prestige, TASP is not on the radar screen of many high school humanities teachers. And many of the top kids are often missed when TASP sends out their invitations. So parents who wait for their kids to be nominated by a teacher without requesting a nomination (as well as parents who wait to see their kid's invitation) may never *see* a nomination—no matter how brilliant and talented the student is.

Be proactive. Have your child nominate herself for TASP if she loves the humanities and you think that that she will thrive in the program. Nominations need to be accompanied by teacher recommendations; speak to the appropriate English or social studies teachers in advance—preferably at the very beginning of junior year to register the notion that your kid is hoping to attend TASP. Don't assign this first notification to your son or daughter. (To a kid, the thought of advising a teacher that she wants to be nominated will sound terribly immodest.) Also, don't talk the program up at school, lest you encourage the teacher to round up a larger crowd of kids to recommend, which may work against you—teachers are only allowed to recommend up to five kids.

SECRET 244 | **The folks who run TASP also direct another smaller program called Telluride Association Sophomore Seminars (TASS).** For rising juniors only, TASS focuses intensively on African American studies. About 300 to 350 students apply each year—most nominated by teachers and other school faculty—and the program accepts about 54 in total to attend its seminars at University of Michigan and Indiana University. TASS participants are then invited to apply for TASP for the following summer.

Building Up Humanities Credentials

A student interested in pursuing a humanities course of study might start during the summer before 8th grade at one of the major talent search programs (as discussed in chapter 2), where humanities-related courses abound. For example, at Northwestern's Center for Talent Development (CTD) program, recent offerings for grades 7 to 9 have included Great American Authors, Shakespeare, Latin, Etymology, Psychology, Philosophy, Geopolitics, and Law. At Duke's Talent Identification Program (TIP), summer humanities options have included a similar array, plus exotic courses such as Appalachian Tales, Mutiny and Piracy in Literature, Existentialism, From Wonderland to Hogwarts, Changing the World Through Theater, Shakespeare and Performance, Dystopian Literature in the Twentieth Century, Revolution and Terrorism, From Frodo to Jon Snow (Fantasy Literature), Greatest Generation (Politics, Culture, and Society at Mid-Century), Ghosts in Literature and Art, Knights in Shining Armor (Fact vs. Fiction), Vikings, and Wisdom of the East (On Knowing Oneself).

Anthropology and Archaeology

SECRET 245 | **The ideal anthropology high school plan should feature minimal coursework and maximum adventure, immersing oneself in different cultures.** While few in-school anthropology courses are offered by high schools, out-of-school programs—especially summer immersion programs and school-year exchange programs—exist that will captivate your child and make her appealing to the top colleges that offer majors in anthropology (most top liberal arts colleges).

You might get your child's feet wet by sending her to live on a Navajo reservation in a month-long immersion program. Unlike drive-by teen tours that drop in on reservations for a day or two and let teens help build something for two days, the Experiment in International Living (a company that has been organizing participatory travel for more than seventy-five years) sponsors a four-week Navajo National Summer "Abroad" Program in which high school students undergo a few days' orientation and then get to live on a reservation and experience a family stay. The program includes community service—building playgrounds, helping with farming chores—and rafting, hiking, and exploration of Anasazi ruins.

In recent years Duke University has offered another intriguing domestic anthropology adventure: Appalachian Tales: Ghosts, Hikers, and Bluegrass, exploring the culture of the Appalachian Trail, from Maine to Georgia, "with particular focus on the customs, ecosystems, and folklore of North Carolina's Blue Ridge Mountains." Readings include ghost stories, hiking journals, and bluegrass lyrics. And students take part in nature field trips and attend local musical performances.

Exotic overseas anthropology expeditions and programs are also readily available to students through organizations like **Global Routes** (which sponsors three- to five-week community service programs in Africa, Asia, Latin America, France, and the Caribbean), **Experiment in International Living** (described above), and **Earthwatch Institute** (which "engages people worldwide in . . . field research," allowing young people to participate in actual ongoing research led by scholars). Note that Earthwatch has also introduced a program in which one hundred teens (sixteen and up) each year are awarded fellowships to work in teams of six to eight students on North American research expeditions—some of them nature bent, and others more anthropological; e-mail EducationAwards@earthwatch.org for more information.

| SECRET 246 | To enrich her experience and credentials, your child might consider founding an anthropology |

club back at school. Members of different ethnicities could become exchange students in one another's homes for celebrations and holidays to experience other cultures. Colleges love kids who are leaders and who pioneer new activities; if, for whatever reason, it isn't possible to set this club up at school, set one up outside of school.

For the student whose interest leans more toward archeology, options are available both internationally and domestically. One of the most alluring programs is offered by the Crow Canyon Archaeological Center's Summer Field School (www.crowcanyon.org), where high school students participate in a Pueblo Indian (Anasazi) dig and lab work in Colorado.

Earthwatch Institute also sponsors digs—for teens and for families—in which lay participants are invited to help archeologists. In recent years, families have participated in a domestic dig studying ancient civilizations on the Mississippi for seven days (children ages ten and over) at Cahokia

Mounds Historic Site in Illinois. Prices of Earthwatch expeditions are comparable to other, more luxurious, vacations; the fee for this particular trip was $2,400 per adult in 2006, $1,995 per child.

SECRET 247 | **Taking part in an archaeological dig can be very impressive to colleges—but only if the student really takes the time to learn lab techniques of archaeologists and the culture of the people being studied.** Drive-by teen tours that include a day or two at a dig site do not impress colleges. A lot depends on how much intellectual energy your kid devotes to the task.

Art History

SECRET 248 | **During high school, an aspiring art historian should plan to take AP Art History to establish credibility with colleges.** If his school doesn't offer it, arrange to have the course introduced before he hits junior year. This may mean speaking with the principal or before a board of education meeting (during your child's sophomore year) or to others who make monetary decisions for the school. If you are told that such a course is impossible—that there isn't enough student interest or budget—try to arrange either an independent study version, a correspondence course, or a local university equivalent.

Some parents worry that colleges might look down upon art courses taken in high school—that colleges would prefer to see physics or Latin on the transcript. But if the colleges to which your child plans to apply offer art history or studio art as a major, and your kid demonstrates a serious interest in majoring in art and has a track record that supports this interest, then art courses will not only be *res*pected but *ex*pected.

While college art history has increasingly begun to encompass non-Western art, an art history die-hard's track record should include AP European History (in addition to AP Art History). Another way to build a strong track record is by taking college art history courses during the summer. Note that some of the art history summer courses offered to high school students also feature trips abroad and visits to museums and galleries (in addition to classroom work) to see actual works and gain impressive expertise. (See a listing of summer options for art history students in the appendix.)

Other ways of demonstrating a serious interest in art history include visiting museums, galleries, sculpture gardens, and homes of famous artists independently, and focusing on these visits in a college essay. In addition, a student's credentials should include internships with an art dealer, museum, gallery, or even at a historic home that contains art treasures. (Find such opportunities through www.Volunteermatch.org.)

SECRET 249 **Many small museums offer students unadvertised docent internships or volunteer jobs in the gift shop or at fund-raising events.** A student who is passionate about art history should make a point of volunteering at art institutions either during the summer or during the school year. (Phone the institution directly.) Or encourage your child to organize student groups supporting the arts or initiate her own fund-raiser. Such experiences and networking opportunities could significantly enhance a student's college resume.

Classics

In a time when many movies and computer games focus on rebuilding ancient Rome and Greece, interest is being renewed in ancient history—and plenty of summer courses and programs that explore classical civilizations and languages are available at the talent search–affiliated colleges (described in chapter 2) and other major universities, including Yale, Harvard, UCLA, and Northwestern.

If your child's high school doesn't offer Latin, ancient Greek, or ancient history, many colleges do; parents can scout out evening classes at nearby colleges or even online ancient Greek courses. *Why would anyone want to study classics?* parents ask me when debating whether their kids should take Latin, Spanish, or French in high school. There are many excellent reasons—not the least of which is that many teachers claim that Latin improves students' verbal SAT scores. But another reason that some choose Latin is to increase their chance of choice college admissions. Once enrolled in Latin and ancient Greek, many students discover the intrinsic value of the classics.

SECRET 250 **Many of the top liberal arts colleges have classics departments, but students willing to major in classics are relatively rare.** While a student needs to be able to demonstrate good grades and test scores, expressing a desire to major in classics can provide a good backdoor entry into very competitive colleges for the student with a genuine interest. In order to be taken seriously, she needs to take Latin or ancient Greek in high school.

| SECRET 251 | **Medaling in the forty-minute National Latin Exam is the main pedigree in classics.** About 148,000 students in Latin Levels 1 to 6 take the exam appropriate for their level each |

March. Levels 5 and 6 represent AP Latin courses, and students who stay with Latin long enough to reach those levels have excellent odds of earning national distinction that will impress colleges. In 2006, for example, only 2,194 students took the Latin 5 exam. Of those, 44 had perfect papers, 190 additional students won gold medals, 292 won silver medals, 319 won bronze medals, and 326 won cum laude. The odds are even better for those students who hang on to complete Latin 6. In 2006, only 215 students took the Level 6 exam, but more than half won awards—123 students. Nine had perfect scores, 23 won gold, 22 won silver, 42 won bronze, and 36 won cum laude.

If your kid's school doesn't offer the National Latin Exam, she can still sign up to take it outside of school as long as you can get a Latin teacher or private tutor to proctor. For an individual child, the total cost is $20; for more than two test takers it's $4 per additional person, plus $10 shipping and handling of the exams; go to www.nle.org.

Fewer students know about the National Greek Exam, which focuses on ancient Greek and is open to high school and college students.

| SECRET 252 | **If you want to make your kid extremely desired by the top colleges, have him study ancient Greek.** As rare as Latin students are, high school students with knowledge of ancient |

Greek are even rarer. "Colleges WANT these kids," a spokeswoman for the national exam stressed, explaining that most liberal arts colleges and major universities have classics departments, but few have enough students to fill them. In total, about 1,500 students nationally register each year to take any of the six levels of the National Greek Exam—introductory, beginning, intermediate, Homeric, prose, or Attic tragedians (most advanced)—but usually only 1,300 kids actually take one of the exams. Of those, 80 percent take the lower levels. For the very top level, Attic tragedians, fewer than fifteen students usually sign up—and these kids do well when it comes time to apply to college. In addition, the top single scorer wins a scholarship, which in recent years has been $1,000. About half the test takers win ribbons:

purple (perfect score), blue, red, and green. Winning a purple ribbon in an advanced-level exam is a big deal. In recent years, the top scorers have applied their scholarships toward tuition to Princeton, Oxford, Yale, Harvard, and University of Texas at Austin. Each test is a forty-question, fifty-minute, multiple-choice exam. Students can get study packets in advance (free) and old exams for $2 apiece; to order contact NGE@ACLClassics.org. For other exam information, contact Dr. Deb Davies at ddavies@brooksschool.org. The annual exam is given during the second week in March.

SECRET 253 If your kid's school doesn't offer ancient Greek, have her take an online course. In fact, the biggest growth in National Greek Exam test takers have been home-schooled kids who take the course on the Internet. Several virtual schools teach ancient Greek online; among the more popular is Kypros-Net, at www.kypros.org/LearnGreek.

SECRET 254 Another rarity desired by top colleges is the student who has studied biblical Greek. Such scholars get to prove their talent through the National Biblical Greek Exams, a series of Internet exams that range from beginner to graduate level: www.greekexam.com/index.php.

SECRET 255 To demonstrate extra interest in classics and to win the chance to stand out nationally and impress colleges, students can join the National Junior Classical League, which sponsors annual conventions. The organization is an umbrella group for students in grades 7 to 12 who study Latin, ancient Greek or mythology. NJCL national conventions take place each summer at different universities. In 2007, it was the University of Tennessee in Knoxville; in 2008 it was to be held at Miami of Ohio in Oxford, Ohio; in 2009, at San Diego State. The only criterion (besides grade level) to be eligible for the convention is membership in NJCL (www.njcl.org), which costs $7 per student, usually paid through school Latin classes, but students may join as at-large members if their school doesn't participate or if they're homeschooled.

One of the most popular events at the convention is Certamen, a quiz-bowl-style contest. The Costume Contest—students dress like classics characters and are quizzed about their characters—is another highlight. Much of the week is spent taking written Latin exams, with certificates, medals, trophies and ribbons awarded. Exam options also include mythology and Greek derivatives.

> **SECRET 256** **Another way to stand out nationally in classics is to take the Medusa Mythology Exam (www.medusaexam.org).** Not as well known as the National Latin Exam or National Junior Classical League competitions, the Medusa Mythology Exam is open to all high school age students—your kid does not have to be enrolled in Latin or Greek. The exam focuses only on mythology. Doing well adds a good credential to a college applicant seeking to pursue classics as a major.

Summer Courses and Programs

Summer courses in classics could include mythology, Greek drama, ancient philosophy, ancient recreation, and ancient theater. (For a sampling of available summer courses, see the appendix.)

Several companies offer trips to Rome for high school Latin students. University of Dallas Summer Programs offers one of the most serious on-site courses, called Latin in Rome. For three weeks in July, participants study what Cicero, Pliny, Virgil, and Horace wrote about Rome as they visit famous sites that these writers referred to. The program includes lectures by college professors, daily language tutorials, discussions, and guided tours of historical sites and museums. To be eligible, students must be rising juniors and seniors who have completed at least three years of high school Latin. The program awards three college credits.

Foreign Language and Linguistics

Combine exotic foreign language study (exotic, meaning anything other than French or Spanish) with international relations or international business to create a very impressive high school résumé—or specialize in a group of languages and linguistics for their own intrinsic value. Either track makes a high school linguist a very impressive college candidate, compared with the vast majority of American students who focus on French, Spanish, or their own native languages exclusively.

Americans are notoriously negligent when it comes to learning to speak foreign languages. For students who want to seriously gain a mastery of a foreign language, however, overseas immersion programs abound. Check out some of the overseas options at www.PlanetEdu.com. Colleges and prep schools also offer intensive foreign language and immersion programs on their U.S. campuses during the summer. Some, but not all, provide college credit as well. While many colleges offer summer French, German, Italian, and Spanish, more exotic language options for summer study can be found as well: Beloit, for example, has in recent summers offered Arabic, Chinese, Czech, Hungarian, Japanese, Korean, and Russian. Boston University has had Arabic, Chinese, Hebrew, and Japanese. Concordia has offered Arabic, Chinese, Danish, Finnish, Japanese, Korean, Norwegian, Russian, and Swedish. Earlham has offered Japanese. Georgetown has had separate courses in Modern Arabic, Egyptian Arabic, and Iraqi Arabic, plus Chinese, Persian, and Russian. Harvard has had Arabic, Celtic, Chinese, Greek, Hindi, Japanese, Latin, Portuguese, Russian, Sanskrit, Spanish, and Ukrainian. UCLA's Summer Language Intensives have included Amharic (Ethiopian) Arabic, Catalan (Spanish), Greek, Hebrew, Iranian (Persian/Farsi), Japanese, Korean, Latin, Quechua (language of the Andes), Portuguese, Romanian, Russian, Swahili (East Africa, Tanzania), and Yoruba (Nigeria). University of Michigan Summer Language Institute has offered Arabic, Chinese, Dutch, Greek, Hindi, Japanese, Kurdish, Latin, Polish, Russian, and Swedish. And Penn Summer Sessions have had Arabic, Chinese, Greek, Latin, Russian, Slavic, and Swahili.

SECRET 257 **The U.S. Government is hoping to encourage students to learn selected undersubscribed languages as part of its National Security Language Initiative (started in 2006).** The gist is this: Scholarships are being awarded to college students for seven to eleven weeks of study abroad for those learning Arabic, Bangla/Bengali, Chinese, Hindi, Korean, Persian, Punjabi, Russian, Turkish, and Urdu at American Overseas Research Centers and affiliated partner locations. High school linguists are much more eligible to receive such scholarships during college if they start learning any of these languages while still in high school.

SECRET 258 **Beware when selecting languages: If your child declares a passion for a rare language that is not offered at the colleges to which he is applying, the colleges may feel that they cannot adequately accommodate him and may deliberately reject him, thinking that they're doing him a favor.** Before your son embarks on learning a new language, check the colleges that you think he's likely to apply to, to see if they offer any follow-up on the language he is considering.

Linguistics courses are relatively rare on the high school level, but several summer programs have offered linguistics in recent years: University of Pennsylvania Pre-College, Johns Hopkins CTY and CAA, and UCLA. A linguistics enthusiast should round out his program by studying multiple languages in high school.

SECRET 259 | **A savvy parent who is eager to put a talented linguist kid on the map nationally might consider starting up a U.S. linguistic Olympiad team.** In the International Linguistic Olympiad, which is considered one of the newest science Olympiads (founded in 2003), participating students are asked questions from the fields of phonetics, morphology, and semantics. Competitions are held in different participating countries each year. The United States has not yet sponsored a team in this Olympiad, so the challenge of founding a team represents a great opportunity for a young American linguist (and her parents) who wants to serve as pioneers. As described in chapter 6, international science Olympiad participants can virtually write their own ticket into any college. Contest sites in recent years have included Russia, Bulgaria, and the Netherlands. Locate the Olympiad at http://olympiads.win.tue.nl/ilo/index.html.

Geography

If your child has a passion for geography, start by enrolling her in AP Human Geography; if the course is not offered at her high school, petition her school or district to offer the course. In addition, you might encourage her to pursue college courses in geography. Of course, the best and most enjoyable way for her to gain impressive geography expertise is to travel—not with group tours or teen tours, but rather independently or with family, so she can interact with the cultures and environments she visits. Camping trips in national parks, for example, can contribute significantly to one's understanding of both geography and geology, as can organized volunteer work in the U.S. National Parks through the Student Conservation Association.

SECRET 260 | **A student who is intrigued by the earth's topography, geology, and population might consider forming a U.S. geography Olympiad competition or team—the opportunity is wide**

open. Since 1996, other countries have been participating in an International Geography Olympiad, but the United States currently has no team. Filling this gap would be a major endeavor—one with far greater rewards than merely getting into a choice college—but it would also require major parental commitment. If your daughter helps to organize a team, she could list herself as a founder. In 2006, twenty-three countries participated in the international event in Australia. (Olympiads are held in alternating years, and the next event was scheduled for 2008 in Tunisia: www.geoolympiad.org/008-2008Tunisia).

SECRET 261   **Since geography is barely touched on in most American high school social studies or earth science classes, any training that your child gains will put him miles ahead of his peers when applying to a college that offers geography or similar subjects.** Not many colleges offer geography majors. But a solid understanding of geography can also apply to geology, geophysics, international relations, natural resources, environmental studies, and majors in various cultural studies.

History

SECRET 262   **There is a national pedigree in history that makes history-buff applicants stand out from the pack when it comes to college admissions.** Let me introduce the National Writing Board. Few parents seem to know about it, but thirty-nine colleges, including some of the most-competitive universities (Harvard, Yale, Princeton, Stanford, Duke, Georgetown, Amherst, Williams, Dartmouth, and others) officially endorse the program, according to the organizer (and welcome students to enclose their NWB submissions along with their applications when applying to college).

Participation comes with a price tag: $200. The gist is this: When a high school student writes an original history paper that she feels merits notice, she submits it (with a check) to the National Writing Board for evaluation—scores and a written assessment. No need to wait for a social studies teacher to submit your kid's paper; this can be done independently of school. The paper should be either short (1,500 to 2,500 words) or long (4,000 to 6,000 words) and may focus on any topic in history, domestic or foreign. In return, the student receives a three-page evaluation from the board. Many students submit that evaluation along with their college applications to demonstrate their talents in history. And even the most competitive colleges say they are impressed by positive feedback from the board. Details on submission are available at www.tcr.org.

SECRET 263 **The National Writing Board is affiliated with the** *Concord Review*, **another extremely prestigious venue for high school students to distinguish themselves in history; in many ways it's the history equivalent of science's Intel Science Talent Search.** Billed as "the only quarterly journal in the world to publish the academic work of secondary students," the *Concord Review* publishes forty-four articles annually and awards five top article writers the Ralph Waldo Emerson Prize (which has ranged in recent years from $500 to $3,000). The top liberal arts colleges say they are indeed wowed by the winners of the Emerson Prize and the other writers of articles that get published each year. In case you're wondering: By early 2007, of more than seven hundred authors who had been published since the journal began a decade earlier, eighty-three went on to become undergraduates at Harvard, sixty-four at Yale, forty-four at Princeton, twenty-six at Stanford, twenty-one at Brown, fifteen at Penn, fourteen at Columbia, twelve at Cornell, ten at Dartmouth, and ten at Oxford. The article submission fee is $40, which includes a one-year subscription (four issues).

SECRET 264 **Encourage your history buff to form a National History Club chapter at his school and have him lead the group in history-related activities.** The national organization is more than 240 chapters strong, with participation in forty states. The aim of the club is to "encourage the reading, writing, discussion, and enjoyment of history" among secondary school students and their teachers. Activities vary from chapter to chapter. A club in Indiana invited a survivor of Sobibor concentration camp as a guest speaker in 2006. A chapter in Maryland studied the history of its high school. A Virginia chapter took a canoe trip down the Potomac to determine the river's impact on local history. Find information on the club at www.tcr.org/nhc/index.htm.

Additional Credentials for History Students

What are other achievements a history student can pursue that will really impress a college? Following is a sample résumé of a fictitious student with a passion for American history. Achievements listed in **bold** are honors that were or are actually available to high school students. (Note that specific opportunities may change from year to year—and in some years, the schedules of different programs may conflict—but the sponsoring organizations tend to offer similar options each year. Also note that the majority of these achievements are not GPA based, yet the résumé presents an outstanding history student.)

REGINALD WALKER

American History Achievements
President's Volunteer Service Award, 2008
U.S. Congressional Award, gold medal, 2009
Concord Review; published original article on Civil War
   (national high school journal of history)
Gilder Lehrman Prize of American History recipient
DAR American History Essay Contest state finalist
Fort Necessity National Battlefield, volunteer crew for Student
   Conservation Association to help restore this Pennsylvania
   battlefield from the French and Indian War (summer 2009)
Camp Evans, Landmark Volunteer, helped to restore National
   Park Service science facility (NJ) where Guglielmo Marconi
   transmitted the first trans-Atlantic radio communication, 2009
Student Challenge Award Project (SCAP), Earthwatch Institute,
   Analyzed structural burning in an ancient Hopi Village
   at state park in Arizona, led by scientists, 2007
Battle of Gettysburg Reenactor, Gettysburg, PA, 2007 and 2008
Battle of Cedar Creek Reenactor, Virginia, 2008 and 2009
Battle of Bull Run Reenactor, Virginia, 2008 and 2009

Education
College of William and Mary, Precollegiate Summer Program
   in Early American History; 4 college credits, summer 2008
Harvard Summer Secondary School Program eight weeks, summer 2007
      The American Revolution (4 college credits)
      History of the U.S. Constitution (4 college credits)
Citytown Public High School, full-time student GPA 3.78 (unweighted)
      SAT I: 700 verbal, 620 math, 670 writing
      SAT II: 800 American History, 720 Global History, 590 Math 1C
      AP Exams: American History 5, European History 5, U.S. Government 5
      President of Citytown Public High School Student Government

Literature

U.S. high schools barely scrape the surface in literature. Rare is the American high school student who has read even one of the following names in European and Russian literature: Tolstoy, Dostoevsky, Chekhov, Goethe, Flaubert, Balzac, Pushkin, Blake, Wordsworth, Coleridge, Byron, Petrarca, Dante, Mann, Kafka, Voltaire, Joyce, Shelley, or Yeats. Most English programs seem to include one Shakespeare play per year and three Charles Dickens novels in total. Plus the class gets to watch a video of a Jane Austen novel. That's it for foreign literature—four Shakespeares, three Dickenses, and an Austen movie. Camus, Victor Hugo, and Molière only pop up in French classes. And only Latin students learn who Virgil was. The big focus in most American English classes is American literature.

| **SECRET 265** | **If your kid is interested in literature, he only needs to open a book by a European author to** |

stand out from the competition. It is startling to hear a teenager quote Goethe or Yeats in the body of an essay—beyond some superficial opening quotation—or in the course of a conversation. (And I can't tell you how many times I've seen college applicants start their essays with overused quotations like "Friends, Romans, Countrymen . . ." or "A rose by any other name" or "Wherefore art thou Romeo." Find a quotation from a Thomas Mann or Chekhov if you want to impress colleges, I tell them. Or at least find a more obscure quotation from Shakespeare that demonstrates that you read and absorbed the entire play—not just the CliffsNotes.)

| **SECRET 266** | **One of the options on the Harvard application has been to list the books that the applicant has read** |

in the past twelve months. In response, I have seen rare well-read applicants list pages of books that they were prepared to discuss if asked about during an interview. The point is, a high school student who reads beyond the bare minimum required in high school can look very impressive to colleges. And achieving this edge doesn't even require paying tuition to an expensive program.

| **SECRET 267** | **To motivate your kid to read, encourage her to establish a book club, either in or outside of school.** |

This demonstrates both a love of literature and leadership skills. Or you might encourage her participation in an already-formed club if one exists. Parents can also explore local English literature college courses and even adult education courses that offer stimulating book discussions.

An early high school student who would like to be well read by the time she graduates might enjoy the (one- or two-week) Great Books Summer Program at a choice of Stanford or Amherst; www.greatbookssummer.com. While such short programs make lengthy books prohibitive, the two-week session does manage to include Plato's *Republic,* Aristotle's *Ethics,* Cicero, Tolstoy's *Master and Man,* Dante's *Inferno,* Euripides' *Trojan Women,* and Sophocles' *Antigone*, in addition to many selections by American authors. The rest of the summer could be devoted to reading lengthier works on the student's own watch.

By later high school, when kids become eligible to take college courses for credit, a student who wants to wow colleges faces a wide array of options that differ from year to year. In a Harvard Summer School 4-credit seminar on twentieth-century authors included Proust, Woolf, Beckett, Bernhard, Nabokov, Pynchon, Calvino, Sebald, and Saramago. At Cornell, a three-week, 3-credit course called Genius and Madness in Literature featured works by Aristotle, Plato, Ficino, Shakespeare, Goethe, Kant, Foucault, Freud, E. T. A. Hoffmann, Buechner, Nietzsche, Wagner, Elinlak, the Brontë sisters, Tolstoy, Ibsen, Kafka, and Thomas Mann. The prerequisite for these programs was the completion of junior year of high school. Compare the kid who is able to discuss these authors' works by summer's end with the applicant who claims to want to major in English but who has relied entirely on his high school curriculum.

Philosophy and Comparative Religion

Few public high schools offer courses in philosophy or comparative religion.

SECRET 268 | **The lack of opportunities in philosophy and comparative religion for young high school students makes a kid who pursues those studies more unique and appealing to colleges.** The nation's major talent search programs are among the only summer schools to offer philosophy to 8th, 9th, and 10th graders. Brown

University also has more than twenty related Mini-Courses that include Skepticism, Existentialism, and The Meaning of Life.

If your child is interested in comparative religion, start him with classes in your own religion's institutions. Such courses tend to be the most accessible and the easiest for parents to help interpret. By junior year, he will be eligible for college religion courses and philosophy courses, of which there are many options. Most liberal arts colleges offer courses in both fields, so pursuing either may be a matter of taking evening courses locally (one night a week during the school year) or choosing from a wide array of summer courses for credit.

| SECRET 269 | **A philosophy or comparative religion student who wants to dazzle colleges might also seek out a university research internship, in the same way that science students conduct research.** |

Science does not have the monopoly on university research. Using the Internet, search college philosophy or religious studies departments and read about the work that individual professors are doing. (Look under "Faculty.") If you and your child are able to locate an ongoing project that intrigues her, have her contact the professor directly (be prepared to send a résumé) to see if there is a way that she can participate. Larger departments are likely to have more professors willing to mentor an ambitious high school student and help develop a research project that leads to writing a paper. Having authorship or coauthorship of a paper published in a professional philosophy or religious studies journal would definitely make a student irresistible to colleges.

★   ★   ★

If your child enjoys the humanities research and investigation process but would prefer to see his or her work (whether unbiased or supporting a particular cause) published in a newspaper or magazine—or have it aired on TV or radio—you might encourage him to explore journalism or advocacy.

CHAPTER 10

Journalism, Media, and Advocacy

Headlining the Front-Page Kid

I want to be a TV news anchorwoman," a student proclaimed at her college interview when asked about career goals.

"Really? And what have you done so far in TV or journalism?" the interviewer asked.

"I'm just a high school student," the girl responded, taken aback by the question. "But I watch a lot of TV news."

In these competitive times, candidates with big dreams and no track record are sounding less and less appealing to colleges—being "just a high school student" is no longer an excuse. Applicants whose journalism and/or advocacy-related dreams are backed up with impressive credentials, however—credentials that demonstrate their commitment and abilities—are earning their way into the country's top undergraduate programs for these fields.

As with the other subject areas in this book, parents can be very instrumental in scouting out and facilitating appealing opportunities for their kids. American high schools tend to be uneven when it comes to journalism and advocacy—some have far more elaborate and sophisticated offerings than others.

Broadcast Journalism

SECRET 270 | **Some high schools have elaborate TV stations with five-day-a-week news broadcasts that rival the quality of professional TV.** While people in these communities are aware of how sophisticated high school broadcasting has become, to the rest of the nation this opportunity is relatively secret.

For a real eye-opener, check out CHSTV, run by Carlsbad High School in Carlsbad, California, at www.carlsbadhigh.com. Since 2002, the school has been broadcasting five days a week, winning several Student Emmies. Participants get their first TV experience in the district's middle school at station VMSTV (Valley Middle School). A winning sample of the high school students' work can be found at www.nationalstudent.tv/play.asp?id=CA-1167-0022.

Compare this form of professional quality, up-to-the-minute journalism to the rinky-dink conventional high school newspaper that comes out once a month or every other week. It's important to see this distinction before letting your kid boast on his college application that he's the news editor of his high school paper.

You don't live in Carlsbad? Parents of kids with a passion for broadcast journalism need to look beyond their kids' high schools to find opportunities at either summer programs or local TV or radio stations (or both), whether your child wants to work in front of the camera or behind it.

TV Internships and Jobs

Public and Community Access TV

Many communities have public or community access TV that allocates a set percentage of local programming to local citizens. The programming in these communities often tends to become monopolized by retirees and other local residents who have daytime hours to devote to producing talk shows without pay—but that doesn't mean a high school student can't become involved. Regardless of who runs the channel, public access stations generally offer classes for local residents in how to use the equipment. If your community has public access television, phone the local station or cable service provider to find out the procedures and any minimum age requirements for having your future talk-show host produce a local access TV show. A public access station could be a great springboard for the aspiring media mogul or news anchor.

Library and Parks TV

Some public library districts and park districts have underutilized TV stations as well. The bulk of programming features taped library, school, or community events and lists of upcoming schedules. But these institutions may welcome additional community-oriented programming. If your daughter would like to try to produce a regularly scheduled series-format show, take a look at the schedule for the local channels to determine in advance if any topics are missing from the lineup that would especially serve the community. Sample ideas: high school team coverage, local politicians speaking about issues, local doctors addressing medical issues, arts and crafts for elementary school kids, excerpts from school performances. Encourage your daughter to initiate more imaginative ideas that complement her interests as well. To keep up with what other localities are producing, check the Global Village CAT, a centralized online source for information about public and community access stations around the world, at www.communitymedia.se/cat.

★   ★   ★

In pitching ideas to the local community administrator or board that runs the local public/community access, library, or park channel, encourage your daughter to draw up an organized outline for the show or series—this will enhance the likelihood of having the show approved and produced. If she is given scheduling options, encourage her not to be overly ambitious at first—don't request that the show appear *too* often or at prime time. Remember, production must coordinate with her high school homework schedule. Offer a once-per-month show at first. Once a go-ahead is received, help her with the background errands, logistics, clerical work, and publicity required to produce the show. Note that a one-episode documentary can be just as rewarding as a multiepisode show in the beginning, and such a report could allow a student the freedom to explore a more focused interest or question.

Local Channels and Public TV

Local channels or public TV stations (as opposed to public *access* TV) are generally run by professional media workers but frequently welcome high school interns or volunteers. Internships range from running errands, to preparing guests who will be appearing on air, to preparing news reports. Depending on how populated your town or city is, however, such internships may be competitive to land. Your kid's odds are better if he has had some prior courses in TV production or a related field.

Underutilized In-School TV

If your kid is lucky enough to be attending a school or school district that has its own TV system but doesn't offer elaborate programming on the scale of Carlsbad, you and your child might become more involved in upgrading the opportunities for the school or community. If the broadcast facility is not located in your daughter's high school building, take her to see that studio—and introduce yourselves to the people in charge. If the facility is located within the school, let her visit and make her own connections independently. School studios and their uses vary. Some schools have short-circuit TV systems reserved exclusively for homebound students or classroom support. Introducing new and perhaps exciting programs to homebound students could represent an excellent opportunity for your future TV producer if the school is receptive to the idea. Other schools only use the service to rebroadcast school performances and athletic games; this also can be viewed as a wide-open opportunity to introduce additional programming.

TV Courses

TV production courses are sometimes offered through local adult education programs, community access TV (as mentioned above), community after-school programs, libraries, or at local universities. The summer before junior year, your TV-aspiring child should take serious production courses at a university or TV production training program. This will reinforce his claim on his college application that he is genuinely interested in TV, journalism, or both.

Here are a few excellent college TV courses available in summer to high school students.

Columbia College

Located in Chicago—not the university in New York—Columbia College's High School Summer Institute offers Television News I: Reporting and Anchoring, a one-month, 2-credit course. To gain additional experience with TV equipment, a student may choose from four other one-month 2-credit TV production courses: Creating a Television Program, Writing the TV Sitcom, Advanced Television Production: Interactive Television, and Advanced Television Production: AVID Editing. (Note that Columbia in Chicago also offers radio journalism courses, including Introduction to Radio Newscasting and Introduction to Radio Sportscasting.)

UCLA

The university's Summer Session offers a 6-credit Undergraduate Television and Video Production course through its College-Level Courses for High School Students. Each student directs a three-camera, live-to-tape production of his or her choice. Options include a drama or sitcom scene; a segment from a cooking, news, or talk show; an infomercial, demonstration video, or "something experimental." Meanwhile, classmates alternate in crew positions to gain studio experience.

Boston University's Institute for Television, Film, and Radio Production

One-month summer courses include Television Field and Television Studio for high school students.

Other outstanding programs are offered by **Indiana University**, Northwestern's **Medill School**, and **Miami of Ohio**.

The TV Producer's College Application

| SECRET 271 | **If your child wants to eventually be involved in a university TV studio at college, help her find internships or jobs at professional TV stations the summer before her senior year.** This will familiarize her with industry practices and give her an edge when applying. |

If your child wants to eventually be involved in a university TV studio at college, help her find internships or jobs at professional TV stations the summer before her senior year. This will familiarize her with industry practices and give her an edge when applying.

When applying for TV internships, your child will need to show samples of her work. That's one reason why it's a good idea for her to start accumulating credentials early. Tape all shows that your child produces, and have her bring copies to TV stations when applying for an internship.

SECRET 273 | **When applying to college, if the school is receptive to receiving additional application materials, submit a taped version of your kid's best show—one that presents your kid as articulate, with no technical glitches, no bad-hair day, and minimal stumbling—if you're confident that the show will wow savvy admissions officers.** As a rule, TV looks impressive. That said, the show should be well edited, without errors. Make sure the kid is credited somewhere prominently during the program, and also make sure that the tape is labeled. Submit copies only: Do not expect to receive the tape or DVD back from the college admissions office.

Before applying to colleges, your child should visit the college TV studios at the universities she is considering to make sure the campus *has* a TV studio, for one, and to ensure that the facilities will be able to accommodate her interests. If the campus has a studio that's underutilized, find out why. Are undergrads not given access? Is the studio controlled by a small clique? Are years of stringent prerequisite courses required before a student may touch the equipment?

You also may want to find out how the college department has been faring in the Academy of Television Arts & Sciences College TV Awards, the most prestigious TV-related awards given to college students. The twenty-eighth annual awards took place in March of 2007 and included entries from the following schools: American Film Institute, Art Center College of Design (California), Ball State University, Brigham Young, CalArts, City College of New York, Clark Atlanta University, College for Creative Studies (Detroit), Eastern Washington University, Emerson College, Florida State University Graduate Film School, North Carolina School of the Arts, Northwestern University, NYU, Ohio University, Robert Morris University (Pittsburgh), Savannah College of Art and Design, St. Cloud State University (Minnesota), University of Oregon, UC Berkeley Graduate School of Journalism, UCLA, University of Florida, University of Texas (Austin), and USC.

SECRET 274 | **On her application, your broadcast aspirant should be able to envision and write intelligently about the particular campus TV studio and curriculum and how she fits in with the university's TV broadcasting system.** Does she envision producing a new talk show for the station? Can she imagine reporting for a new college sports show? Does she plan to major in broadcast journalism or TV production? (Does the college even offer such majors?)

| SECRET 275 | **The most desired TV applicant is the student who is already a sure thing, having won recognition like** |

the Cannon Memorial Scholarship or a Student Emmy for producing TV shows and other related work while still in high school. The Foundation of the National Academy of Television Arts and Sciences awards a $40,000 John Cannon Memorial Scholarship each year to one high school senior who plans to major in communications at a four-year college. Judging is a three-tiered process. In 2007, a total of 258 applicants entered; that got whittled down to 28 semifinalists, then 10 finalists, then one Emmy winner of $40,000 (the other nine runners-up win $1,000 each). To enter, one must be able to submit creative TV/broadcast/journalism work (radio and student newspaper writers and editors are eligible). The 2006 winner was from Kenosha, Wisconsin; the 2005 winner was from Springfield, Missouri.

Applications can be obtained at www.emmyonline.TV/emmy/scholarship.html. The deadline is in mid-December. Although the winner doesn't get to attend the Emmys we see on TV, there is a separate ceremony (held in a different place each year) where the winner (who is informed in advance—no surprises) receives a trophy. This award has become the highest pedigree for high school students to aim for if they consider communications their thing.

Print Journalism

Although TV and print differ in many ways, print is still often considered the backbone of journalism—and a student who aspires to a career in broadcast journalism should probably get some experience in both. A student with a solid track record in multiple forms of journalism generally looks more appealing and more versatile to colleges that offer journalism as a major.

| SECRET 276 | **Most student editors know little more about journalism than what they've learned by working on** |

their high school or middle school newspaper. So if your child takes even a single outside journalism course, he or she is likely to be far ahead of the game and far more knowledgeable than the other staffers.

SECRET 277   **Many high school newspaper advisers know little about journalism, have never worked for a news organization, and have never had any journalism education.** High schools generally assign the task of faculty sponsor to English or social studies teachers who don't know much more about journalism than what they might have gleaned from reading their daily newspaper. It's important to know this so your kid is not dependent on an adviser for all her journalism knowledge.

"My daughter deserved to be made editor-in-chief," the mother whined. "She put in all those years on the school newspaper selling ads for them with the idea that if she worked without complaining they would eventually reward her with a plum editorship senior year. Instead, they made her a copy editor. When she asked the advisor how this could have happened, he told her that she had no writing or editing experience. Well, of course she didn't—they never let her write or edit in previous years! Meanwhile, the top editor job went to someone who had great positions all the way through. And that new editor had the audacity to tell my daughter that the reason she wasn't made editor was that her writing wasn't good enough. Now what do high school students really know about good writing, editing, or journalism? It's just a popularity contest."

I've heard this speech many times from parents all over the country whose kids have gotten burned by school newspapers. Transcend school politics by having your kid step outside the box—or even *above* the box. Yes, high school appointments may be arbitrary, but even if your kid lands a coveted position, this will only take him so far on a college application—most kids whose sole print journalism experience has been through their high school graduate with minimal credentials or real journalism experience, and colleges know this. Your child will be much more impressive if he obtains legitimate print journalism experience and/or training offered by universities.

Columbia (University) Scholastic Press Association (CSPA)

CSPA offers aspiring high school journalists three major opportunities: a five-day intensive workshop in New York for newspaper and yearbook editors (limited to 350 participants and 30 per school), a Fall Conference for student editors and faculty advisors (focusing on "writing and editing, staff organization and motivation; design and layout . . . legal and ethical concerns"), and a three-day Spring Scholastic Convention (hundreds of students and faculty members attend more than three hundred lectures, work-shops, and sessions, choosing from seven journalism sequences: newspaper, yearbook, magazine, online media, video/broadcasting, law and ethics, and advising). Participation—college applicants who are able to discuss what they learned and how they applied that information when writing their application essays—rather than mere attendance is what impresses colleges.

A highlight of the Spring Scholastic Convention is the announcement of the Gold and Silver Crown Awards "for top publications" from among the finalist publications. Finalists are announced before the convention. (In 2007, for example, 1,860 high school publications were considered by the judges; more than 40 newspapers were named finalists, as were more than 30 year-books and more than 30 magazines.) At the March convention, the Gold Crown Awards for top individual students are also announced. Winning these competitions can help put a high school student on the map with colleges.

Print Journalism Summer Programs

In addition to the CSPA programs, some of the very best undergraduate journalism programs in America offer summer courses that give high school students enough of an edge to publish in real-world newspapers, blowing away the competition in colleges' eyes.

Medill School of Journalism

For a student who wants to seriously pursue journalism during the summer and possibly gain an edge for a high school editorship, Northwestern University's High School Institute at Medill offers an intensive one-month residential program at one of the nation's top undergraduate journalism colleges. Admission is very competitive—only eighty-eight rising seniors are admitted. To qualify, students must rank academically in the top quarter of their high school class, submit a current transcript and letter of recommendation, submit PSAT scores, "meet a high standard of character, dependability, and intelligence," and "give evidence of special ability or interest in the chosen field."

Indiana University High School Journalism Institute

A series of five-day summer programs, offered through the Indiana University High School Journalism Institute, trains students and teachers in the areas of newspaper/newsmagazine, television news, photojournalism, yearbook, and business advertising. (After one five-day newspaper/newsmagazine session, a student probably will know enough to outdo the rest of the school newspaper staff. Go to www.journalism.indiana.edu/hsji.)

Other top summer journalism programs for high school students are offered by **Syracuse's S. I. Newhouse School** and the **University of Missouri** (both among the nation's very top undergraduate journalism programs). For suggested four-year summer plans in journalism, see the appendix, page 274.

Outlets to Give Your Kid a Voice

| SECRET 278 | **Parents should note that students need not be dependent on high school sponsored or high school** |

originated publications to have a voice within your community. Many out-of-school venues exist. If your kid is not made an editor and wants to have a voice, try some of the following:

- Have him start his own blog and start publishing immediately (more on blogs below).
- Get hold of a book called *The Writer's Market*, which lists writing contests, literary agents, magazine publishers, and book publishers—so he may proceed independently of school.
- Check out www.FastWeb.com, which lists student competitions, awards, and scholarships, many of them for young writers.
- Encourage him to write and submit articles to a very local newspaper—write about the school sailing team, or crew team, or something that nobody else covers for the local newspaper.
- Help him to start his own out-of-school publication (a literary magazine, sports magazine related to whichever sports he plays, or a foreign language literary magazine in which students contribute poems in whatever other languages they speak), stapled together for in-school distribution.

- Have him enter samples of his work into the Scholastic Art & Writing Awards (grades 7 through 12) to compete for a writing scholarship. (See pages 167 and 193 for more information about this competition.)

Blogs

SECRET 279 **Blogging in itself is a best-kept secret for high school students.** If your child launches a blog, instantly he is the editor-in-chief of an international publication. Blogs sometimes are more widely read than school newspapers and magazines, and there's less bureaucracy, no cost, and no wasted paper. Your daughter can start her own blog from home and be her own editor. In addition, blogging often comes more naturally than newspaper writing to students brought up in a time of IMing, Googling, and e-mailing.

If you have no idea what blogging is, don't be intimidated! Explore this avenue with your child. Your first step should be to read sample blogs online and then to visit www.blogger.com/start, which will take your child step by step through the process of organizing a blog.

Before she sets up a blog, brainstorm with her on potential niches to cover—in the way that you would if she were writing a newspaper column. Also talk with her about publishing ethics. She shouldn't be using a blog to bad-mouth or libel anyone, for example. And she should assume that anything that she publishes could potentially be read by admissions officers who are making decisions about her. You might want to agree to see all blog entries in advance—not as a censor, but more as a protector. While blogging is a relatively new form of journalism, a well-thought-out blog with a sizeable audience can be extremely impressive to colleges.

Journalism Contests and Awards to Put Your Kid on the Map

An aspiring journalist showed me an article she had written during her sophomore year for the high school newspaper, asking if it would be okay to include in her college application, given that it was written back then. She had won some journalism awards, and this particular article had apparently been a prize winner.

I wasn't impressed. In short: I advise kids *not* to submit their journalistic works with their college application unless the works were published professionally. Putting articles in the hands of admissions counselors who may not get what's so good about them is not a risk worth taking. Instead, such an award-winning journalism aspirant should list some of the competitions won as a way of documenting her journalistic talent.

Contests in journalism vary. Some require teacher-initiated nominations (meaning parents can't nominate their own kid) and most require participation on a school publication. That said, parents can spark the process by telling a teacher or faculty advisor that they'd like their kid to be nominated.

For listings of print journalism awards and contests, go to www.Publish ingstudents.com/Awardprograms.html. Among the most prestigious is winning an award from **Quill and Scroll International Honorary Society for High School Students**, of which more than 14,000 high schools internationally are members. The organization gives out a total 170 awards, 24 of which are National First Place Awards, in its two contests—a yearbook competition and a writing/photo contest. All of the yearbook entries and most of the writing/photo entries are faculty nominated, although an independent student may enter the writing/photo contest without faculty support as long as his work is published somewhere—not necessarily a school publication. Winning Quill and Scroll will add a significant credential to your child's college application; going on to publish professionally will make him a shoo-in.

Journalism After High School

For students planning to continue studying journalism in college, note that relatively few of the most-competitive colleges offer majors or minors in journalism, media studies, or communications. But the University of Pennsylvania (Annenberg), Cornell (College of Agriculture and Life Sciences), and Stanford all offer communications; and Northwestern (Medill School) and NYU have journalism majors. To pursue a career in journalism at all other *most* competitive colleges, the route generally entails getting an undergraduate degree and expertise in something else, and then pursuing graduate work in journalism.

A top student who wants to pursue journalism as an undergraduate major might also consider some *competitive* colleges especially known for their outstanding journalism programs, particularly the University of Missouri, Syracuse (Newhouse), and USC (Annenberg).

Advocacy and Public Service

Students who would rather invest their voices in advocacy or public service will find that opportunities abound. Many service organizations are eager to find caring and able high school students to assist. And such volunteering can significantly improve a student's résumé for college—depending on the nature of the experience and what the student learns from it.

| SECRET 280 | **Your child should avoid volunteer experiences where intellectual growth is not likely to occur or** |

where there are no new skills to gain. The major rewards of community service tend to be learning, enrichment, innovating, the satisfaction of helping others, supporting a cause you believe in, and enjoyment—not pay. And the big side benefit for a high school student is that successful advocacy can be very impressive to colleges, particularly if it can be quantified in some way. Is your daughter able to state how much money was raised for lymphoma research as a result of the speech she gave at the fund-raiser? Is your son able to determine how many more children were clothed as a result of the clothing drive he organized?

As a general rule, the more the student enjoys an advocacy assignment, the more successful he'll be. Students who take on dull, unrewarding volunteer jobs in which they feel they aren't making a significant contribution, aren't challenged intellectually, and their voices aren't being heard are usually the first to quit—no matter how noble the cause. I've had students complain to me that their parents made them do tedious filing every weekend at the local hospital, or wash dishes at a senior center, or hand out campaign materials on a street corner—all as volunteers whose input wasn't welcomed. This is not advocacy. Parents naively thought that such tasks would help their kids eventually get into college, medical school, or law school—by demonstrating long-term commitment or even compassion, despite the dullness of the task.

| SECRET 281 | **For the benefit of those parents, I want to emphasize that a student who sticks with a boring** |

task—without innovating or adding some insight or improvement—does not impress colleges. In addition, such dead-end volunteer jobs often backfire—I can't tell you how many students I've met with whose boring tasks at medical offices turned them off from pursuing medicine.

| SECRET 282 | In choosing a local cause to advocate while in high school, your child should check the advo- |

cacy groups offered at each college that she may consider—to get a sense of which volunteer activities various colleges value. Not every campus will welcome every cause. But if your daughter's advocacy work matches the values of the college and her grades and test scores are in the college's range, active participation in a particular cause could help get her in.

If your child is up in the air about which cause to devote herself to in high school, avoid heavily political or religious causes that tend to be controversial—and advise your child to avoid writing about such causes in the college application essay. Instead, encourage her to pursue nondivisive causes that entail disease prevention, public health, public safety, the environment, tutoring, literacy, education, soup kitchens, fund-raising for botanical gardens, zoos, and museums, and entertaining at senior centers or children's day care centers.

| SECRET 283 | Advocacy and community service can help your child build invaluable leadership skills and give |

him the chance to take intellectual risks. The types of challenges posed may include delivering a speech at a fund-raiser or rally, designing a fund-raiser from scratch, developing leadership skills by organizing other volunteers, interacting with and learning from strangers, developing new methods to distribute needed goods, devising new teaching or tutoring methods, or learning how to bridge social gaps with a new population.

Please advise your child that when describing his advocacy work on his college application, he should focus on the positive—the intellectual growth as a result, and the improvement to society. Advise him not to write about his failures unless the story ultimately has a happy ending— whining essays don't impress. One most-competitive college, for example, has asked applicants to describe a time when it seemed like "the end of the world." An unsuccessful service or advocacy attempt could make a good topic—but only if the kid demonstrates that he has learned from the experience and went on to perform the service successfully. (Understand that your kid gets one chance to convince colleges that he's the kid they want. Using the essay to describe a failure is not likely to be convincing—no matter how kindhearted you imagine the admissions officers to be.)

SECRET 284　Find out what social service clubs and advocacy organizations your kid's high school offers, and have her join the ones that interest her most when she's still in 9th or 10th grade to give her the best shot at an elected leadership role down the road. Let her build a track record, so that by 11th or 12th grade, if she wants to lead a school club, she will have seniority, and if she's interested in advocacy outside of school, she'll have accumulated good résumé items and experience.

The Community Service Requirement

Does every child need to do community service? It's not a bad idea if you want your child to grow up to be a caring adult. However, parents need to think creatively about interpreting what constitutes service. Conducting science research to end cancer is community service enough—you don't have to make that research-oriented kid clean the floors of a day care center for it to count as service. Similarly, if your violinist child performs at a local senior center, that's community service. Or if your horticulture enthusiast plants a garden at a local tourist attraction, that qualifies. Service should not be equated with suffering or tedium.

SECRET 285　Contrary to what many kids think, being an officer of an advocacy group in itself is not very impressive—successfully *using* that office to initiate events like new and innovative fund-raisers and social service campaigns, however, will make a student extremely desirable to colleges. With or without holding office, a student can organize drives, including food or clothing collections for the homeless, a charity costume ball for cancer research, an innovative cleanup campaign for a local park (or beach or botanical gardens), a performance tour for hospitalized children or bedridden seniors, or a tutoring program for underprivileged children.

SECRET 286　A community service–focused student should establish an overall theme in his work to become more appealing to colleges. The theme might be health, environmentalism, international relations, or raising money for the arts. Discourage your child from dabbling in too many unrelated good causes at the risk of appearing unfocused and uncommitted and never earning leadership opportunities.

In helping her to choose a cause (keeping in mind the suggestions offered in Secret 282), start with an activity or institution that she enjoys most. She likes botany? Find out what opportunities exist at a local garden or plant nursery. He likes computers? Find out which local organizations can use help with their computer needs. A great place to research community service options is VolunteerMatch.org, which lists opportunities online. Type in your zip code and the distance you're willing to let your child travel to volunteer. Opportunities are more plentiful in large urban and suburban areas. But online options and exchange student–hosting possibilities exist even in the most remote areas. Select your kid's theme of interest. Choose from the following: advocacy and human rights; animals; arts and culture; board development; children and youth; community; computers and technology; crisis support; disabled; education and literature; emergency and safety; employment; gay, lesbian, and bi; health and medicine; homeless and housing; hunger; hurricane relief; immigrants and refugees; international; justice and legal; media and broadcast; politics, race, and ethnicity; religion; seniors; sports and recreation; and women.

To give you a sense of the range of volunteer opportunities offered to teens, check out the following 2007 listings from VolunteerMatch.org: A museum in New York sought a curatorial team member and newsletter writer; a Los Angeles rabbit shelter wanted volunteers to help assist in animal adoptions; a Virginia after-school program wanted a chess expert; an Ohio cancer research fund-raising group sought party planners; a Midwest hospice wanted birthday cake bakers; a New Mexico wilderness project sought "apprentice ecologists"; and Salem, Massachusetts, wanted volunteers for its annual October Haunted City. Participation in any of the above could make excellent college application essay topics—but more importantly they offer outstanding community service experiences for high school students.

A high school student who has pursued advocacy and community service as her primary talent can be very desirable to colleges, particularly if she demonstrates leadership, original input, results, and significant time commitment. To give you an even better idea of the types of winning credentials your child should strive to earn, I've provided a sample résumé for a student with a passion in this area, that would be very impressive to colleges. Note that items in **bold** are genuine opportunities.

AMY RIVERS

Racial Equality Advocacy and Community Service

Desmond Tutu Peace Foundation, administrative assistant, part time, during school year, New York City, 2008–09

Religions for Peace—USA, publicity volunteer, wrote press releases/speeches, 2007

Delivered a speech at **9/11 Unity Walk Rally**

Congress of Racial Equality, writer, volunteer, 2008

Contributed articles to organization newsletter

Advocacy speech writer; worked in the office of local congressman and helped draft speeches, 2007–08

Project Ghana, Global Routes, helped build a health clinic in small village outside Cape Coast city, four weeks, summer 2008

Winner, Patricia M. McNamara Memorial Scholarship, 2009

ACT-SO (Afro-Academic, Cultural, Technological, and Scientific Olympics), Oratory Award, 2009

Toyota Community Scholars Program, $20,000 Scholarship

US Congressional Award, Gold Medal, 2009

Education

TASS, Telluride Association Sophomore Seminars, Indiana University, Civic Engagement and African American Youth, six weeks, summer 2006

Central High School, class of 2009, GPA: 4.0

Courses included: **AP World History, AP U.S. History, AP Comparative Government and Politics, and AP Human Geography**

NAACP School Chapter,

President, 2008–09

Member, 2006–07 and 2007–08

UCLA, Elementary Yoruba (language of Nigeria), eight weeks, summer 2007, 12 credits, final grade: A

Stanford University Summer Session, Liberty and Justice for All? Law and Inequality in American Society, summer 2005, four units

Athletic Achievements

Central High School Girls' Track and Field Team Thrower

Captain 2007–08 and 2008–09

Scholar-Athlete Award 2009 in discus and javelin

No. 1 in county in javelin, 2008

Advocacy and Additional Public Service Courses

Older students (grades 10 to 12) who previously qualified for a national talent search in younger grades should consider applying to the Civic Leadership Institute, a three-week summer program offered by Johns Hopkins University, or the program it was modeled after, Northwestern University's Civic Education Project (CEP). The Hopkins program features a course in Civic Engagement & Contemporary Social Issues, and aims to provide "tools and strategies for community development and positive social change." Students work with community organizations, and each student gets to focus on a topic of particular interest to him (world poverty, criminal justice, school reform, etc.). Evening colloquia feature guest speakers, and a daily recreational program helps students network with other student advocates.

| SECRET 287 | **For a student interested in environmental advocacy, the Student Conservation Association—a** |

best-kept American secret with no tuition—helps provide an entry to many top colleges (when accompanied by top grades and test scores). Participants work on summer crews in U.S. national parks, where they contribute tangibly to the environment, learn about ecology, meet students from all over America, and learn teamwork.

★   ★   ★

Journalism and community activism are two ways for a student to develop leadership skills in high school. For a student who prefers to focus directly on leadership, however, many opportunities exist for high school students in government and politics as well.

CHAPTER 11

Government

*Building a Political Leader
from the Ground Up*

My dream is to become president of the United States someday," the girl said in her campaign speech for 8th grade class president. "But this is where it starts. I'll need your support now and in all four years of high school."

Sure enough, for the four years of high school that followed, the girl proceeded to be elected class president, until senior year, when she was voted president of the entire school. She worked hard and maintained top grades, after which, surprising no one, she got into Yale, a college that values leadership.

Sure, you can point to a legendary leader like Mohandas Gandhi, who began as a shy adolescent and shy young adult and much later in life emerged as a great leader. But there are many more examples of leaders who were either born into a royal family—or were treated as if they were—and who learned to lead confidently from the get-go. Parents can be instrumental in setting their kids up for a career of leadership (not necessarily exclusive to politics).

| SECRET 288 | **Competitive colleges prefer candidates who demonstrate a track record of leadership—not limited to** |

student government, but also in the arts, math, humanities, community service, and sports. And, as some college administrators point out, leaders are differentiated from mere title holders. Everybody knows at least one kid who gets elected, let's say, vice president of a student club, and never lifts a finger because he only intended to use this credential to bolster his college application—not to *do* anything. Colleges call them place holders, title holders, or dead wood, because these students don't *do* anything more than hold an office that another student could just as easily fill, and they show no leadership or passion for their position. But to get elected and actually innovate or effect improvement—that can win a student lots of points in the admissions office.

"If everyone at a top college is a leader, who will the followers be?" a mother asked me. "Don't these colleges need worker bees, too?" That would seem to make sense. But the most-competitive colleges are drawn to leaders nonetheless. And demonstrating leadership in any given field is important for getting into a top college.

SECRET 289
Leaders don't necessarily hold offices. They are movers and shakers, however, and this is apparent to anyone they meet. They initiate new clubs; they affect their school's curriculum; and they pioneer new ideas in their community. They're innovative. They're energetic. They're optimistic, and their enthusiasm is contagious. They're the kids that colleges are seeking. Many of these student leaders tend to be drawn into politics and student government.

SECRET 290
When searching for formal leadership training for your child—which is not necessarily required for every potential leader—inquire about specific skills taught and methods used. Lots of very different types of programs profess to teach children to lead, ranging from leadership sleepaway camps to college-style political science or business management courses. Some programs espouse that proficiency at rock climbing or sensitivity training (fall back into someone's arms and trust that they'll catch you) will increase your daughter's leadership confidence or abilities. Decide for yourself. Might she prefer a more directed approach, perhaps, like a class called something like Leadership Skills, which provides specific management techniques, or Public Speaking? I have known many kids who attribute their high school success to Dale Carnegie courses that gave them the confidence—and techniques—to speak in public. To find current offerings in your area, go to their Web site, www.dalecarnegie.com.

SECRET 291
Leadership roles are commonly grandfathered in from middle school (at schools that draw the same progression of students). Don't neglect your child's middle school years if she envisions becoming a political leader in high school. Even if she plans to attend a separate private or prep school for high school, she is much

more likely to become a leader if she has gained some leadership experience (and confidence) by the end of 8th grade.

Building a Convincing Track Record in Government

As I mentioned previously, a college application that states that the student wants to become a leader is much more credible if the student has shown some experience actually *leading* in high school, rather than just holding an office.

"I am hoping to major in government, having had a taste of politics," one applicant wrote to Yale, Princeton, and Harvard. "I was elected vice president of the Student General Organization this past year, and secretary the year before." He didn't get into any of the three colleges. His credentials didn't stand out, because his essay never discussed what he *did* in those offices.

Such a student may feel confident that he is earmarked for the most-competitive colleges or even the White House, but holding an office in high school is not the kind of ambition that particularly wows people at the most-competitive universities. With 27,000 high schools in America, assume that each has a student government president, vice president, secretary, and treasurer—more than 100,000 students who are high school *office holders*. If your son wants to impress admissions officers with his background, in addition to encouraging him to make the most of a school office, find out-of-school opportunities in government and challenging courses (some are described in this chapter) that make him stand out nationally. A lot depends on which area of government or politics interests him.

"I spent the summer working in Congress," a student boasted in a back-to-school class discussion. "I conducted vital research on global warming."

"How did you get *that* job?" other classmates asked, completely awed.

"Getting the job was very competitive," the kid responded without revealing a clue. "But they liked my credentials."

| SECRET 292 | High school students *do* get internships in Washington, and the "big secret" is that the first step in |

landing such jobs is simply to apply. Most people assume that the only way to get a government internship is through family or friend connections. But connections aren't necessary. Something that *will* give your kid an edge over the competition, however, is applying directly to a government official rather than to a bureaucratic office of employment or student internships, and building up enough credentials beforehand to create an impressive résumé.

SECRET 293 **For high school students interested in domestic politics, the best internships are secured by contacting specific government leaders, offices, and programs in your home state or district directly.** Your representative to Congress will favor a supporter from her own district. In many areas, even the most populated, the competition isn't so stiff, because other students don't know to apply. Contact the offices of local politicians whom you endorse and ask how your child may volunteer. It's okay for parents to make the initial phone call to find out about application procedures. Before the parent phones, however, his or her child should have a résumé ready to e-mail or fax.

SECRET 294 **A student who wants to work in a national government office should start building a solid résumé in government in 9th grade.** By junior and senior year, students with appealing government-related credentials may be eligible for positions as congressional pages. Apply through your senator's office. Minimum age is sixteen. Pages serve largely as *informed* messengers within the congressional buildings. They also attend the United States Senate Page School, accredited by the Middle States Association of Colleges and Schools. And, even though the position largely consists of errand running, many pages report that this "Inner Beltway" experience can be very exciting, and pages are well received by colleges. Imagine college essays in which your kid gets to talk about her conversation with Senator X and Senator Y, and how that influenced national policy. (In the case of a Senate page, dropping names is considered justified on an application.)

Of course, a lot depends on how your kid handles the job. I have worked with students who knew how to initiate discussions with senators and were thereby able to feel a sense of influencing policy. I have also worked with very reticent students who did the bare bones minimum of being a messenger. The latter is not necessarily desired by colleges, which often can tell just by the essay if the kid was simply a place holder.

SECRET 295 **Other government agencies bring in high school interns as well.** For students who live in the

Washington, D.C, area or who are able to relocate to the capital for the summer, opportunities are available at Smithsonian museums (www.si.edu/ofg/intern.htm) and other government institutions. Check for availabilities with the specific agency that interests your child. For a listing of some agencies that take interns, UC San Diego has a helpful Web site: career.ucsd.edu/sa/GovInternship.shtml.

Government students who want to make themselves irresistible to colleges should also develop some knowledge and skills in related fields, particularly law, business, economics, American history, public speaking, and debate—while still in high school. Such students should also read the local newspaper and other news sources daily, so they can discuss politics and politicians intelligently and know who's who.

To build a résumé for a page position or other internship, a student might attend the Choate Rosemary Hall John F. Kennedy Institute of Government (Connecticut) four-week program during the summer before 9th grade. Then, the following summer, she could enroll in the four-week Junior Statesmen program at Georgetown in Washington, D.C. The next summer, she should attend the ten-day George Washington University Summer Session's Mini-Course on Election Politics: Building a Campaign and, in addition, Barnard College's Young Women's Leadership Institute one-week program. The summer before her senior year, she could attend Geogetown's American Politics and Current Affairs and the Presidential Classroom Scholars (one-week) Program in Washington, D.C. By senior year, she should be very qualified for the Page Program.

Such a summer plan should be accompanied by in-school college-level government-related courses, including AP American History, AP U.S. Government and Politics (taken at Junior Statesmen), AP Comparative Politics (taken at Junior Statesmen), AP Economics, and AP European History, as well as active participation in the high school debate team, Model Congress, We the People, or other speech-related clubs. Your child's high school doesn't offer such a wide selection of AP courses? Check out the local college evening courses to supplement her high school curriculum.

Other Impressive Credentials

Boys Nation and Girls Nation: Another way to gain impressive national leadership experience is through Boys Nation (www.legion

.org/boysnation) and Girls Nation (girlsnation-auxiliary.com), programs that are unevenly publicized in different parts of the country. The two "nations" are sponsored by the American Legion (boys) and the American Legion Auxiliary (girls). Boys Nation was originally founded as Boys Forum of National Government in 1946; Girls Nation was founded a year later. Participation is cited on résumés for students as diverse as Intel Science Talent Search finalists and the *USA Today* Academic First Team winners. Each year, high school junior delegates are chosen by local units and posts of the American Legion and Auxiliary to attend their state's convention.

SECRET 296	**To qualify for selection, your kid needs to contact a nearby post and apply—don't wait for your kid to**

be nominated. If you think this activity might interest your child, don't expect someone else to single him out; contact the post yourself. Participants are chosen on the basis of grade point average, volunteer work, and possibly an essay, résumé, or interview (each post chooses differently). There are 15,000 posts in the United States; to find the nearest, look in a local phone book.

The state-level event usually takes place in June at a university campus; students apply to the Legion or Auxiliary much earlier in the school year. Although the American Legion motto is "For God and Country," organizers emphasize that participants of both "nations" are of "all different colors, shapes, sizes, politics, *and religions.*" The state program teaches about state and local government. Of each state's delegates (tens of thousands of students participate), two boys are then elected (by their peers) to attend the Boys Nation convention, and two girls are elected for the Girls Nation convention.

The national conventions, held in Washington, D.C, teach about *national* politics—the participating students write national senatorial resolutions. Former President Bill Clinton was once a delegate. At the beginning of the national conventions, delegates are divided into two parties randomly, and each convention ultimately elects a president and vice president—both officers must be of the same party. During the weeklong event, described by Girls Nation as "a national government training program," the candidates campaign and also get to meet real Washington officials.

Law Camp: UCLA Law School, the Foundation of the State Bar of California, and the Constitutional Rights Foundation together offer a one-week intensive Summer Law Institute for high school students considering a pre-law track or political science major in college. The program includes shadowing an attorney, visiting law firms, having lunch with a judge, and attending workshops on the First Amendment, capital punishment, using law to create social change, and the media's effect on the justice system. The cost in 2007 was $1,200, including room and board. Scholarships were available; go to http://crf-usa.org/law_government/sli.htm. While this credential alone isn't likely to make your kid a shoo-in to college, attending this camp along with other law- or leadership-related programs can add a nice credential.

Debate and Forensics Teams

Another completely different but potentially impressive route for students interested in politics, government, and law is the speech and debate approach. Thousands of high schools sponsor debate teams—even the lowest budget schools, since debate does not require expensive labs or funding beyond compensating a faculty advisor.

Intensive training programs exist throughout the United States to help students stand out. (See below for more information about these programs.) But most students who participate in high school debate view it as a school-year-only activity and assume that participation alone will impress colleges; they never polish their skills beyond what the school team offers. In reality, debate at the school level only is not particularly impressive. Remember, there are 27,000 high schools in this country, many of which have debate and/or speech teams. But once a student stands out on a state level—not just getting into a state contest, but winning—he starts to look impressive to colleges.

"I tried the debate team," a 9th grader told her mother. "But two of the kids were so sophisticated, I couldn't understand what they were saying. These two boys who've won multiple state championships dominate the team. So I thought it was boring and left."

While debate can be very intimidating to the novice observer, there's generally a huge gap between the kids who win state and regional events and the rest of the team for a good reason—but it's not brains; it's training.

SECRET 297 **High school debate should be treated like any other high school sport—excellent training and coaching create a winner.** No matter how smart the kid is or how good he is on his feet, there is no substitution for learning oratory and research skills if he wants to be a debate champion. Send your kid for formal training in the summer if this is an important activity to him.

| SECRET 298 | **For the trained student who would like to walk away with local recognition for debate—even in the** |

most competitive states—the state awards are practically his for the taking. Having moderated at many high school debates—even in some of the most competitive counties—I have found that few kids know how to conduct original research or come up with their own persuasive approaches to issues. These are very intelligent kids, but most are intimidated, since they have no outside training. In many cases, the students never fully understand the issues they debate—issues of global economics, national education standards, policing other countries, use of torture for national security, for example. And parents who are frequently called in to judge often have little or less understanding—and have been known to select winners based on what the kid is wearing, how confident the kid looks, and so on. At the same time, it's not uncommon to see team members dependent on their captain or faculty adviser to tell them which points to make and whom to quote.

If a student attends a serious summer program that teaches her how to first analyze the issues—being able to take both sides of an issue, as many debates require—then develop logical opinions to support each side, and find the most relevant sources to back her arguments, she has an enormous edge in local and state pools.

Do you want to put your kid in the most competitive league? The most rigorous training program is offered by the Dartmouth Debate Institute in New Hampshire.

| SECRET 299 | **Dartmouth's four-week summer program for high school seniors claims to have trained "the winners** |

of most national tournaments including seventeen of the last [2006] nineteen Tournament of Champions and NFL Nationals." (NFL, in this case, stands for the National Forensic League.) Dartmouth's approach is serious, and they cover all aspects of cross-examination policy debate.

"You probably have not experienced as intense and demanding an academic setting as the Dartmouth Debate Institute," their promotion teases. "Students are required to attend classes from about 8:30 a.m. until 5:00 p.m., Monday through Friday, and there are usually classes on weekends."

For rising sophomores and juniors interested in intensive debate, Dartmouth offers a three-week Debate Workshop. The curriculum teaches "theory, strategy, and skills, along with a considerable amount of research."

Another very serious training program is offered by the **National High School Coon-Hardy Debate Scholars at Northwestern University**. Only thirty-six students are accepted into this program each summer (based on grades, recommendations, and past tournament history), to keep lessons individualized and tailored to the needs of the accepted students, and to encourage "substantial interaction among students and staff."

Also at Northwestern, the **Championship Debate Group** is a five-week program for an even more select group of high school seniors—limited to sixteen students, selected from the applicant pool. Championship Debate also offers four-week sessions for rising high school sophomores and juniors—limited to twenty-four students total.

At **Stanford University's National Forensic Institute**, "accelerated students are guaranteed 20 critiqued rounds during the course of the camp. Other special programs include a novice program and a 4th week extension that allows even more critiqued practice rounds."

For serious debaters, additional training camps have been offered at Baylor University (Baylor Debate Workshops), Berkeley (Cal National Debate Institute), Cameron University (Speech-Debate-Broadcast Camp), Gonzaga (Gonzaga Debate Institute), Miami (Miami Debate Institute), Michigan (Michigan Debate Institute), three Midwest campuses (Missouri-Kansas Scholars Program), Michigan State (Spartan Debate Institutes), University of Houston Debate Institute, University of Richmond National Debate Institute, University of North Texas Mean Green Workshops, Wake Forest University Debate Workshops, Whitman National Debate Institute, and University of Vermont (World Debate Institute).

A student who participates in some of the most challenging summer debate programs need not worry about whether or not he is elected or appointed captain of his high school debate team. He will have impressive credentials that transcend school politics—particularly if he starts winning debates. Have him spend four full summers focusing on debate if he wants to be a national champion, or have him focus on debate one summer early in high school—to get the basic background and win the edge in debating—and then spend his other high school summers focused more on content studies: American government, economics, or international relations, for example.

National-Level Debate and Speech

The credential that ultimately makes a debate or speech student most desirable to colleges with debate teams is winning on a national level. Two major debate and special competitions provide such national venues.

The Tournament of Champions features a Lincoln-Douglas Debate, Policy Debate, Public Forum, and Student Congress, and takes place over three days each May at the University of Kentucky. Individuals are named national winners, and winning is extremely prestigious and appealing to colleges. To be eligible, a student must win bids at any two designated qualifying tournaments, which are held throughout the country.

| SECRET 300 | **The tournament organizers allow students with only one bid to apply for an additional at-large** |

bid. The recipients of at-large bids are decided in early spring, "based upon their records in comparison to the records of everyone else applying for the at-large bid within the region." The deadline to apply in recent years has been the very beginning of March. For rules and guidelines to the tournament, see www.uky.edu/Provost/ChellgrenCenter/Debate/champions.htm.

The National Speech Tournament, the other major national debate venue, is run by the National Forensic League (NFL) and features winners from 103 districts throughout the United States that hold qualifying tournaments. The weeklong national event includes a Student Congress, Lincoln-Douglas Debate, Policy Debate, Public Forum Debate, International Extemp, U.S. Extemp, Original Oratory, Dramatic Interpretation, Humorous Interpretation, Duo Interpretation, and Supplemental/Consolation. More than $130,000 in scholarships is awarded. The competition takes place in different locations each year. To locate a local qualifying tournament, see www.nflonline.org/DistrictInformation/TournamentDates.

International Relations

Some students who aspire to a career in government and politics take a completely different path, incorporating international relations and diplomacy into their high school studies.

For a high school student interested in international relations, what follows is an exemplary résumé. If this potentially is your child's interest, create a four-year plan by picking and choosing from some of the programs and opportunities printed in **bold** on this fictitious student's résumé. Note that quality of the programs varies, and mentioning them in no way represents an endorsement. Also note that the résumé is somewhat padded (loaded with extra credentials) and some of these activities might meet at conflicting times. The aim is to give parents an idea of some of the credentials that their children can pursue. (In planning out your child's four high school years, you should also check out the four-summer plan for international relations in the appendix.)

BRENDAN O'REILLY

International Relations Experience and Honors

United Nations Internship, eight weeks, summer 2010

Global Scholar, Washington and Lee University, summer 2010

Cross Cultural Solutions, volunteered in China, eight weeks, 2009

U.N. National High School Essay Contest, semifinalist, 2007

Global Routes; four weeks as volunteer in Tibet and China, 2008
    Taught English to young Tibetan children

Model U.N., President of school chapter 2008, 2009, and 2010

Yale Model U.N., represented United Arab Emirates, 2007

Student Cultural Exchange Club; created and led (2007 to current)
    local club in which students experience cultural celebrations
    in one another's homes; began with 10 members; up to 100

EF Foundation for Foreign Study, hosted an international
    exchange student from Argentina during winter of 2008

Education

Georgetown International Relations for High School Students
    Intensive eight-day program on international law, economics,
    policy, and crisis simulation, summer 2008

University of Pennsylvania Model UN, four weeks, summer 2007
    Foreign Policy, International Relations and Global Politics

**University of Pennsylvania International Relations Theory and
    U.S. Grand Strategy**, summer 2009

Columbia University, U.S. Economy and Globalization, summer 2008

Concordia College, Chinese Language Village (Minnesota) Chinese
(four-week immersion; one year of high school Chinese credit), 2007
Concordia College, Arabic Language Village (Minnesota) Arabic
(two-week immersion), 2006
Citytown Public High School; expected to graduate May 2010
      Grade point average 3.75 (unweighted)
      SAT I : 670 verbal, 670 math, 690 writing
      SAT II: Global History 730, American History 690, English
          Literature 680, Biology 590
      AP Exams: European History 5, American History 4, World
          History 4, Comparative Government 5, U.S.
          Government 4, Economics (Macro and Micro) 5,
          English Composition 4, Math I C 2.

SECRET 301 | **To strengthen an international relations student's résumé and provide a strong edge, parents should encourage development of at least one sought-after foreign language, preferably two.** Among the most sought-after languages are Arabic, Chinese (Mandarin), Russian, and some specific languages of India. (See "Foreign Language and Linguistics" in chapter 9.)

Students who want to specialize in international relations should plan to take in-school AP Comparative Government and Politics, AP European History, AP World History, AP U.S. Government and Politics, AP Economics, and at least one foreign spoken language taught in school, preferably on an AP level.

SECRET 302 | **If your child's high school does not offer a complete array of AP social studies or language courses, negotiate a way for your kid to get credit for learning the material independently or at a local college.** Could your daughter, for example, take the already existing social studies course and be given extra materials to prepare for the related AP exam? Could your son take AP courses independent study in place of the school's social studies program? When your child is in 8th grade, try to determine which social science AP courses he is likely to want to take and which year he will take which course.

As of 2007, the AP social science options included the following: U.S. History, World History, European History, Comparative Government & Politics, U.S. Government & Politics, Macroeconomics, Microeconomics, Human Geography, and Psychology. Related topics included: Statistics, AP

Art History, Chinese Language & Culture, English Language, English Literature, French Language, French Literature, German Language, Italian Language & Culture, Japanese Language & Culture, Latin Literature, Latin Virgil, Psychology, Spanish Language, Spanish Literature.

| SECRET 303 | **If there are social studies courses that your kid will likely want to take that are not offered** |

through her school, another option is to try to negotiate with the board of education (or the school's funding organization) to set up such a course at least *a year in advance.* Don't wait until your kid is ready to take the course; you have to give the teachers a year to study up to teach such a course. Also, you're more likely to be successful if you round up some parents whose kids would also be interested in taking the course to justify the addition of the course economically.

In proposing a new course, consider which course the district could eliminate to free up a teacher to teach the AP course—so when you're told that the school doesn't have enough staff or space, you can explain how you'd free up a teacher and a classroom.

| SECRET 304 | **As a rule, never suggest eliminating a remedial or more basic course in favor of an advanced course—** |

if you do, you'll surely make enemies among parents and teachers, and you won't achieve what you're hoping to achieve. Nor will you necessarily want the teacher of the remedial class—who may be an expert on working with learning disabilities—to turn around and teach the advanced class, the curriculum of which she might not be familiar with. You'd be smarter to suggest a plan in which AP offerings are switched from year to year, and instead of two sections of, let's say, Comparative Government, the school offers one section on Comparative Government and one section on U.S. Government.

★   ★   ★

For the student who would rather become a leader in business than a leader of politics, courses and programs are available to high school students in multiple business disciplines. Some students may also want to combine studies in high school government with business opportunities.

CHAPTER 12

Business

Marketing the Future Mogul

"W hy would Penn ask its applicants to name professors with whom they'd like to study or conduct research?" asked the father of a 12th grader who was phoning me for advice on his daughter's college applications. The girl had just been rejected Early Decision from the Wharton School, and he wanted to know how to guide her in her next round of applications. "How would a high school kid know *that*?"

"How could a potential business major be expected to write about his 'business experience'?" the mother of another student questioned similarly. "How could a high school student possibly have any meaningful experience in business?"

★ ★ ★

These are the most common kinds of queries I hear from parents of children who want to pursue an undergraduate degree in business at universities or business colleges. Most business programs leave the application essay open-ended, so the kid doesn't have to write about business. But admissions officers look for essays that demonstrate an interest or even a track record in business.

There are many exciting opportunities for high school students with an interest in business, and by the time the prospective business student reaches senior year of high school, he should have experienced at least *some* of them. (If not, he could wait until after college to pursue an MBA, after all. College is not his last chance to learn business.) For example, university summer courses are plentiful enough that a teenager could specialize in finance, entrepreneurial studies, or marketing, and build up a significant track record of credentials (both in an out of the classroom) by the time she applies to college business programs. And a student could work in a local business during the summer or explore entrepreneurship while still in high school.

Why do business colleges and departments want to see that students have already taken business courses? you might wonder. *Isn't the point of attending business school to expose the student to business subjects?*

Imagine the novice business student who enrolls in the required introductory accounting course and realizes, after a week, that he doesn't like the subject as much as he had expected—in fact, he loathes it. And his college program requires that he take at least two more semesters of accounting. Or imagine that after a month as a business undergrad, your daughter suddenly decides that she would like the opportunity to pursue a medical career, and she is attending, let's say, Babson, Bentley, or NYU Stern (business colleges), which don't specialize in turning out medical doctors.

| SECRET 305 | **Before your kid applies to any program with a single specialized focus (such as business, pharmacy, or dentistry), he needs to have already had some experience in the field to know that he will be happy with such a focused program of study.** Such |

colleges are more impressed with kids who have had at least some related experience—this is part of the reason they ask students to explain why they think they're "the best fit" or "the perfect match" for the school. If your child hasn't proven interest and aptitude in any of the subjects in which the school specializes, the college may believe it is doing him a favor by rejecting him.

Start at School

In helping your child to gain a suitable background in business, the best place to start is at her high school. Many schools offer business courses and business-related clubs. Start by exploring the course options. At some schools, high school business courses such as Business Law, Entrepreneurship, and Basic Bookkeeping are very serious; at others, classes with the same names are catch-alls for behavior-problem kids. Educate yourself about these courses (speak with the guidance counselor and parents of older kids) before enrolling your kid in any of them. At a minimum, an AP

Economics course is guaranteed to be serious, and your kid should plan to take it during her high school career in whichever grade (most commonly junior or senior year) it is offered.

There are two business associations for high school students that are major players internationally: Delta Epsilon Chi (Association) (DECA) and Future Business Leaders of America (FBLA). They both offer a wide array of exciting activities to lure your child into business. DECA claims five thousand chapters and more than 180,000 members. The aim is to "prepare future leaders in . . . business administration, and management, entrepreneurship, finance, marketing, sales and service; and hospitality and tourism." The organization sponsors competitive events and role play to improve students' understanding of business operations and show students what's exciting about business. Among the highlights, DECA sponsors an annual Sports and Entertainment Marketing Conference. The 2007 conference was at Disney World's All-Star Sports Resort.

FBLA, which claims to be "the largest business-based student organization in the world," also offers engaging business competitions, challenges, and community service projects.

For both organizations, find out if a local chapter exists when your child is in 8th grade if possible. If no local chapter exists, you might consider going through school channels to find out how to help set up a school chapter. If a chapter of either organization *does* exist, you should encourage your business-interested child to join once she arrives in 9th grade, in time for her to get the benefit of four full years' membership.

While business colleges may not care about exactly how many years your kid belonged to a club, these clubs usually offer lots of good experience to use as grist in writing application essays and gaining additional business-related credentials.

SECRET 306   **When your child is searching for business opportunities outside of school, parents can be extremely helpful in locating options.** Aim for variety in the younger years to familiarize your child with different aspects of business (finance, marketing, entrepreneurship, etc.). Encourage your child to fine-tune her interest as she reaches junior year. In addition to summer coursework, a student could pursue experiences in a variety of business settings (a retail store, a fundraising event, an entrepreneurial enterprise, a local business office, etc.), take evening courses, and even develop her own products and business plans.

Business Internships and Jobs

Unpaid internships and volunteer work are tricky in business, as businesses tend to be much more tightly structured than other institutions: Your kid is either working in a paid position or not there at all. There are several ways to find business-related internships, however. The easiest is to find out if any companies or government agencies list opportunities with your child's high school—some high schools have youth employment offices, and some post opportunities in the guidance office or school internship office (if one exists). If none of these resources is available, parents can sometimes find appealing opportunities listed in books like *The Internship Bible* (Princeton Review), *Internships* (Peterson's), or *Vault Guide to Top Internships*. Many internship listings specify that they want college students or grads, but some employers will make exceptions for an impressive high school student with needed skills. My students have found better luck applying directly to the companies or institutions for whom they most want to work (without waiting to see a job or internship listing in a book or newspaper)—local government offices, investment companies, banks, and other businesses. And my most successful students have told me that they got the best internships by applying directly to a person in the department in which they wanted to work—rather than contacting the personnel office to find out generically about any openings.

Sometimes a high school student can gain excellent business experience by working for a volunteer organization and offering to help in business-related functions like fund-raising, bookkeeping, and media relations.

When helping your child to find an internship, beware of business internships that go nowhere. You know that kid (a.k.a. fund-raising intern) who is selling chocolate bars to raise money for the rehab center? The young telemarketer (a.k.a. retail intern) who interrupted your dinner the other night to try to sell you chimney-cleaning service when you don't have a chimney? And the girl (a.k.a. marketing intern) who handed you a flyer for a gym opening in your neighborhood? While vaguely business related, internships such as these (which kids with an interest in business often take because they think they will look good on a résumé) are dead-end jobs—not very impressive to colleges—paid or not. In addition, such experiences become boring very quickly and don't give students any greater understanding of how businesses work; they don't challenge the mind and don't teach anything about business responsibility or enterprise. Often they turn students off to business. Much more useful are internships in which students grow intellectually. Similarly, working in a local retail outlet can provide a good first experience, but working in the same store year after year is no more impressive than working there one summer unless the child is promoted to a job that teaches new skills.

If your child is unable to land a challenging internship, your best bet may be to have her take business courses during the summer instead and to temporarily explore entrepreneurship—to start her *own* business.

Entrepreneurs

Among the businesses that high school students I have worked with have started successfully are creating and selling jewelry, performing as party magicians, designing Web pages, repairing computers, selling manure for fertilizer, performing in rock bands for parties, creating and selling greeting cards, designing clothing, working as a local tour guide, and running farm stands. Launching and running any of these endeavors can help to teach your kid how to run a small business—and an enterprising kid with a creative concept and successful business can be very impressive to business colleges and business departments who seek students with energy and enthusiasm. Conventional "kid businesses" like babysitting, tutoring, shoveling snow, and dog-walking probably won't impress colleges nowadays, as students are creating more elaborate and sophisticated businesses—unless your kid starts a babysitting collective or organizes a lucrative tutoring circle. Encourage your child to think creatively when pursuing entrepreneurship. Imagine how impressive he'll be when he applies to business colleges with three years of successful entrepreneurial experience. Note that in many communities, organizations of retired business executives eagerly offer free entrepreneurial advice to young novices. To learn how to create a successful business, your child may also want to take classes for at least a portion of each summer.

Entrepreneurial Studies

The summer before 9th grade could feature three weeks at Duke University's Talent Identification Program (TIP) Center studying Strategic

Entrepreneurial Leadership. The summer before 10th grade could include two weeks at Boston University's Summer Challenge Business course, which provides instruction on how to set up a professional business plan. The summer before 11th grade could feature four weeks at USC's Summer Exploring Entrepreneurship (for 3 college credits) or nineteen days at the University of Maryland Young Scholars Program, Discovering New Ventures and Foundations of Entrepreneurship. And the summer before senior year could be spent at Wharton School's Management & Technology Summer Institute, with one week at the Presidential Classroom, Entrepreneurship and Global Business Program. (See the appendix for a fuller listing of summer course options.) By the time this student becomes a senior, he has accrued three college courses and a background in entrepreneurship.

Investment and Finance

For students more interested in investment and finance, many options also exist for summer study. (A fuller listing of some of the best opportunities is provided in the appendix.) One of the most intriguing investment immersion programs is offered at Bentley College in Massachusetts. Bentley's Wall Street 101 one-week summer program for high school juniors and seniors simulates real-world business trading in the business college's "state-of-the art Trading Room," which features real-time data like a real trading floor. While admission to "Camp Bentley" is by application, what will wow colleges most about a student who gets in is his newfound ability to talk intelligently about investment with any college interviewer.

Wharton School at the University of Pennsylvania offers a four-week Leadership in the Business World program. Participants "work in teams to design, prepare, and formulate an original business plan presentation to be judged by . . . venture capitalists." They probably also get a good sense of who their competition will be in applying to college business programs. Admission is very competitive: Wharton admits only sixty rising seniors each summer, based on transcript, test scores (with official reports), demonstrated business commitment (business credentials), two teacher recommendations, and leadership.

International Business

For students who want to delve into international business and economics, the Knowledge Exchange Institute (a travel group that partners with universities, research facilities, art academies, companies, and professional organizations to offer subject-specific educational opportunities) runs a summer program called European Capitals, which visits ten European cities: Amsterdam, Berlin, Bruges, Brussels, Geneva, London, Luxemburg, Paris, Prague, and Vienna. The five-week economics–politics–culture-focused program is based at the International Management Institute in Brussels and is conducted in English. Students earn 3 college credits (or 3 additional credits for studying French). Transcripts are issued by the International Management Institute and Clark Atlanta University.

Note that *students especially interested in international business can strengthen their college applications by mastering a foreign language in addition to learning about business.* Such a student should devote time in the earlier summers of high school to language immersion—either an intensive live-abroad program or one of several programs offered at domestic universities—so that by the later years he may focus on business courses or a combination of business and foreign language. (Course options are listed under "Foreign Languages and Linguistics" in chapter 9.)

The Fed Challenge

| SECRET 307 | **To help your child earn top credentials for business school or a business or economics major, reg-** |

ister her interest in the Fed Challenge with her high school social studies department. It's likely that nobody from school will announce this opportunity or notify your child that the opportunity exists, since the program is very competitive, and only a few may represent each participating high school as a team. If economics is something that your child might like to pursue, initiate discussion with your child's social studies or economics teachers—early in her high school career. Don't wait for them to come to her, and don't invite parents of her friends to join your campaign. State her interest early to lay claim to participation or put the social studies teachers on notice—before they pass her over and hand the opportunity to someone else. This is one of those programs where teachers are asked to hand-pick kids, and you don't hear about it until you read about the end result in the local newspaper.

The Fed Challenge is sponsored by participating reserve banks and the board of governors of the Federal Reserve System. The gist is: High school teams prepare and present monetary policy recommendations to current members of the Federal Open Market Committee (FOMC) first on the local and district levels. District winners then go on to the semifinals and then the national finals in Washington, D.C., in May. The contest began in 1994, and each year Citibank awards a total of almost $200,000 to winning teams from all parts of the nation. Individual students can win up to $7,000. The national round is sponsored by seven reserve banks and branches in the federal system.

Résumé for Business

Following is a sample résumé for a student interested in business, which will give you an idea of the credentials a serious business student can acquire by senior year of high school. Parents should especially note the credentials marked in **bold**, which represent actual opportunities, and note that the résumé may be a bit overloaded to cram in as many credentials as I could, thus giving you a fuller idea of what's out there. Using this résumé, pick and choose opportunities for your own child.

RALPH HAWKINS

<u>Business-Related Experience and Achievements</u>

Federal Reserve, Fed Challenge Winner, 2010

Wharton School, University of Pennsylvania, summer 2009

Management and Technology Summer Institute

> three-week program; one of only fifty students selected nationally

Georgetown University, summer 2008

Gateway to Business Program for High School Juniors

> five-week, 3-credit intensive program exploring finance,
> marketing, accounting, management, communications,
> strategy, planning, organizational behavior, and business law

Brown University, summer 2007

> **International Financial Markets & Investments**, three weeks
> **Financial Markets & Investments**, three weeks

DECA

> **Earned "Exceeds Expectations" score**
> **Business Law & Ethics Management Team**
> **Decision Making Event**, score 100 in 2010
> **Sports and Entertainment Management Team**
> **Decision Making Event**, score 98 in 2009
> President of school DECA Club 2009–10
> Vice president of school DECA Club 2008–09

Future Business Leaders of America

Business Achievement Award winner, 2009

NLC Banking and Financial Systems Award, 2010

Stock Market Game Club, National Winner 2010

> Organized and led a schoolwide investment club for students to gain
> an understanding of the stock market, 2008, 2009, 2010

<u>Education</u>

Middledale High School, class of 2010

GPA 3.6	SAT I: 700 math, 620 verbal, 620 writing	
AP	**MicroEconomics**	4
	MacroEconomics	5
	U.S. History	3
	Calculus A	4
	Statistics	4

Business courses at Middledale High School:

> Business Law, Business Writing, Sports Marketing

Applying to Business Programs

Who should pursue business programs for college? Only students who are genuinely interested in business.

"I wasn't good at biology," a student wrote on his application. "So I decided against premed. I also found law books to be incredibly boring, so I eliminated law. But I'd like to make a good salary, so I thought I'd try business."

That's the beginning of a loser essay for business programs. An application should be based on positive reasons, not process of elimination. No college wants to hear that your son is applying to their school because he can't succeed anywhere else. And such a statement does not give the reader any reassurance that the applicant will persist if his interest wanes slightly or if the coursework gets difficult.

In contrast, a student I worked with wrote about how he was invited to sit in on a meeting with a famous clothing designer and got to contribute his marketing input, which he incorporated into his future clothing lines. Another of my students wrote about working in a retail store and resolving a customer dispute that the manager was unable to settle. Yet another wrote about how he successfully developed and marketed an innovative drain pipe. These upbeat essays were much more appealing to admissions officers, demonstrating genuine passion for business and real-life experience that was relevant to the particular programs to which these students were applying. As a result, all of these students were offered admission into prestigious business programs.

| SECRET 308 | The perfect application essay for business school or a business program focuses mostly on a single |

business-related experience that was influential in the applicant's life. The same can be true in any number of fields, but generally speaking, colleges are not quite as concerned if a potential philosophy major arrives at a liberal arts college and wants to switch to political science or anthropology. In contrast, at many college business programs, once accepted, students are locked into business. The essay needs to convince colleges that the interest is deep-rooted and not fickle or likely to change. That said, the essay should lightly mention additional experiences as well, so it doesn't appear that the interest is based solely on a single incident. But in order to be able to write such an essay, the student needs a collection of experiences from which to draw.

| SECRET 309 | **In addition to enriching your child's business interest with courses and learning experiences,** |

make sure your child is familiar with the business basics, too. A kid with a professed business interest should have enough experience/background to know, for example, the difference between a stock and a bond. Your daughter should be familiar with what *finance* means, what marketers do, and what *entrepreneur* means. At an interview for a business college, she will be asked what field of business she is hoping to study. Her response should be based on her repertoire of knowledge and her initiative to explore the possibilities. It bears repeating that colleges are unimpressed with the complete novice who demonstrates no prior track record, the dabbler who seems unfocused, and the unmotivated student who asks the admissions interviewer to explain the different fields of business.

★　★　★

The gist is this: In business, as in other fields, your child should arrive at senior year having explored a whole repertoire of captivating experiences in the subjects that interest him most. High school has become a time of opportunity—with so many options available. In these competitive times, the kid who has no idea what he wants to study in college looks very unappealing, and is viewed as less likely to take advantage of a university's vast resources when compared with the applicant who is focused and motivated. You want to help your child find that focus—and some mastery of his field of choice—by the end of high school.

A FINAL NOTE

In sharing with you the many opportunities that are available to high school students, I don't want you to worry that you haven't been doing enough for your children. Instead, the aim has been to show you the rich array of creative possibilities—especially the ones that high schools don't tell you about—to help your children pursue those that interest them most. And the fact that you've picked up this book to read demonstrates that you're a caring parent. As a consumer of education, you are entitled to know what is out there, how your kid is being judged, what kind of credentials will help your child earn competitive college admission, what special opportunities exist that competitors may not want you to know about, and how, by listening to your kid's deepest aspirations, you can guide your high school children's young careers more successfully.

Once you've read this book, keep it by your bedside. Refer to it throughout your child's high school days. Feel free to e-mail me if you have questions about how to help your kid achieve that special academic or artistic dream (visit my Web site at www.WhatHighSchoolsDontTell You.com). And share with me any opportunities that your kids have outgrown that are not already mentioned in the book; that way I may share them on my Web site, and you can have a part in helping others. As I mentioned previously, a lot of the current college admissions frenzy has been the result of parents not knowing how many wonderful opportunities exist and in how many different disciplines. Parents have felt pressured to enroll their kids in the few opportunities of which they were aware. But, as you now know, so many more inspiring opportunities are available than most parents imagine.

I hope that this book helps you to transcend high school politics and the college application frenzy, and provides you with the secrets you need to help your children's dreams come true.

APPENDIX

Four-Year Summer Plans
for Forty Different Interests

Listed alphabetically by subject

For parents seeking to structure a four-year high school summer plan tailored to their children's interests, this appendix provides potential summer plans for forty of the goals that my students have asked about most. This is not all-inclusive—there are many more topics that are especially popular among students—nor is this appendix meant to endorse or promote any particular program or course of study. Instead, the aim is to give parents a sense of some of the many opportunities that exist; these lists should serve as a launching point for your own investigation of what options and programs would be suitable for your children. I created this appendix because summers are key in giving your child the educational and experiential edge and in creating a convincing and well-focused track record for college. My intention is to save you significant time in this process and to help you direct your children toward success. You'll notice that more programs and courses are readily available for some pursuits than for others; this should not be interpreted as a value judgment of which subject is more or less important.

When crafting your own child's four-year summer plan, pick and choose. While very few of the programs individually guarantee your child entrance into her first-choice college, combining programs—spending each summer absorbing all the lessons from a variety of intensive programs—along with the right range of grades and test scores together create a powerful résumé and the strongest possible case for admissions for any college applicant. In reading the following listings, please note that Summer 1 refers to the summer *before* 9th grade, and CAA, CTD, CTY, TIP Academy, and TIP Center refer to summer gifted programs with competitive admissions requirements—usually standardized tests taken in 7th and 8th grade—as described in chapter 2. And please be aware that all listed programs are subject to change or even cancellation from year to year—depending on available funding, popularity of the program, and availability of qualified instructors.

Aeronautics and Aerospace

Summer 1: University of Illinois, Illinois Aerospace Institute
Camp Kennedy Space Center
Duke University TIP, Above and Beyond: Astronomy,
    Physics and Astrobiology, PARI Observatory
Embry-Riddle Aerospace Engineering Summer Camp

Summer 2: Westminster College, Salt Lake City, Aviation Camp
Duke University TIP Academy/Center Aerospace
    Engineering
University of Illinois, Illinois Aerospace Institute

Summer 3: Oklahoma State Aerospace Education High School
    Summer Academy
North Carolina State Aerospace Engineering Workshop

Summer 4: Embry-Riddle Prescott Campus Summer Flight Program
NASA Goddard research internship (Opportunities
    within NASA change from year to year, depending
    on government funding. Check with the individual
    NASA branch early in the year to find out which
    internship opportunities, if any, are offered for high
    school students that year.)

Imagine that you're a college admissions officer comparing two students who both claim to have a passion for aero/astro. If both students came from similar demographics, would you take the one who only read about it? Or would you prefer the student who had designed vehicles for flight and had interned at NASA?

Anthropology

Summer 1: Duke TIP Academy, Appalachian Tales: Ghosts, Hikers, and Bluegrass; Trips to Blue Ridge Mountains
UCLA Culture and Society

Summer 2: Experiment in International Living, Navajo National Summer Abroad Program
Global Routes Project Thailand

Summer 3: Harvard Summer School, Introduction to Social Anthropology
Experiment in International Living, South Africa

Summer 4: Washington University High School Summer Scholars, Introduction to Cultural Anthropology
Global Routes Project Costa Rica, four weeks

Archaeology

Summer 1: Johns Hopkins CTY, Archaeology
Duke TIP Center, Stones & Bones: Archaeology & Anthropology
Brown University Summer Mini-Course, Introduction to Archaeology

Summer 2: Cornell University, Archaeology 100: Explorations in Ancient People and Places
Earthwatch, Ancient Civilizations on Mississippi River family dig
Crow Canyon Archeaological Center, High School Field School

Summer 3: Penn State, Introduction to Archaeology
Archaeological Institute of America international dig

Summer 4: Washington University, High School Summer Scholars, Introduction to Archaeology
Gunston Hall Archaeology Project dig
Stanford, Introduction to Statistical Methods (archaeology)
University of Pennsylvania, Introduction to Archaeology

Depending upon which programs you choose, your child could accumulate 9 to 11 college credits and experience domestic and overseas digs by the time he or she finishes high school.

Architecture

The American Institute of Architects lists many summer architecture education programs for high school students. When creating a four-year plan, be sure to visit their Web site, www.aia.org/ed_k12programs. The plan below represents a very small sampling of programs available.

Summer 1: Duke University TIP Academy, Architecture
Summer 2: Penn State University, Introduction to Architecture
Summer 3: University of Pennsylvania, Penn Summer Studio in
          Architecture
          Cornell Explorations, Introduction to Architecture
          (Studio and Lecture)
          University of Illinois, Discover Architecture
Summer 4: Syracuse Summer Pre-College, Architecture (portfolio
          help)
          Ball State College of Architecture & Planning Summer
          Workshop
          Roger Williams (Rhode Island) Summer Academy in
          Architecture

In four years a student could accumulate enough building and structure designs and models to assemble a very appealing portfolio and could receive guidance in the process of assembling a portfolio.

Art: Drawing and Painting

Summer 1: California State Summer School for the Arts, InnerSpark
          Interlochen Arts Camp, Painting (portfolio required)
Summer 2: North Carolina School of the Arts
          Kansas City Arts Institute, Summer Studio Intensives,
          painting

Summer 3:   Knowledge Exchange Institute (KEI), Venetian Art
                History (in Italy), with two studio courses in painting
                or drawing
                Art Institute of Chicago
                Otis College Summer of Art, Los Angeles, four weeks
Summer 4:   Rhode Island School of Design (RISD), painting or
                drawing
                Massachusetts College of Art (MassArt), Summer Youth
                Program; students develop portfolios during program
                UCLA Design Summer Institute; portfolio assistance

This four-summer program should complement art courses at school
and culminate in the creation of a quality portfolio and courses in AP Art
History and AP Studio Art. In addition, an art student could initiate a local
exhibit of her works and works by fellow art students at adult centers, libraries, and other public spaces.

Art History

Summer 1:   Duke TIP Center, Art History
                Johns Hopkins CTY, 20th Century Art
Summer 2:   Duke TIP, Art and Soul: Architecture and Art History—
                Rome and Florence, Italy
                Brown University Pre-College Mini-Courses, Survey of
                Art History: Italian Renaissance to the Present
                Penn State, Renaissance to Modern Art
Summer 3:   UCLA: Art of India and Southeast Asia *or*
                Renaissance and Baroque Art
                Barnard College Pre-College, Masterpieces of Western
                Art, including trips to major New York City museums
Summer 4:   AIFS Summer Advantage: History of Russian Art,
                taught in St. Petersburg, Russia, along with Russian
                Language
                NYU, Introduction to Galleries and Museums of
                New York

Most programs include museum and gallery visits. Many universities also offer summer art history courses overseas.

Business: Entrepreneurship

Summer 1:   University of Wisconsin, Youth Entrepreneur Camp
                 Money Camp, info@themoneycamp.com

Summer 2:   Boston University Summer Challenge, Business Seminar
                 USC Summer, Exploring Entrepreneurship

Summer 3:   University of Maryland Young Scholars, Discovering
                 New Ventures—Foundations of Entrepreneurship

Summer 4:   Maritime Academy, Camp Venture, Vallejo, California
                 Presidential Classroom, Entrepreneurship and Global
                 Business

A student who is interested in entrepreneurship should also give serious consideration to devoting a portion of each summer to starting up small businesses and possibly carrying those businesses into the school year if successful. Colleges are very impressed with successful young entrepreneurs.

Business: Finance, Investment, and Marketing

Summer 1:   Westminster College, Finance Camp, Salt Lake City
                 Choate Rosemary Hall, Wall Street

Summer 2:   Stanford University Education Program for Gifted
                 Youth, Topics in Business
                 Brown Mini-Course, Financial Markets and Investments

Summer 3:   Bentley College, Wall Street 101, Camp Bentley,
                 Massachusetts
                 Columbia University Summer Program for High School
                 Students, Introduction to Business Finance and
                 Economics
                 Northwestern University College Prep, Principles of
                 Marketing

Summer 4:   Georgetown Gateway to Business for High School
                 Juniors

Syracuse Summer Pre-College Management
Miami University of Ohio, Junior Scholars,
     Introduction to Business and
     Principles of Marketing

Business-interested students could devote some time during the summer to gaining real-world business experience, taking a job or internship at a business or a commerce-related government agency.

Choreography and Dance

Summer 1: American Ballet Theatre Summer Intensive, University
         of Texas (Austin)
         Interlochen, Intermediate Dance program
Summer 2: Cornell University Dance 210: Beginning Dance Com-
         position
         USC SummerDance
         Northeast Louisiana University, Dance
Summer 3: University of Michigan Summer Dance Institute
         UCLA Dance Theater Intensive
Summer 4: NYU Tisch Summer Dance Residency Festival
         Alvin Ailey Summer Intensive

To be considered for most serious college dance programs, students will need to have some experience in ballet, and/or modern—even if the student wants to specialize in contemporary or ethnic dance. Summers are the ideal time to pursue dance experience outside the student's specific dance preference—exploration time—to complement the yearlong dance program in which the student focuses only on his dance preference. To locate other quality summer dance opportunities, check out *Dance Magazine* (www .dancemagazine.com) and Cyberdance (www.cyberdance.org/summer.html).

Codes and Encryption

Summer 1: Brown University Mini-Course, Cryptography
         Introduction to Egyptian Hieroglyphics

Rocky Mountain Talent Search, Cryptography,
University of Denver
Summer 2: Cornell University, The Art of Secret Writing
Duke TIP Center, Spy 101: Cryptology and Number
Theory
University of Michigan, Math and Science Summer
Scholars, Codes, Ciphers and Secret Messages
Summer 3: University of Connecticut Mentor Connection,
Cracking the Code
Summer 4: Harvard Summer Seminar, Lost Languages and
Decipherment
Johns Hopkins CTY, Advanced Cryptography

If a high school student chooses to focus on codes and encryption, he should also try to gain mastery of sophisticated mathematics (at programs like Ross and PROMYS—see "Mathematics" below), crucial for more advanced encryption.

Debate

Summer 1: Duke University TIP Center, State Your Case, the Art
of Debate,
Summer 2: Case Western CTD Equinox, Public Speaking and
Debate Honors
Phillips Exeter Academy, Debate and Argumentation
Summer 3: Dartmouth Debate Institute
Northwestern National High School Coon-Hardy
Debate Scholars
UCLA Mock Trial Institute
USC Summer Argumentation and Debate
Summer 4: Dartmouth Debate Institute
Northwestern National High School Coon-Hardy
Debate Scholars **or** Northwestern's Championship
Debate Group

So your kid wasn't named head of the school debate team. That's no problem if he follows this four-summer plan. By senior year he should be winning every debate locally and on a grander scale as well.

Drama

Summer 1: American Academy of Dramatic Arts Summer Program
(New York and L.A.)
Interlochen
Summer 2: UCLA Acting and Performance Institute
Carnegie Mellon School of Drama (Pittsburgh)
Summer 3: NYU Tisch, Drama at Lee Strasberg Theatre Institute
Northwestern, Acting I, *and* Stage Makeup
Summer 4: Yale Summer Conservatory for Drama

Drama students who have substantial résumés should consider auditioning for local and professional productions, too, as part of their high school experience.

Energy Science

Summer 1: Duke TIP Academy, The Science of Energy, Fueling the
World for the 21st Century (Texas A&M)
Johns Hopkins CAA, Nuclear Energy
Brown University Mini-Course, Harnessing the Giant:
Our World of Energy
Summer 2: University of Michigan, Michigan Math and Science
Summer Scholars, Cars, Energy and Chemistry
Summer 3: North Carolina State Young Investigators' Program in
Nuclear Technology
University of Connecticut Mentor Connection,
Chemical Engineering: Securing a More
Energy-Efficient Future (conducting research)
Oklahoma State, Exploring the Science, Technology,
Engineering & Mathematics of Wind and Oil Energy
in Oklahoma
Summer 4: University of Connecticut Mentor Connection, Fuel
Cells (conducting research)

Students interested in energy should also seek internships in professional labs to conduct original research that could then be entered into science research competitions. Energy and nuclear energy courses go undersubscribed at some top colleges and tech schools, making a student who is interested in (and knowledgeable about) energy very appealing.

Engineering

Summer 1:   Duke TIP Center, Nanotechnology; Engineering
                Problem Solving
Summer 2:   North Carolina State, Engineering Workshops
                Rensselaer Polytechnic Institute (RPI), Why Plastics?
                (chemical engineering)
                Widener University Engineering Summer Camp
                (Pennsylvania)
Summer 3:   George Washington University, Explore Engineering
                (lab experience)
                University of Connecticut, Mentors, Calling All
                Inventors (original inventing) **and** Biological
                Engineering
                Michigan State High School Engineering Institute
                American Society of Metals Materials Science Research
                Camp
Summer 4:   George Washington University, Applied
                Pre-Engineering Experience
                Vanderbilt University, PAVE Pre-College Program
                Cornell Summer Explorations, Topics in Engineering;
                Digital World and You
                North Carolina State, Materials Science & Engineering
                Workshop
                MIT Women's Technology Program
                MIT Minority Introduction to Engineering and
                Sciences (MITES)

This four-summer plan exposes the potential engineer to nanotechnology, chemical engineering, mechanical engineering, biological engineering, and independent invention. Combine these courses and programs with creative and independent tinkering, and students should be able to enter science and engineering competitions with original projects by junior year. Many more programs exist, including engineering programs especially created to interest women or minorities, who tend to be underrepresented in the field. For additional listings, check: http://tbp.mit.edu/highschool.

Fashion

Summer 1: Williams College, Excel Pre-College, Putney, Fashion Design

Summer 2: Penn State, Fashion and Design

Savannah College of Art and Design, Designing for the Runway: Fashion Basics

Art Institute of Chicago, Fashion Design and Fashion Construction

Columbia College in Chicago, Chicago Fashion Industry

Summer 3: Parsons New School of Design, New York, Fashion Design

Parsons New School of Design, Fashion in Paris (in France)

Pratt Pre-College, New York, Fashion Design

University of the Arts, London College of Fashion, Creating a Customized Collection (five days)

Summer 4: Syracuse Summer Pre-College, Fashion and Textile Design

Rhode Island School of Design Pre-College Program, Fashion

Instead of spending four summers hanging out at the mall, a high school student could potentially emerge with her own line of designer clothes after four summers of studying serious fashion design. High school fashion students could also accrue up to 18 college credits—more than a semester's worth—and study in London and Paris.

Forensic Science (Detective Work)

Note: This does not *refer to debate.*

Summer 1: Duke TIP Center, Forensic Science
Brown University Mini-Course, Art of Forgery in the
Age of Photoshop
Summer 2: Syracuse Summer Pre-College, Forensic Science
SUNY Stony Brook, Investigations in Forensics Camp
Summer 3: University of Miami, Forensic Investigation
Vanderbilt University, Forensic Anthropology
Summer 4: Yale University, Forensic Anthropology
Northeastern University, Crime Scene Investigation

This background is not only useful for future law enforcement special-
ists but also for future mystery writers, criminal lawyers, forensic medicine
experts, and laboratory scientists. A student aspiring to careers in any of
these fields can dazzle admissions officers with knowledge of forensics.

Game Programming

Summer 1: Penn State, Introduction to 2-D Game Design,
Animation and Web Development
Vanderbilt Program for Talented Youth, Digital
Storytelling: Narration Through the Web, Graphic
Design and Video
Rensselaer Polytechnic, Computer Game Development
Academy
Duke TIP Center, Java for Video Games
Summer 2: Case Western CTD Equinox, Introduction to
Computer Game Design
Penn State, Advanced 2-D Game Design
Northeastern University (Boston), Video Game Design
Fundamentals
Summer 3: Columbia University Summer, Computer Graphics
through Game Programming

UCLA Design/Media Arts Summer Institute, Game
Design
USC Summer Session, Introduction to Video Game
Design

Summer 4: Johns Hopkins, Discover Hopkins Pre-College,
Machinima
Carnegie Mellon, National High School Game Academy

This four-summer plan invites students to create their own games (and eventually enter the National High School Game Academy Awards competition at Carnegie Mellon during the final summer). Imagine how much more appealing these artists, innovators, and creators are to colleges and tech schools than students who spent their four summers of high school merely *playing* games.

Genetics

Summer 1: Johns Hopkins CTY, Genetics, *and* Genomics
Brown, Summer Studies, Genetics and Human Behavior
Summer 2: Case Western CTD, Genetics and Biotechnology Honors
Phillips Exeter Academy, Genetic Engineering/
Molecular Biology
Summer 3: Penn State, Genetics, Ecology & Evolution
Brown, Techniques in DNA Based Biotechnology
and Molecular Basis of Human Disease
Summer 4: University of Michigan, Math-Science Scholars Program,
Genes to Genomics
Northwestern College Prep, Genetics & Evolution
Genetics research at a university or laboratory

Such a four-summer program requires careful coordination with high school coursework, making sure that the student has enough high school biology and chemistry background—in some cases AP courses—to be able to benefit from the specific summer opportunity. By junior or senior year, the student should have a sophisticated enough understanding of genetics to be able to conduct summer research and enter high school science research competitions.

Government

Summer 1: Choate Rosemary Hall John F. Kennedy Institute of Government

Summer 2: Junior Statesmen Program

Georgetown University Summer, U.S. Political Systems

Summer 3: Harvard Summer School, Introduction to American Government

George Washington Summer Mini-Course, Election Politics: Building a Campaign

Summer 4: Presidential Classroom Scholars Program, Washington D.C.

University of Connecticut Mentor Program, Adventures in Saving the World

Government internship

This plan provides the student with a solid educational background and real credentials for internships in government or on a political campaign the summers before junior or senior year. Courses in politics are not enough to dazzle a college, but what the student does with those programs through internships or campaigns can make the student a shoo-in.

Industrial Design

Summer 1: Johns Hopkins CAA, Principles of Engineering Design

Auburn University (Alabama) Industrial Design Workshop

Duke TIP Academy, Shaping the Future, Product Design for the New Millenium

Summer 2: UCLA Summer Session, Nature of Design

Summer 3: Columbia Summer, Engineering Design via Community Service

Pratt Institute, New York, Pre-College Program, Interior Design

> Parsons New School of Design, New York, Product
> Design
> Rhode Island School of Design, Pre-College Industrial
> Design (or Furniture Design)

Summer 4: Pratt Institute, New York, Pre-College Industrial Design
> Carnegie Mellon Pre-College Fine Arts Program in
> Design

For the young artist whose doodles include pictures of new cars as well as for the kid who fantasizes about improving the design of everyday appliances and other items, these summer opportunities offer college credits and experience at some of the most famous engineering design programs.

International Relations

Summer 1: Dickinson College, Comparative Law and International
> Relations
> Auburn University World Affairs Camp (Model U.N.)
> Duke University TIP Global Dialogues Institute (at
> Wake Forest University)

Summer 2: Johns' Hopkins CTY Princeton, Global Politics: Human
> Rights & Justice
> Putney Student Travel Global Awareness trips to El Sal-
> vador, Malawi, India, Madagascar, Cambodia, or U.S.
> Gulf Coast
> Duke TIP, World Politics: Diplomat's Perspective—
> London

Summer 3: Georgetown, International Relations Program for High
> School Students
> Harvard Summer School, variety of international
> relations courses
> Tufts, Ethics and Global Citizenship
> Presidential Classroom, Future World Leaders Summit
> Washington and Lee University, Global Scholar High
> School Program

Summer 4:   Yale, International Dimensions of Democratization
American Field Service internship in orphanage in
Ghana
Johns Hopkins CTY (Princeton), Global Issues in the
21st Century

A student pursuing some of these courses and programs could potentially amass 14 college credits, more than a full semester of college, and gain expertise in international relations at universities that include Georgetown, Harvard, Yale, and Johns Hopkins. She should also spend some time traveling independently for a course or community service overseas (not with a teen tour).

Journalism

Summer 1:   Syracuse University Summer Pre-College, Public
Communications
Summer 2:   Indiana University Summer High School Journalism
Institute, newspaper/newsmagazine, TV news,
photojournalism
George Washington University Photojournalism
Summer 3:   Presidential Classroom, Media and Democracy Program
University of Missouri, *full menu* of summer journalism
classes
Summer 4:   Miami University of Ohio, Junior Scholars Program,
News Writing and Reporting for All Media
Northwestern Summer High School Institute, intensive
journalism (eighty-eight students)

Regardless of whether your child is named editor of the high school newspaper, she can know twice as much as any other student—and possibly the faculty advisor—about journalism by the time she graduates from high school if she follows a four-summer plan similar to the one above. The courses on this plan will prepare any high school student for an editorship or plum reporting position in college, in addition to providing a semester's worth of credits and a solid foundation in photojournalism, media ethics, and nonfiction writing. To complement this program, the student should also write articles and seek publication in professional outlets to dazzle colleges.

Landscape Design

Summer 1: University of Michigan Math and Science Summer Scholars Program: Why Here? Reading Diverse Landscapes

Summer 2: Penn State Architecture-Landscape Architecture Camp USC, Designing the Architectural Landscape of Tomorrow

Summer 3: Ball State University College of Architecture and Planning (CAP) High School Summer Workshop on Environmental Design

Parsons New School of Design, New York, The Edge of the City: Architecture and Landscape

Barnard College, Urban Landscapes, Exploring New York Cityscapes

Summer 4: Harvard Summer School, Crucial Issues in Landscape Creation and Perception

University of Miami School of Architecture, Explorations in Architecture and Design (including landscape)

In addition to gaining expertise in the emerging field of landscape design, the background that this subject provides is also useful in eventually pursuing majors in architecture, virtual landscape design for computer games, city and town planning, or park administration.

Law

Summer 1: Johns Hopkins CAA, Great Cases: American Legal History

Brown University Mini-Course, Law and Criminality in American History

Duke TIP Center, Criminal Law and Mock Trial

Summer 2: Case Western Reserve CTD, Equinox, Law & Politics
Honors

Furman College, Mock Trial: Who Kidnapped Bailey
Reynolds?

Summer 3: Northwestern College Prep, Introduction to Philosophy
of Law

UCLA's Mock Trial Institute and Summer Law
Institute

Cornell University, Freedom and Justice

George Washington University Mini-Course, Law and
Evidence, Inside Criminal Law

Summer 4: Columbia University, Summer Program for High
School Students, Constitutional Law or Leadership in
Law

University of Pennsylvania, Law and Society; Criminology

University of Chicago, American Law and Litigation

Presidential Classroom, Law and Justice in a Democracy

Literature

Summer 1: Great Books Summer Program (Stanford or Amherst
campuses)

Duke TIP Center, From Frodo to Jon Snow, The
Evolution of Fantasy Literature, **and** From
Wonderland to Hogwarts

Summer 2: Harvard, Shakespeare

Brown University, Russian Short Stories from Karamzin
to Chekhov

Summer 3: Duke TIP Center, The Play's the Thing, Performance,
Popular Culture and Shakespeare's Dramatic Works

Cornell University, Genius and Madness in Literature

Cornell Explorations, Imaginative Argument in English
Literature

University of Dallas, Shakespeare in Italy

Summer 4: TASP (Telluride Program)

University of Pennsylvania, 18th Century British
Literature, Satire

These four-summer options give students expertise in a broad range of literature, from Shakespeare to Harry Potter, and exposes them to literature courses at Harvard, Stanford, Duke, Cornell, and Amherst. In addition, the University of Dallas program in Italy focuses on the works of Shakespeare in Venice, Padua, Sicily, and Verona. Regardless of which programs the student selects, he should plan to spend the bulk of the remainder of each summer reading literature to build up a repertoire of books read.

Marine Biology and Ocean Science

Summer 1: Johns Hopkins (CTY and CAA) courses in Hawaii:
Oceanography, the Hawaiian Pacific
The Life Cycle of an Island: Hawaii
Earthwatch, Grey Whale Migrations (family trip),
British Columbia

Summer 2: Johns Hopkins CAA, The Blue Crab, The Chesapeake
Bay Oyster, *or* Whales and Estuary Systems
Earthwatch, Belize Reef Survey
Oceanic Society Expeditions, Marine Mammals (in
Belize)
Students on Ice, Youth Whale-Watch, Gulf of
St. Lawrence
Duke TIP courses: Coastal Ecology, Marine Biology,
Marine Zoology, Oceanography, *and* Physiological
Ecology in North Carolina Outer Banks

Summer 3: Duke TIP, Beneath the Surface: Marine Biology and
Neuroscience, Sarasota Bay, New College of Florida
Earthwatch, Bahamian Reef Survey, San Salvador Island
Apply to Student Challenge Awards Program (SCAP)
Stanford, The Oceans: Introduction to the Marine
Environment
Brown University, The Hidden Island,
Marine Science (Kohala, Hawaii)

Summer 4: Cornell, Oceanography of the Gulf of Maine, living
aboard a ship and on Shoals Island to conduct
research

> USC, Oceanography of the Southern California Bight,
> living aboard ship and on Catalina Island to conduct
> research
>
> Student Conservation Society, volunteer at choice of
> national parks

These plans allow students to pursue valuable marine biology and environmental research at some of the world's most beautiful beaches. Some of these programs offer college credit and all are impressive when applying to colleges with marine science, oceanography, conservation, or zoology programs.

MATH (Number Theory or Olympiad Training)

Summer before
8th grade: Stanford University, Math Olympiad Problem-Solving
                (grades 8 to 10), Education Program for Gifted Youth
Summer 1:   Awesome Math Summer Program (Olympiad)
                Enroll: Art of Problem Solving online courses for fall
                (Olympiad)
Summer 2:   Canada/USA Mathcamp
                Enroll: Art of Problem Solving online courses for fall
                (Olympiad)
Summer 3:   Ross Program at Ohio State University, Number
                Theory
                PROMYS at Boston University, Number Theory
                Hampshire College Summer Studies in Math, Number
                Theory
                Enroll: Art of Problem Solving online courses for fall
Summer 4:   Ross Program at Ohio State University, Combinatorics
                Enroll: Art of Problem Solving online courses for fall

For a student who would like to be among the handful of top high school mathematicians in the world, this four-summer plan is based on the route that other math winners have taken. Contrary to what an outsider might think, mathematics is exhilarating at these programs, where students come head-to-head with the small circle of top competitors—the international who's who of mathematicians their age. Do well at these programs and write your own ticket to any college.

Medicine

Summer 1: Johns Hopkins CTY, History of Disease; Neuroscience; Introduction to Biomedical Sciences

Johns Hopkins CAA, Pharmacology & Toxicology; Biotechnology

Duke TIP Academy, Introduction to Medical Science

Duke TIP Center, Medicine in America; Disease and Immunology

University of Michigan Math/Science Scholars, Mysteries of Embryology

Summer 2: Duke TIP Center, Biology of Cancer; Neuroscience; Medical Ethics

Brown University Mini-Courses include Introduction to Medicine, Medical Microbiology, Epidemiology, Waging War on Cancer, Nervous System Function, Sport Physiology, Bio-Medical Science, Molecular Basis of Human Disease, Research Techniques in Biomedical Fields

Summer 3: Duke TIP, Tropical Medicine and Ethnobiology, Costa Rica

University of Pennsylvania, Penn Summer Science Academy, Biomedical Research Program: Frontiers & Challenges

University of Kansas School of Pharmacy Summer Camp

University of Connecticut Mentor Connections, Drug Development

Summer 4: UCSF Department of Pediatrics High School Summer Internship

Jackson Laboratory, Bar Harbor Maine, summer research

National Institutes of Health (NIH) Summer Internship in Biomedical Research

Many, many summer programs exist for motivated high school students seeking to explore medicine and research cures for diseases. The general aim should be to have students conduct *original* medical research by their junior or senior year—to be able to enter the nation's top science and medical research competitions. In addition, a student taking some of these courses could potentially become an expert in diseases or other special areas of medicine, and all of these credentials could be helpful years later in applying to medical school (in addition to college.)

Meteorology

Summer 1: Weather Academy, University of Missouri

            Brown University SPARK program, Forces of Nature: Monster Storms, Global Warming, and the Science of Weather

            Penn State University Weather Camp

            University of Michigan Math and Science Summer Scholars, Modeling Daisyworld (controlling climate)

Summer 2: University of Missouri, Introductory Meteorology online course, Center for Distance and Independent Study (CDIS)

            University of Wisconsin, Madison, Meteorological Cooperative Institute for Meteorological Satellite Studies Summer Workshop on Atmospheric, Earth, and Space Sciences for High School Students

            Brown University BELL program (environment leadership, global warming)

Summer 3: Furman College (South Carolina), Understanding and Using GIS and GPS,

            Northeastern University, Disasters, Nature's Violence, and the Human Threat

Summer 4: University of Connecticut Mentor Connection, Earth From Above, Exploring Our Environment via Remote Sensing

            Johns Hopkins Discover Hopkins Program, Global Warming

Johns Hopkins Pre-College Program, Introduction to
  Meteorology
Internship with the National Weather Service

These programs give students expertise in meteorology and an impressive familiarity with the tools used by meteorologists, including remote sensing equipment and satellite studies.

Mythology and Folktales

Summer 1: Brown University Summer and Continuing Studies,
  Mythology *and* Classical Roots of Western Literature
  Duke TIP Center, Mind and Myth
Summer 2: Cornell Explorations, Greek Mythology; Intensive
  Ancient Greek
Summer 3: Harvard, two concurrent courses: Gods & Rituals in
  Greek Tragedy *and* Fairytales: Their Tellers, Hearers
  & Interpreters *or* Introduction to Irish Myth and
  Folklore
Summer 4: Miami University of Ohio, Junior Scholars, Classical
  Mythology
  University of Missouri, Columbia, Classical Mythology
  Brandeis University, Adolescent Literature from Grimm
  to Voldemort
  Duke TIP Pre-College, Fairy Tales: Grimm to Disney

If you thought that myths and fairytales were just for little kids, note that Harvard offers an undergraduate *major* in folklore and mythology. For a student interested in ancient Greek and Roman mythology, a good selection from the four-summer plan described should make her expert enough to enter some of the most prestigious national contests like the National Mythology Exam and the Medusa Mythology Exam.

Neuroscience

Summer before
8th grade: Brown University SPARK program, From Brain to
                  Sensation
                  Johns Hopkins CTY, Neuroscience
Summer 1:   Brown University, three courses: Brain Basics from
                  Biology to Behavior, Vision: A Glimpse of the Brain
                  and The Brain from Neurons to Behavior
Summer 2:   Case Western Reserve CTD, Neuroscience Honors
Summer 3:   Brown University Summer Courses Pre-College,
                  Introduction to Neuroscience
                  Harvard University Summer, Neurobiology
Summer 4:   University of Connecticut Mentor Connection, Brain
                  Power: Unraveling the Development of the Cerebral
                  Cortex, research

Neuroscience is currently one of the most cutting-edge fields of medical research, and universities are offering high school students the opportunity to study the brain and also to conduct original brain research through summer programs. This is just a sampling of summer opportunities. By senior year, the high school student pursuing this path will have studied at some of the top research universities and accumulated college credits—and should have conducted actual original neuroscience research that can be entered into major science and neuroscience competitions, including the American Academy of Neurology Neuroscience Award competition.

Paleontology

Summer 1:   Johns Hopkins CTY, Paleobiology
                  Earthwatch, family trip Mammoth Graveyard, Hot
                  Springs, South Dakota
                  Royal Tyrrell Museum, Alberta, Canada, family one-day
                  digs (age four and up)

Summer 2: PaleoWorld Research Foundation Montana Dinosaur
Expedition (for families)
Colorado College, Geology of the Pike's Peak Region
Summer 3: UCLA, Dinosaurs and Their Relatives
Landmark Volunteers, Paleontological Research
Institution
Volunteer at Rocky Mountain (bird) Raptor Program
Summer 4: University of Chicago Stones and Bones Paleontology
(Chicago classes, Wyoming digs)
Volunteer at the Smithsonian Institution National
Museum of Natural History or Dinosaur National
Monument

A creative four-summer plan for a student with an interest in paleontology could include excavations in Canada, South Dakota, and Wyoming, and visits to Dinosaur National Monument in Colorado and Utah, with an internship at the Smithsonian Institution National Museum of Natural History in Washington, D.C. A student pursuing this path could accumulate 11 college credits by the time the college application process starts.

Philosophy

Summer 1: Duke TIP Academy, Philosophy of Mind *and* The
Philosophic Quest: In Search of Wisdom
Johns Hopkins Talent Search choices include Ethics,
and Logic, Principles of Reasoning, Philosophy of
Mind, Philosophy, and Introduction to Logic
Summer 2: Duke TIP Academy, Existentialism and Beyond
Johns Hopkins Pre-College Introduction to Political
Philosophy
Johns Hopkins Pre-College Introduction to Moral
Philosophy
Brown University Pre-College Mini-Courses: Giants of
Philosophy, Themes from Existentialism, Meaning of
Life, and more

Summer 3: Harvard Summer Session, Introduction to Philosophy
concurrent with Harvard Introduction to Deductive
Logic

UCLA, Introduction to Philosophy of Mind

Summer 4: Stanford Summer choices include Philosophy East and
West, Introduction to Moral Philosophy, The
Perception of Others, and Logic, Reasoning &
Argumentation

Georgetown University, Introduction to Ethics

While other fields may give students "something to show" for four summers of work, the serious philosophy student should keep a running notebook of thoughts and ideas and possibly a blog. In addition, a philosophy student should probably pursue university level social science research with a philosophy-related focus, mentored by a philosophy professor.

Poetry

Summer 1: Interlochen, Intermediate Level Creative Writing
Summer 2: Sarah Lawrence College (New York), Free Verse Poetry:
Reining In & Letting Loose

Brown University, Pre-College Mini-Course, Creative
Writing/Poetry

Summer 3: Susquehanna University (Pennsylvania), Writers
Workshops (poetry)

University of Arizona Poetry Center, Get Your Verse
On: Poetry Workshop for High School Writers

Iowa Young Writers' Studio (poetry)

Summer 4: Columbia University, Creative Writing Master Classes
in Poetry

Barnard College, Poetry in New York

Johns Hopkins, Introductory Workshop in Poetry

Yale, Writing the Lyric

Students who pursue this path are bound to reach senior year with volumes of work to refer to on their college applications. Poets should contribute to their high school literary magazines—or found such publications if none exists. In addition, they should enter national poetry contests—find a listing in the annual *Writer's Market* book. Also check *Poets & Writers* magazine. They might also consider publishing their work through greeting card companies, whose information can also be found in *The Writer's Market*. Many children's magazines accept verse written by kids. Parents should purchase the *Children's Writer's & Illustrator's Market* as well. In addition, many local newspapers publish an occasional poem on the op-ed page, and specialty magazines are often willing to publish a poem relevant to their subject matter; students should submit to these outlets as well. Students who write in their own ethnic language should seek to have their poems published in ethnic newspapers and magazines.

Psychology

Summer 1: Duke TIP Center program, Abnormal Psychology
Johns Hopkins CTY, Cognitive Psychology
Johns Hopkins CAA, Foundations of Psychology
Brown University Mini-Courses offer a wide range
    of topics including Genetics and Human Behavior,
    Addictive Behaviors, Abnormal Psychology, Mood
    Disorders, Introduction to Clinical Psychology

Summer 2: Northwestern College-Prep, options include Social
    Psychology, Introduction to Psychology,
    Developmental Psychology, Research Methods
University of Chicago, Developmental Psychology,
    Theories and Techniques
Brown University Summer, Controversies in Mood
    Disorders (and many more psychology options)

Summer 3: University of Pennsylvania Introduction to
    Experimental Psychology

Summer 4: Harvard Summer Seminar, Behavior and Behavior
    Modification
Stanford, a wide range of options includes Social
    Psychology, Cognitive Psychology, Developmental
    Psychology, Personality, Self and Identity

University of Connecticut Mentor Connection offers
multiple research opportunities in autism and also
memory

Most universities that offer summer courses for high school students feature psychology as one of the options—many, many courses exist for high school students. To truly impress colleges, a student with a serious interest probably should aim to conduct psychology research under the supervision of a lab professional that can be entered into science research competitions by junior or senior year of high school. But in order to get there, the student should take college-level courses in the earlier summers of high school.

Religion

Summer 1:   Duke TIP Center, World Religions
UCLA, Introduction to the Philosophy of Religion
Summer 2:   Johns Hopkins CTY, Islam
Brown University Mini-Courses offer a wide range of
options, including Buddhism, Meaning of Life, Religious Traditions
Summer 3:   Harvard University, Perspectives of Islam: Religion,
History, and Culture
Washington University, Science Fiction & Religion:
May the Force Be with You
Vanderbilt University, Comparative Religions
Summer 4:   Stanford University, American Evangelicalism
Washington University, Introduction to the World's
Religions
Brown University, Philosophy of Religion

Comparative religion course offerings seem to vary more from year to year than course offerings in other fields. When looking for summer courses at any given university, if you don't find any listings under *R* (religion), look for *C* (comparative religion). For the student who wants to delve into the teachings of any particular religion, check out seminaries, pilgrimage tours, and religious institutions in addition to universities.

Robotics

Summer before

8th grade: Rensselaer Polytechnic Institute, LEGO® Robotics
Academy

Summer 1:   Stanford University's Education Program for Gifted
Youth, Introduction to Computer Programming, Java
& Robotics

Lake Superior State University (Michigan), Robotics
Summer Camp

Cybercamps (locations across America)

iD Tech Camp (locations across America)

Rocky Mountain Talent Search, Robotics (University of
Denver)

NASA Alliance Robotics Course Project Vex online

Vanderbilt Summer Academy, Robotics

Summer 2:   Case Western Reserve Equinox, CTD, Introduction to
Robotics

USC Summer, Introduction to Robotic Design

Brown University Mini-Course, Robot Rover Derby

Summer 3:   Stanford University, EPGY, Java and Robotics

North Carolina State, Autonomous Robotics Workshop

Arizona State, ROBOTS Camp for Girls

Summer 4:   Harvard Secondary Program, Engineering Sciences
S-160 Mobile Robot and Embedded Programming

The key to becoming a real expert in robotics by senior year is learning enough math and computer programming. Ideally, robotics studies should be coordinated with in-school math courses and extracurricular activities including an in-school computer club, school math team, out-of-school Internet-based USA Computing Olympiad, and an in-school *FIRST* team in robotics.

Rock and Roll (and Popular Music)

Summer 1: Rock and Roll Camp, ends with campers' rock concert
Battle of the Bands, Explore Camp, Queens University
(Charlotte, North Carolina)
Brown University Mini-Course, Hip-Hop, Punk and
Country

Summer 2: Penn State University, Music: The History of Rock 'N
Roll
USC Summer Seminars, Electric Guitar—Jazz, Rock
and Beyond
Columbia College in Chicago, Fundamentals of Record
Production

Summer 3: UCLA Design/Media Arts Summer Institute, Music
Video
Northwestern University College-Prep, two courses:
The Beatles, A Multidisciplinary Mystery Tour, *and*
Rap Music

Summer 4: Northeastern University (Boston), The Entertainment
Industry Rock 'n Roll Fantasy Camp (child attends
with parents)

This plan gives the rock-and-roll musician or pop star experience performing, a sense of the music industry, and a cultural education that includes history, music theory, repertoire, and music appreciation. A student who pursues this program should be able to speak intelligently about rock and roll at a college interview. Plus, for the right kid, it's just plain fun.

Science Fiction (and Other Fiction)

Summer 1: Simon's Rock College (Great Barrington, Massachusetts)
Summer Young Writers Workshop, three-week program (not sci-fi)
Johns Hopkins CTY, The Critical Essay: Science Fiction
(writing *about* science fiction)
Duke TIP Center, Science Fiction (reading)

Summer 2: Duke TIP Academy, Science Fiction and Society:
Interstellar Battleships and Beyond
University of Kansas, Science Fiction Writers Workshop
(also available as online course Science Fiction,
English 506)

Summer 3: Iowa Young Writers' Studio (fiction)
Washington University, Science Fiction & Religion:
May the Force Be with You

Summer 4: Duke University TIP, Creative Writing Ghost Ranch;
write novella

In addition to the works he pens at organized programs, the student science fiction writer should try to write at least one novella each summer after attending a program. By the end of this four-year plan, the student should have written three science fiction novellas and accrued up to 6 college credits. Parents should help the child find publishing opportunities and children's fiction-writing contests, and also locate a local mentor (local journalist, writer, English teacher) able to provide editorial input to help improve the manuscripts. To help your child pursue publishing his work, get a copy of the latest *Children's Writer's & Illustrator's Market*.

Screenplay Writing/Playwriting

Summer 1: Interlochen Summer Camp, Playwriting
Duke University TIP, Screenwriting

Summer 2: Northwestern University College Prep, Foundations of
Screenwriting
Barnard College, Columbia University (New York),
Fiction Film: Page to Screen

Summer 3: Yale University Summer Program, Screenwriting
University of Pennsylvania, Pre-College Screenwriting
Workshop
USC Summer Screen/Playwriting (complete
twenty-page play)

Summer 4: Harvard Summer, Beginning Screenwriting
NYU Tisch, Dramatic Writing for High School

Students (Summer Screenwriting and Summer Play
Writing)

Most of these programs could help a student assemble a portfolio of
screenplays ready to produce by the time he graduates from high school. If
you were on the admissions committee of a prestigious university that offered film production as a major, wouldn't this student look far more appealing to you than his peer who watched TV for four summers and has a
bunch of screenplay ideas (but has never actually written any)?

INDEX

Academic calendar, 70–71, 119

Academy of Applied Science, 159

Academy of Television Arts & Sciences College TV Awards, 220

Acceleration (skipping), 55–59, 57–59, 114–117, 131

ACTs, 30, 67

Advocacy and public service, 215, 227–232

Aeronautics and aerospace summer programs, 260

Alliance for Young Artists & Writers, 167

All-USA First Academic Team (*USA Today*), 66–67

All-USA High School Musicians, 186

Alvin Ailey Junior Division Summer Intensive Program, 191

American Academy of Neurology Competition, 127

American Invitational Mathematics Exam (AIME), 88, 91–94, 100, 101

American Legion, 238

American Mathematics Competitions (AMC), 88, 90–95, 98, 99–101

American Regions Math League (ARML), 88, 95, 103, 105, 111, 113

Amherst College, 105, 106

Andreescu, Titu, 101

Anthropology, 200–202
  summer programs, 261

AP (Advanced Placement) courses, 51–53, 57, 116, 122, 123, 168, 202, 204, 208

Apathetic teenager, 9

Archeology, 200–202
  summer programs, 261–262

Architecture summer programs, 262

Art history, 202–203
  summer programs, 263–264

Art Institute of Chicago, 170

Art of Problem Solving, The (Rusczyk and Lehoczky), 94, 98, 100

Art of Problem Solving Foundation, 93–94, 100–101

Arts, 163–196
  creative writing, 192–196
  dance, 165, 166, 181–184, 188–191
  drama, 165, 173–181
  fine arts, 168–172, 262–263
  music, 164, 165, 181–192

Arts (*continued*)
　national awards, 166–168
　out-of-school lessons, 164–166, 168,
　　182–184, 188–191
　portfolio, 171–173
　recording performances, 191–192
　talent agents, 179–181
Association of Talent Agents (ATA),
　180
Astronomy summer programs, 152–153
Auditions, 174–181
AwesomeMath, 101–102

Ballet School of Chapel Hill, 165
Baylor University, 153
Bentley College, 251
Blogs, 224, 225
Boston University, 207, 219
　PROMYS (Program in Mathematics
　　for Young Scientists) Program, 89,
　　103, 104–105, 109
　Tanglewood Institute, 189–190
Boys Nation, 237–238
Broadcast journalism (*see* Journalism)
Brown University, 39, 214
Buck, Kavin, 168, 172, 173
Business, 246–256
　application essay, 255–256
　basics, 256
　entrepreneurship, 250–251
　high school courses, 247–248
　internships and jobs, 249–250
　investment and finance, 251
　résumé for, 253–254
　summer programs, 246–247,
　　250–251

Calculus, 87, 116
Camps, summer, 27–28, 36
Canada/USA Mathcamp, 89, 103, 106
Cannon Memorial Scholarship, 221

Carlsbad High School, California, 216
Carnegie Mellon, 176
CASPER (Center for Astrophysics,
　Space Physics and Engineering
　Research), 127, 153
Center for Excellence in Education,
　150
Christopher Columbus Fellowship
　Foundation, 161
Classics, 203–206
Clay Mathematics Institute, 27,
　107–109
Clubs, founding, 60–62
Codes and encryption summer
　programs, 266
College Board, 33
College courses, supplementing,
　52–54
College drama programs, 178–179
College visits, early, 6–7
Colorado College Summer Dance
　Intensive, 190
Columbia College, 218–219
Columbia University, 196
Columbia (University) Scholastic Press
　Association (CSPA), 222–223
Community access TV, 216, 218
Community service (*see* Advocacy and
　public service)
Comparative religion, 213–214
　summer programs, 286
Competitions and contests, 57, 62–64
　arts, 166–168, 188
　journalism, 225–226
　mathematics, 88, 89–103
　science and engineering, 113,
　　117–124, 126–129, 131–135, 145,
　　153–162
Computing
　summer programs, 43–44, 270–271
　USA Computing Olympiad, 113,
　　117, 118, 122–124
Concord Review, 210

Congressional pages, 236, 237

Contests (*see* Competitions and contests)

Cornell University, 213, 226

Courses, summer, 36–40. (*see also* Summer programs)

Creative writing, 192–196

Crow Canyon Archaeological Center, 201

Dance, 165, 166, 181–184, 188–191
 summer programs, 265

Dartmouth Debate Institute, 240–241

Davidson Fellows Award, 193

Davidson Institute, 30*n*, 127

Davies, Deb, 205

Debate, 239–242
 summer programs, 266

Delat Epsilon Chi (Association) (DECA), 248

Denver, University of, Rocky Mountain Talent Search, 29

Doherty, Gillian, 123

Down time, 25

Drama, 165, 173–181
 summer programs, 176–177, 267

Duke University, 201
 Talent Identification Program (TIP), 29

Earthwatch Institute, 201–202

Energy science summer programs, 267–268

Engineering (*see* Science and engineering)

Entrepreneurship, 250–251
 summer programs, 264

Experiment in International Living, 200, 201

Extracurricular opportunities, 60–62. (*see also* Summer programs)

Family calendar, 70–71, 119

Family vacations, 45

Fashion summer programs, 269

FastWeb.com, 63

Fed Challenge, 252–253

Feynmann, Richard, 39

Fields Medal, 88

Field trips, 10

Fine arts, 168–172
 summer programs, 262–263

FIRST Robotics Competition, 61, 160–161

First Step to the Nobel Prize in Chemistry, 127

First Step to the Nobel Prize in Physics, 127

Foreign language, 206–208

Forensic science (detective work) summer programs, 270

Forensics teams, 239–242

Foundation of the National Academy of Television Arts and Sciences, 221

Four-year academic plan, 4, 5, 47–75
 acceleration, 55–59
 AP courses, 51–53, 57
 contests and scholarships, 62–64
 designing ideal, 64–67
 extracurricular opportunities, 60–62
 family calendar, 70–71
 grades, 47–49
 IB program, 51–52
 local college courses as supplement, 52–54
 sample résumés, 72–75
 short-term refrigerator goals, 67–70
 starting early, 54–55
 starting résumés early, 71–72
 staying on tracks and avoiding derailments, 49–51

Future Business Leaders of America (FBLA), 248

Game plan, (*see also* Four–year
  academic plan; Goals and passions;
  Summer programs)
  coordinating with school, 76–82
  elements of, 5
Game programming summer programs,
  43–44, 270–271
Garcia Program, 151, 152
Genetics summer programs, 271
Geography, 208–209
George Mason University, 118
Georgetown University, 39, 207
Girls Nation, 237–238
Global Routes, 201
Goals and passions, 3–20
  abandoning, 18–19
  apathetic teenager and, 9
  creating, 9
  dazzling and ambitious, 11, 12
  describing, 11
  early college visits and, 6–7
  identifying, 10–16
  list of, 13–14
  motivation and, 5–6, 16–17
  multiple interests and activities,
    10–11
  parental disapproval of, 14–15
  short-term, 5, 67–70
  supporting and taking seriously,
    12–13, 16, 18
  use of as bargaining chips, 68
  in writing, 16–17
Government, 233–245
  building track record in, 235–239
  debate and forensics teams,
    239–242
  international, 252
  international relations, 242–245
  internships, 235–237
  leadership roles, 233–235
  summer programs, 237–241, 272
Grades, 52–54, 53, 59
Great Books Summer Program, 213

Hampshire College Summer Studies in
  Mathematics (HCSSiM), 89, 103,
  105–106
Harvard-MIT Mathematics
  Tournament (HMMT), 96–97
Harvard University, 96–97, 109, 149,
  176, 207, 212, 213
History, 209–212
Humanities, 197–214
  anthropology and archeology,
    200–202
  art history, 202–203
  building credentials, 200
  classics, 203–206
  foreign language and linguistics,
    206–208
  geography, 208–209
  history, 209–212
  literature, 212–213
  philosophy and comparative
    religion, 213–214
  summer programs, 198–199, 206,
    213

IB (International Baccalaureate)
  Diploma programs, 51–52
Idyllwild Arts, 176
Imagine (Johns Hopkins magazine), 64,
  110
Indiana University, 199, 219
  High School Journalism Institute,
    224
Industrial design summer programs,
  272–273
Intel International Science and
  Engineering Fair (ISEF), 57, 89,
  106, 113, 127, 154, 158–159
Intel Science Talent Search (STS), 57,
  89, 105, 111, 113, 127, 132, 137,
  150, 151, 154–156
Interlochen Arts Camp, 170, 189, 196
International business, 252

International Geography Olympiad, 208–209
International Linguistic Olympiad, 208
International Mathematical Olympiad (IMO), 87, 88, 90–92, 95, 98, 101, 103
International relations, 242–245
  summer programs, 273–274
Internships, 25–26, 63, 130. (*see also* Summer programs)
  business, 249–250
  government, 235–237
  journalism, 216–220
  science and engineering research, 141–144, 147
Investment and finance, 251
  summer programs, 264–265
Iowa, University, 95
Iowa Young Writers' Studio, 196

Jobs (*see* Internships; Summer programs)
Johns Hopkins University
  Center for Academic Advancement (CAA), 30, 32, 208
  Center for Talented Youth (CTY), 29, 30, 32, 33, 89, 110, 123, 208
  Civic Leadership Institute, 232
Journalism, 215–226
  blogs, 224, 225
  contests and awards, 225–226
  in-school TV, 218
  print, 221–225
  summer programs, 274–275
  TV internships and jobs, 216–220
  TV production courses, 218–219
Juilliard School, 178–179
Junior Engineering and Technical Society (JETS) TEAMS, 61
Junior Science and Humanities Symposium (JSHS), 113, 127, 159–160

Kansas City Art Institute, 170
Kelly, David, 105
Kernan, Karen, 151
Knowledge Exchange Institute (KEI), 170, 252

Landscape design summer programs, 275
Law summer programs, 275–276
Leadership roles, 233–235
Lehoczky, Sandor, 94, 96, 100
Library and parks TV, 217
Linguistics, 206–208
Literature, 212–213
  summer programs, 276–277

Mandelbrot Competition, 88, 96
Mandell, Eduard, 150
Marine biology and ocean science summer programs, 44, 277–278
Maryland, University of, 118
Massachusetts Institute of Technology (MIT), 91, 96–97, 106, 109, 127, 149, 150
Mathcamp, 89, 103, 106
Math circles, 102–103
MATHCOUNTS, 88, 94–95, 101
Mathematical Olympiad Summer Program (MOSP), 88, 91, 94, 100, 101
Mathematical Reflections (journal), 102
Mathematics, 87–110
  contest track, 88, 89–103
  curriculum gap, 112
  math circles, 102–103
  number theory/combinatorics track, 88–89, 103–107
  practice resources, 99–100
  research track (*see* Research track in mathematics)
  summer programs, 278–279
  training classes, 100–103

Mathematics Camp (SUMaC),
  Stanford University, 89, 103,
  106–107
Math Olympiad Problem-Solving
  Institute, Stanford University, 101,
  102
MathScore, 101, 102
Media (*see* Journalism)
Medicine summer programs, 279–280
Medill School of Journalism, 219, 223,
  226
Medusa Mythology Exam, 206
Meteorology summer programs,
  280–281
Michigan, University of, 199, 207
  Department of Theatre & Drama,
  179
Michigan State High School Honors
  Science-Math Engineering
  Program, 152
Minority Introduction to Engineering
  and Science Program (MITES),
  127
Missouri, University of, 224, 226
Model Congress, 61
Motivation, 5–6, 9, 16–17
Music, 164, 165, 181–192
  summer programs, 288
Mythology and folktales summer
  programs, 281

National Association for Music
  Educations (MENC), 186–187
National Biblical Greek Exam, 205
National Forensic League (NFL), 240,
  242
National Foundation for Advancement
  in the Arts (NFAA), 166–168
National Gallery for America's Young
  Inventors, 127, 161–162
National Greek Exam, 204–205
National Junior Classical League, 205

National Latin Exam, 204
National Merit Scholarship Winners,
  67
National Portfolio Day Association, 173
National Security Agency (NSA), 93,
  94
National Security Language Initiative,
  207
National Speech Tournament, 242
National Writing Board, 209–210
Navajo National Summer "Abroad"
  Program, 200–201
Nebraska, University of, 91, 119
Neuroscience summer programs, 282
Nevada, University of, at Reno, 30n
New England Young Writers'
  Conference at Bread Loaf, 196
New York Tech, 165–166
New York University, 176, 226
North Carolina School of the Arts,
  170, 176
Northwestern University, 219, 223,
  226
  Center for Talent Development
  (CTD), 29, 200
  Championship Debate Group, 241
  Civic Education Project (CEP), 232
  National High School Coon-Hardy
  Debate Scholars, 241
  School of Music, 176–177, 190
Number theory/combinatorics
  mathematics track, 88–89,
  103–107

Ocean Sciences Bowl, 61
Ohio State University Ross Program,
  89, 103–104, 109
Ojai program, 27, 113, 127, 152–153

Paleontology summer programs,
  282–283

Parent–faculty relationship, 77–82
Passions (*see* Goals and passions)
Patents, 126, 151, 162
Penn State University, 39, 95, 105, 207
Pennsylvania, University of, 208, 226, 251
Philosophy, 213–214
  summer programs, 283–284
Photography, 172
Play writing summer programs, 289–290
Poetry summer programs, 284–285
Portfolio, 171–173
PreCollege Research Abroad Program (PRAP), 150–151
Presidential Scholars, 67, 166–167
Princeton Mathematics Competition, 97
Princeton University, 48
Print journalism, 221–225
PROMYS (Program in Mathematics for Young Scientists) Program, Boston University, 89, 103, 104–105, 109
PSATs, 67
Psychology summer programs, 285–286
Public TV stations, 217–218
Publishing, 126, 151, 162, 192–193, 195, 224–225
Punishment, 68
Putnam Competition, 95

Quill and Scroll International Honorary Society for High School Students, 226

Rafailovich, Miriam, 151–152
Ralph Waldo Emerson Prize, 210
Rejections, 68, 69

Religion (*see* Comparative religion)
Research Science Institute (RSI), 27, 127, 149–150
Research track in mathematics, 88, 89, 107–110, 112–113, 125–162
  patents and publishing, 126, 151, 162
Research track in science and engineering, 112–113, 125–162
  basics, 128–132
  competitions, 113, 117–124, 126–129, 131–135, 145, 153–162
  finding research, 135–136
  finding winning project, 137–140
  home-based, 130
  in-school programs, 132–134
  internships, 141–144, 147
  lab opportunities, 129–130, 135–136, 141–145
  owning the project, 145–146
  science fairs, 127–128, 131
  summer programs, 134, 146–153
  university opportunities, 142–143, 148–149
Résumés, 5
  business, 253–254
  government internships, 236, 237
  layout and wording of, 75
  for research track in science and engineering, 142–143
  sample, 72–75, 210–212, 231–232, 253–254
  starting early, 71–72
  theatrical, 173, 180
Rhode Island School of Design, 169
Robotics, 61, 160–161
  summer programs, 287
Ross, Arnold, 105
Ross Program, Ohio State University, 27, 89, 103–104, 109
Rusczyk, Richard, 94, 96, 98, 100
Russian Academy of Science, 150

San Jose State University, 95
Sarah Lawrence, 176, 191
SATs
  prep courses, 32–33
  scores, 32–34, 67, 203
  taking in 7th grade, 30, 32–34
SCATs, 30
Scholarships, 62–64, 66–67
Scholastic Art and Writing Awards,
  167, 193–194, 224–225
School of American Ballet, 191
Science and engineering, 111–162
  curriculum gap, 112
  essential coursework, 114–117
  most prestigious competitions, 113
  research track (*see* Research track in
    science and engineering)
  Science Olympiad track (*see* Science
    Olympiad track)
  summer programs, 134, 146–153,
    268–269
Science fiction summer programs,
  288–289
Science News magazine, 138
Science Olympiad track, 112–113,
  117–124
  basics, 119–120
  Chemistry Olympiad, 113, 117, 118,
    121
  Computing Olympiad, 113, 117,
    118, 122–124
  Physics Olympiad, 113, 116–118,
    121
  studying for, 120–121, 124
Scientific American, 138, 144
Sciserv.org, 64
Screenplay writing summer programs,
  289–290
Seaborg SIYSS Awards, 158
Siemens Competition in Math, Science
  and Technology, 113, 127,
  157–158
Siemens Foundation, 157

Simons, Jim, 151
Simons Program, 151, 152
Socorro program, 27, 113, 127,
  152–153
South Carolina, University of, 226
Spatial Test Battery, 30
Stanford University, 196, 226
  Education Program for Gifted Youth
    (EPGY), 29–30, 102, 197–198
  Mathematics Camp (SUMaC), 89,
    103, 106–107
  Math Olympiad Problem-Solving
    Institute, 101, 102
  National Forensic Institute, 241
Student Conservation Association, 232
Students with Exceptional Talent
  (SET) program, 34
Summer programs, 5, 19–46
  aeronautics and aerospace, 260
  anthropology, 261
  archeology, 261–262
  architecture, 262
  art history, 263–264
  business, 246–247, 250–251,
    264–265
  camps, 27–28, 36
  codes and encryption, 266
  comparative religion, 286
  dance and choreography, 265
  debate, 266
  down time, 25
  drama, 176–177, 267
  energy science, 267–268
  family vacations, 45
  fashion, 269
  fine arts, 170, 262–263
  forensic science (detective work),
    270
  game programming, 270–271
  genetics, 271
  government, 237–241, 272
  humanities, 198–199, 206, 213
  ideal four-year plan, 35–36

independent projects, 45–46
industrial design, 272–273
international relations, 273–274
journalism, 223–224, 274–275
landscape design, 275
law, 275–276
list of four-year plans, 259–290
literature, 276–277
marine biology and ocean science,
    277–278
mathematics, 278–279
medicine, 279–280
meteorology, 280–281
multiple activities in, 24–25
music and dance, 189–191
mythology and folktales, 281
neuroscience, 282
paleontology, 282–283
philosophy, 283–284
poetry, 284–285
psychology, 285–286
remediation and, 40–41
robotics, 287
rock and roll and popular music, 288
sample four-summer plans, 43–44
science and engineering, 134,
    146–153, 268–269
science fiction, 288–289
scouting out activities, 26–27
spending with friends, 41–42
talent searches, 29–36
teen programs and tours, 28–29
unstructured, 23–24
writing, 195–196, 288–290
SUNY Stony Brook, 151–152
Susquehanna University, 193
Syracuse University S.I. Newhouse
    School, 224, 226

Talent agents, 179–181
Talent searches, 29–36
Tanglewood Institute, 189–190

Teachers, relationships with, 77–82
Teen programs and tours, 28–29
Telluride Association Sophomore
    Seminars (TASSS), 199
Telluride Association Summer
    Programs (TASP), 27, 198–199
Texas, University of, in Austin, 54
Texas State Technical College, 153
Time capsule, creation of, 17
Tournament of Champions (debating),
    242
Track record, creating, 8, 22–25
Tutoring, 40, 49, 50, 78

University of California at Berkeley,
    176
University of California at Los
    Angeles, 207, 208, 219
    Acting and Performing Institute, 176
    Design Summer Institute, 170
    School of the Arts and Architecture,
        168, 169
    World Music Summer Institute and
        Music Academy, 190
U.S. Air Force Academy, 118
U.S. Congressional Award Program,
    69–70
USA Biology Olympiad, 57, 113, 117,
    118, 150
USA Chemistry Olympiad, 113, 117,
    118, 121
USA Computing Olympiad, 113, 117,
    118, 122–124
USA Mathematical Olympiad
    (USAMO), 88, 91–94, 100, 101,
    113, 118, 119
USA Mathematical Talent Search
    (USAMTS), 88, 93–94
USA Physics Olympiad, 113, 116–118,
    121
USA Today, 66–67
Usborne Books, 122–123

Vandervelde, Sam, 96
VolunteerMatch.org, 63, 230
Volunteer opportunities, 63–64,
    227–230

Wharton School, 246, 251
Wisconsin, University of, 54, 118
Women's Technology Program, 127

WOOT (Worldwide Online Olympiad
    Training) course, 101
Writer's Art, A: Creative Writing, 195
Writing, 192–196
    summer programs, 195–196,
        288–290

Yale University, 91

ABOUT THE AUTHOR

Elizabeth Wissner-Gross, who is also the author of *What Colleges Don't Tell You (And Other Parents Don't Want You to Know)*, is an educational strategist who, for more than ten years, has helped hundreds of families of 7th to 12th graders create early individualized "game plans" for gaining admission into the country's most-competitive colleges—including Harvard, MIT, Yale, Princeton, Stanford, Berkeley, Caltech, Columbia, the University of Pennsylvania, Northwestern, Dartmouth, Cornell, Brown, Duke, the University of Chicago, Amherst, and Williams. She also successfully used the secrets in this book in raising her own kids, Alex and Zach (each of whom was named among the top twenty high school students in America by *USA Today*), who were offered admission into Harvard, Princeton, Yale, and MIT.

Ms. Wissner-Gross, a graduate of Barnard College and the Columbia University Graduate School of Journalism, began her career as a professional journalist; her articles have appeared in the *New York Times*, the *Boston Globe*, the *Washington Post*, *Newsday*, and more than one hundred publications in the United States and abroad. She has also been very actively involved in issues of education, including leading a school district parent committee on gifted and talented education for fifteen years, until her sons went off to college. She and her husband, Sigmund, reside on Long Island and in Bloomfield, Connecticut. Visit her Web site at www.WhatHigh SchoolsDontTellYou.com.